Baedeker
Lisbon

Baedeker's

LISBON

Imprint

106 illustrations, 6 inner city plans, 4 ground plans, 3 drawings, 1 general map, 1 large map at end of book

Original German text: Eva Missler

Editorial work: Baedeker, Stuttgart
English language edition: Alec Court

Cartography:
Günter Unterberger, Stuttgart
Gert Oberländer, Munich
Falk-verlag GmbH, Hamburg (city map).

Source of Illustrations: Baedeker-Archiv (1), Bohnacker (1), Borowski (20), Brödel (1), Gall-Beermann (17), Historia-Photo (2), Lade (Fotoagentur) (2), Missler (58), Rudolf (Diaarchiv) (1), Schuster (Bildagentur) (1), Thiele (1)

General direction: Dr Peter Baumgarten, Baedeker Stuttgart

English translation: Julie Bullock, Brenda Ferris, Julie Waller

Following the tradition established by Karl Baedeker in 1844, notable buildings and works of art, natural features and views of particular interest, as well as hotels and restaurants of particular quality are distinguished by either one or two asterisks.
To make it easier to locate the various places listed in the "A to Z" section of the Guide, their co-ordinates on the large city map are shown at the head of each entry.
Only a selection of hotels, restaurants and shops can be given; no reflection is implied therefore on establishments not included.
In a time of rapid change it is difficult to ensure that all the information given is entirely accurate and up-to-date, and the possibility of error can never be entirely eliminated. Although the publishers can accept no responsibility for inaccuracies and omissions, they are always grateful for corrections and suggestions for improvement.

1st English edition 1993

US and Canadian edition
Prentice Hall General Reference

Distributed in the United Kingdom by the Publishing Division of the Automobile Association, Fanum House, Basingstoke, Hampshire RG21 2EA

A CIP catalogue record of this book is available from the British Library

Printed in Italy by G. Canale & C.S.p.A – Borgaro T.se –Turin

ISBN UK 0 7495 0593 1
US and Canada 0–671–87130–7

Library of Congress Catalog Card Number: 92–083958

Contents

The Principal Sights at a Glance

Preface

This pocket guide to **Lisbon** is one of the new generation of Baedeker guides.

Baedeker pocket guides, illustrated throughout in colour, are designed to meet the needs of the modern traveller. They are quick and easy to consult, with the principal features of interest described in alphabetical order and practical details about location, opening times, etc., shown in the marigin.

This city guide is divided into three parts. The first part gives a general account of Lisbon, its population, economy, transport, art and culture, famous people and history. A brief selection of quotations leads into the second part where the principal places of interest in and around Lisbon are described; the third part contains a variety of practical information designed to help visitors to find their way about and to make the most of their stay. Both the sights and the Practical Information section are given in alphabetical order.

Baedeker pocket guides, which are regularly updated, are noted for their concentration on essentials and their convenience of use. They contain many coloured illustrations and specially drawn plans, and at the back of the book will be found a large plan of the city. Each main entry in the A to Z section gives the co-ordinates of the square on the plan in which the particular feature can be located. Users of this guide, therefore, should have no difficulty in finding what they want to see.

POLLUX

Facts and Figures

Coat of Arms
Lisbon

General

Lisbon, in Portuguese Lisboa (pronounced "Lishbóa"), capital of Portugal for more than 700 years and its seat of government, is also the chief town of the district of the same name, one of the three "distritos" in the historic province of Estremadura. Centuries of centralised government have meant that the city has long enjoyed the greatest concentration of Portugal's major administrative, economic and cultural functions.

Lisbon's importance was at its height in the late 15th and early 16th c. when it became the centre of the world's trade. The discovery of new trade routes and the founding of overseas colonies speedily created a boom that brought it a relatively brief period of great prosperity and a cultural golden age.

Thanks to its wonderful location Lisbon is rightly numbered among Europe's most beautiful cities. The panoramic vista of the "white city" is still a memorable sight for ships entering Lisbon harbour, and much has been written and sung of its setting on the Tagus amid undulating hills, that special "Atlantic light", and the faded charm of what was once a glittering metropolis.

◀ *View of Baixa and Castelo de São Jorge*

General

Geographical location

On 38°42′ latitude north and 9°7′ longitude west, Lisbon is Europe's most westerly capital, and the furthest south after Athens. The uplands on which it is built are foothills of the Estremadura Plateau extending north of the city, which has its highest point at 113m/371ft.

Tagus

Lisbon's vital artery has long been the Tagus, or Tejo in Portuguese (Tajo in Spanish), which flows into the Atlantic about 15km/10½ miles beyond the original centre of the city on its north bank. North-east of Lisbon the Tagus opens out into the Mar de Palha ("sea of straw"), 13km/8 miles across at its broadest but narrowing down again to an estuary only about 2km/1¼ miles wide west of the city, forming a fine sheltered natural harbour. At about 1100km/684 miles the Tagus is the longest river on the Iberian Peninsula.

Earthquakes

Its geology has rendered the Lisbon region prone to earthquakes down the centuries. The worst were three close together in the mid-14th c., then two more in 1531 and 1755. Minor tremors are frequent, and it is feared that another big one could happen in the foreseeable future.

Climate

Lisbon and its region enjoy a climate that is Mediterranean but with Atlantic maritime influences (see Table p.214). The Gulf Stream means that the temperature almost never gets below 0°C/32°F. The south-west continuation of the Serra da Estrela protects the area in the north, tempering the cold north and north-easterly winds and holding at bay the rain and snow they bring with them. Generally speaking there is little rainfall during the pleasantly hot summer months. From May to October the average highest temperatures are over 20°C/68°F, and in July and August, the two hottest months, they average 26°C/79°F but can climb to 30°C/86°F and above. Even at this time of year the evenings tend to be relatively cool. Between November and March, the winter months, temperatures are generally quite mild, and in December to February on average do not fall below about 8°C/46°F, but rainfall is quite heavy – averaging 111mm/4¼in. in January compared with only 3mm/⅒in. in June. In terms of sunshine August gets 357 hours and January 161. Water temperatures tend not to get above an average 18°C/64°F even in the hottest summer months.

Population and surface area

The city of Lisbon, bounded by the suburbs of Loures, Sintra, Amadora, Oeiras in the north and west, and the Tagus in the south and east, has a population of about 850,000 in an area of 87.44 sq.km/32½ sq.miles, while the population figure for Greater Lisbon, which also includes Oeiras, Cascais and Sintra, is about 1.9 million. Lisbon county, which extends north almost to Peniche, has 2.1 million people – 21% of the population of Portugal (*c.* 9.7 million) living in only 3% of its total area (88,944 sq.km/34,332 sq.miles not including Madeira and the Azores).

Administration

Itself the capital of one of Portugal's 22 administrative counties, Lisbon is subdivided into 53 wards (freguesias). The City Council is the Câmara Municipal de Lisboa (CML). Lisbon county has 15 district councils with a total of 211 ward councils. A notable feature of the capital, i.e. the large number of administrative buildings, is due to the virtually unfettered centralisation of the functions of government in Lisbon.

City friendship links

Lisbon has friendship ties with several cities formerly in Portugal's overseas territories, including Rio de Janeiro, Macao, Praia (Cape Verde), Bissau and Sao Tomé, as well as formal co-operation and friendship treaties with Madrid, Zagreb, Rabat and Miami.

Urban development

Most of Lisbon's oldest buildings date from the second half of the 18th c., after the destruction wrought by the great earthquake of 1755. The few survivors from the 16th and 17th c. are only to be found in old quarters such as Alfama and Mouraria which were left almost unscathed. A few churches and palaces also remain from pre-1755, especially from the first half of the 16th c. Lisbon's oldest church is the Cathedral, Sé Patriarcal.
In the 20th c. a highly individual architectural style, owing much to the German architect Albert Speer, was developed in the "Estado Novo"

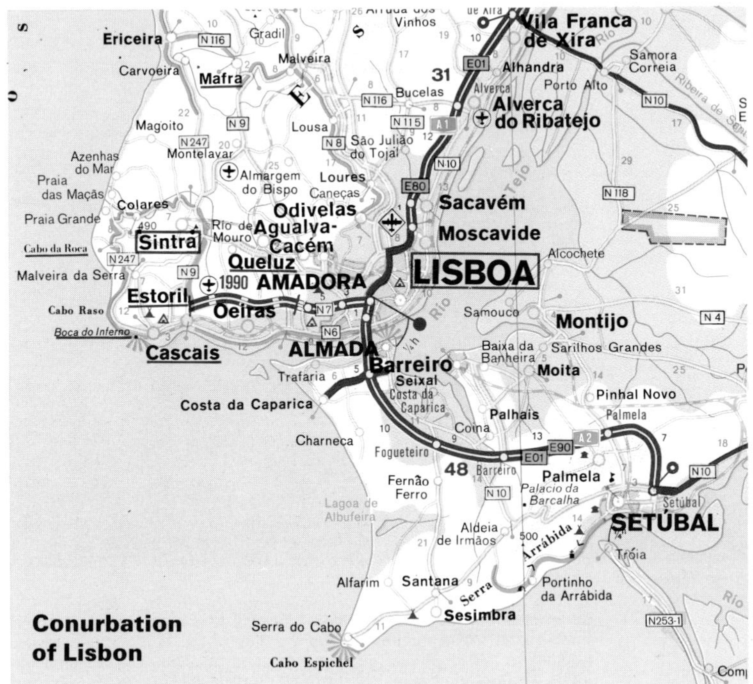

period (1933–74) when, during the Salazar dictatorship, Duarte Pacheco was the Minister responsible for the construction of the "Avenidas Novas" in the north of the city centre, a residential middle-class development built in the monumental style.

Since then virtually the whole cityscape bears the signs of the building boom begun in the 1980s. Apartment blocks ring the city and even the centre has its share of high-rise buildings, especially in the big Avenidas, towering over neighbouring mansions and townhouses built in the eclectic style of the 19th c.

For Lisbon the conservation and preservation of its buildings presents an enormous problem. Empty houses, dilapidated façades and ruined buildings are everywhere in the inner city, and this urban blight is intensified by speculation, lack of financial resources, a rent act that was a disincentive to the renovation of old houses, and a recent past with no feeling for conservation. It was the end of the 1980s before greater measures were taken to try and reverse this situation. An urban renewal programme is currently under way in the very oldest quarters, Alfama and Mouraria, to improve the dreadful housing conditions. Buildings in the lower town are also undergoing total renovation, in some cases behind the old façades.

Population

Growth

Lisbon's first city walls, after Portugal's emergence as an independent state, enclosed about 16ha/40 acres. When the city's population reached

River Tagus, the artery of Lisbon

about 60,000 in the 14th c. a new city wall was built encircling about three-quarters of a square mile. By the time of the 1755 earthquake the population had doubled, but then remained at about 150,000 until the influx of countryfolk from the surrounding rural areas between 1860 and 1890 increased the numbers from 200,000 to 300,000. Further growth between 1920 and 1940 from 500,000 to 700,000 meant that Lisbon's population actually more than tripled within the space of 80 years.
Since 1950 the city as such has experienced relatively little population growth. In fact, since 1970 this has only amounted to around 8%, but in the satellite suburbs and the unofficial shanty towns on Lisbon's perimeter it has shot up by as much as 54% (see General, Population and surface area).

Composition

A great array of different peoples have lived on this site over its two thousand years of history, starting with the Lusitanians, a Celtiberian tribe, and followed by Phoenicians, Carthaginians, Greeks and Jews, Romans, Visigoths and Arabs. As Portugal's empire grew Africans, South Americans and Asians also entered this melting pot. The population of Lisbon county today is 97.5% Portuguese, with Cape Verde Islanders the largest foreign minority.

Religion

The vast majority of the inhabitants are Roman Catholic. Constitutionally there is no established church and since no tithes are levied clerics have to be funded locally. Lisbon is one of Portugal's three ecclesiastical provinces, and since 1393 has been the seat of an Archbishop.

Housing situation

Despite the many satellite towns that have sprung up around Lisbon in the last decade the acute housing shortage is one of the city's major problems. Portugal experienced a massive housing shortfall in the 1970s when rural depopulation was aggravated by the influx of over 600,000 citizens from the country's former overseas territories. Consequently shanty towns of corrugated-iron shacks, the "bairros de lata", grew up in and around

Lisbon in highly inappropriate places for housing – on steep slopes, under flightpaths, along busy main roads. Most of the people living in the 25,000 to 30,000 "bairros de lata" are usually out of work or too poor to pay high rents. They tend to be elderly or have moved here from the provinces or the Cape Verde Islands in search of better living and working conditions. Most of these slums have electricity, but they often lack paved roads, drainage, a domestic water supply, or heating for the cold wet winters. Yet Lisbon has quite a lot of empty housing – old buildings due for demolition or houses that are for sale but not for rent.

Amendment of the Rent Act in 1985 caused confusion in the housing market. Prior to this rents could only be raised when the tenancy changed hands, which meant that the same family could have been living in the same accommodation for generations, and in fact there are still many long-established tenants paying rock-bottom rents. The new Rent Act was intended to encourage landlords to invest in maintaining their property values, but rents have also soared skyhigh, putting them virtually beyond the means of low-income families.

Residential areas

Most of the highrise flats, and some of the shanty towns and slums, are concentrated in the north-west (Amadora), north-east (Chelas, Olivais), and in the south on the opposite bank of the Tagus (Almada). The traditionally upmarket residential areas, with their villas and family homes, are in the west of the city, in Restelo, Estoril, and Cascais.

Economy

Portugal is one of Europe's poorest countries, and, in terms of gross national product per capita, bottom of the league for the European Community, some way below Greece. Since joining the Community in 1986, however, Portugal's fortunes have taken a distinct turn for the better, and in 1987 and 1988 its economic growth was well above the EC average. The capital taken out of the country after the 1974 revolution is gradually flowing back and has helped boost the sharp upturn in investment since 1986. Although there may still be considerable concealed unemployment the official number out of work has fallen to below 5%. Inflation is running at only about 8.5%, compared with figures of 22% in the early 1980s.

The state-owned sector of about 1000 undertakings proved a major obstacle to development when it came to adjustment to Community membership, since the fact that some prices were set arbitrarily ran counter to free market principles and hence EC interests. In 1990 privatisation legislation initiated by Cavaco Silva was passed by the Constitutional Court, despite opposition from Mário Soares.

Because of its relatively small domestic market Portugal's economy has always had to rely on its international exports. Low wages have increasingly made the country more attractive as a production base for British, American, French, Spanish and German companies – Portuguese workers get only a fifth of the wage of their German counterparts. Now, however, there is the fear of competition from even cheaper exports from the countries of Eastern Europe, and the diverting of financial support from Brussels.

Industry

The decentralisation of industry had already begun under Salazar but despite the fact that Oporto, Setúbal, Aveiro and Braga are also important centres for industry Lisbon's harbour and good communications still make it the leading industrial location. The city's industry is mostly south of the Tagus and in the north-east, running along the river on a line between Lisbon and Vila Franca de Xira.

The big foreign companies – in petroleum, electrical goods, cars, chemicals and pharmaceuticals, and electronics – prefer to be located in and around the capital. The main Portuguese sectors sited here include chemicals, textiles, engineering, leather goods, timber, cork, and food processing.

Tourism

Portugal's income from tourism has grown at an extraordinary rate in recent years with Lisbon and the Algarve accounting for two-thirds of tourist facilities. While southern Portugal is very much favoured for the longer beach resort holidays, Lisbon is predominantly a destination for shorter sightseeing trips. There is little foreign tourism along its nearby coastal area. The majority of foreign visitors are from Spain, followed by the British and the Germans.

Communications

Port

Although Lisbon has not managed to maintain its earlier position as the biggest port on the Iberian peninsula, it is still the most important one in Portugal and, like the other Portuguese ports, has grown considerably in terms of its European significance since EC entry. Since this upward trend is expected to continue in the years to come, substantial investment in the port is planned, and it is being enlarged to take the giant vessels.

Airport

"Portela de Sacavém", Lisbon's international airport, is about 13km/8 miles north of the city centre, and is served by about 20 foreign airlines. TAP (Transportes Aéreos Portugueses), the national airline, operates domestic flights as well as flying to many of Europe's major cities, the former colonies, South Africa, and North and South America. Another large airport is due to be built 80km/50 miles south of Lisbon.

Rail

Portugal's rail network is as yet relatively underdeveloped, compared with the many long-distance bus routes, but the whole system is due to be overhauled in the next few years. It will be more closely linked with its Spanish counterpart, the international gauges will be realigned, and high-

Lisbon's trams – more than just a means of transport

Lisbon's trams – the "eléctricos" – look ready for the museum and probably are, but despite this fact, or perhaps because of it, the cityscape would be unthinkable without them. They are practical too, climbing gradients which cars would find difficult to negotiate in first gear, slipping with ease round hairpin bends, and gliding through narrow streets with the horrifying possibility of meeting oncoming traffic.

The system had its beginnings back in 1872 when needless to say the trams were horsedrawn. Many private carriages were also able to make use of the 1435mm/56in. gauge tracks, slotting their wheels into the tramlines, if they were the same distance apart, and enabling their horses to pull passengers and loads through the streets with a minimum of effort. That came to an end at the turn of the century when the gauge was reduced to 900mm/35in. The system was electrified in 1901/1902, and expanded in the years that followed, reaching its limit to date of 76km/47 miles in 1958.

A gradual decline set in the following year when the first metro stations were opened and other routes were abandoned in favour of buses. By 1972 it was actually felt that these curious old tramcars could be phased out altogether by 1977, but the new set of political circumstances meant that it was no longer the end of the line for Lisbon's up and downhill form of transport. Lisbon's population explosion in the mid-1970s, with the influx of people from the former overseas territories, meant the city could not afford to be without this traditional form of transport. The operators embarked on a modernisation programme, and many of the old trams were completely overhauled or replaced by new ones. Despite this ongoing programme of renovation and renewal trams which look virtually as they did when they first entered into service in 1906 can still be seen on the streets of Lisbon.

With luck it is possible to take a ride around Lisbon on one of these old trams – and experience just what it would have been like 85 years ago. Line 28 will provide a cross between a sightseeing tour and a trip on a rollercoaster, starting in the Graça quarter, passing the Igreja de São Vicente and carrying on down through the winding lanes of the Alfama. The first chance to breathe again comes after passing the cathedral where reassuringly the road opens out. Dashing through the Baixa the vehicle starts to climb up the 13.5% gradient, before brushing aside the heavy traffic on the Largo do Camões and moving on through the Calĉada do Combro. Soon comes the fine view of the Palácio de São Bento then the towers of the Basílica da Estrela loom up ahead and finally, after one last steep ascent, the journey ends at the terminus at the Prazeres cemetery.

The people of Lisbon have a very special relationship with "their" trams and are not prepared to do without them, even though they run practically at a loss. Since people have also become aware of their value as a tourist attraction there is a chance that the trams could be trundling around the streets of Lisbon for decades to come.

speed trains are to be introduced. Santa Apolónia, Lisbon's international station, is also to be extended. There is still no direct rail link between the capital and the south of the country, it being necessary first to take the ferry to the Barreiro station on the south bank of the Tagus.

Motorway, trunk roads

Portugal has developed a good network of fast main roads around the larger towns and cities. The only stretches of motorway around Lisbon are the A1 to the north and the A2 south to Setúbal. The motorway system is being extended, but currently there are only about 355km/220 miles of "auto estrada". These are tollroads that have been privately built and operated. A large number of national highways connect Lisbon with the country regions of Estremadura province to the north and west. The road directly south still has to negotiate the bottleneck of the extremely busy bridge over the Tagus.

Inner city public transport

Lisbon's buses are the main form of public transport in the inner city, carrying at least 400 million passengers around its 554km/344 miles of streets every year. Although the Lisbon underground, the Metro, which opened in 1959, is by far the fastest form of transport, its 16km/10 miles of track to date only cover a relatively small sector, and there have long been plans for its extension and modernisation. Lisbon's transport operator, Carris, makes its biggest losses on the antiquated trams, the "eléctricos" (see below), but these are likely to continue in service in the foreseeable future, particularly over the hilliest routes. Lifts and funiculars have also been in use for over a century to negotiate the steepest gradients.

Suburban public transport

Commuter traffic is mostly carried by buses and out-of-town trains running out of Rossio and Cais do Sodré stations. The ferries over the Tagus are another much used means of transport, taking about five million people a month from eight landing stages between the city and the southern shore.

Art and Culture

In something of a backwater from the European mainstream, Lisbon has for centuries been Portugal's cultural centre. It houses the country's leading museums and theatres, as well as the National Library, with over two million volumes, and the national archive in the Torre do Tombo. Within Greater Lisbon there are over 400 arts venues, plus 70 galleries and about 40 archives. Of Portugal's 1200 libraries just under 500 are to be found in and around the capital. Although traditionally Coimbra is Portugal's main university city Lisbon has, since 1911, also had a university again. Its original foundation was moved to Coimbra in 1308, 18 years after it was first established in Lisbon. The city also has public and private colleges of further education.

The Fundação Calouste Gulbenkian, wealthily endowed by oil millionaire Calouste Gulbenkian (see Famous People), plays a leading role in Lisbon's cultural life as well as that of Portugal as a whole. He has been responsible for a major museum, a centre for Portuguese modern art and performance venues in the city, not to mention an orchestra, a choir and a ballet company.

Portugal's music, art and literature have remained almost unknown beyond its frontiers. As the nation's capital, Lisbon has always been the meeting place for leading figures in the arts world, but many of them, through formative years spent abroad, mostly in France, Italy and Germany, have also drawn on the cultural mainstream flowing through the rest of Europe.

Music

Classical

Classical music in Portugal developed along similar lines to the other European countries until well into the 18th c. Most of the works then performed were Italian, and the change did not come until the founding of the Philharmonic Academy and the Lisbon Conservatoire in the 19th c., from which time Portugal increasingly developed its own national music. In fact, between 1793, when it reopened, and 1910 the opera house staged over 60 operas by Portuguese composers. In the 20th c. the most outstanding composers have been Luís de Freitas Branco and Ruy Coelho, both influenced by Schönberg, Frederico de Freitas and Fernando Lopes Graca. Jorge Peixinho, who studied with Luigi Nono and Pierre Boulez, and worked with Stockhausen, is probably the most important of the younger composers, and was the founder in 1970 of the Lisbon Contemporary Music Group. Of instrumental performers, the pianist Maria Joao Pires in particular has become internationally famous.

Rock and Pop

Portuguese rock and pop, although it has much in common with what is played by other western groups, also owes something to its national folk music. The top singers and groups are Fausto, Sérgio Godinho, Vitorino, and José Afonso, and Tovante, GNR, Delfins, Peste e Sida, Mler Ife Dada and Madredeus, while Maria Joao has won a name for herself abroad as a jazz singer.

Fado

The fado – usually described as a type of melancholy Portuguese folk song – traditionally plays an important role in Portugal, and in Lisbon it has assumed a character all of its own. Its origins are still a matter for dispute among the experts. One likely theory is that it evolved from an African dance, the lundum, that was taken by slaves to Brazil and then finally became known in Portugal, where the basically musical elements were converted into song. Another view is that the expressions of yearning and sadness often found in the fado's words and music indicate that it originated among Portuguese seafarers, sung by them on their long voyages away from home.

In the early 19th c. the fado spread through Lisbon's poorest quarters, Alfama, Mouraria and Bairro Alto, earning itself a shady reputation that lasted until it became socially acceptable during the 20th c., not least because it was taken up and interpreted by a member of the nobility. The solo fadista, male or female, is accompanied by two guitarists, one supplying the rhythm on the six-stringed viola, and the other playing the melody on the special fado guitar with English origins, the twelve-stringed guitarra. The songs are often about life in the cities, sometimes rather seamy little tales, or perhaps ballads of love, city streets and the Portuguese people. Fado from Lisbon is quite different from the fado of Coimbra. Although the Lisbon fado in particular still keeps mainly to its fatalistic and melancholy image, there are also some very lively and jolly songs as well.

Great interpreters of the fado always enjoyed a special status. Severa, the most famous fadista of the 19th c., became a kind of legend. She died at the age of 26 and a fado museum is due to be installed in the house in Mouraria where she lived. In this century Alfredo Marceneiro was very popular in Lisbon. Nowadays Amália Rodrigues (see Famous People) is perhaps the most celebrated of all the fadistas, even abroad, while Carlos do Carmo has written new fados many of which deal with the themes of everyday life in Lisbon, Carlos Paredes combines purely instrumental fado with elements from classical music, and jazz musician Rao Kyao plays fado on the saxophone.

History of Art

Portugal's artistic development began with its emergence as a nation in the 12th c., and throughout the centuries it has absorbed the lasting influences of Moorish culture, and then of its territories overseas in India, Africa and South America, as well as other European countries, and France and Italy in particular.

Although Portuguese Romanesque architecture (Sé Partriarcal) clearly

drew on that of France and Spain, the Manueline style (see below) is a typically Portuguese expression of Gothic in the transition to Renaissance. The architecture of the Renaissance never really established itself in Portugal because of the long continued use of Manueline features, and the country's economic and political decline. The chief architect of this period was Filippo Terzi, the Italian responsible for Lisbon's Igreja de São Roque. Renaissance artists of note included Nuno Gonçalves, Grão Vasco, Gregório Lopes, Cristóvão de Figueiredo and, somewhat later, Cristóvão de Morais. The great monastery-palace at Mafra is a monumental example of Portuguese Baroque. The work of two German architects, Johann Ludwig and his son, who trained in Rome, it also influenced late Baroque buildings such as the Basílica da Estrela. This period also saw the full flowering of the talha dourada, an ornate form of decorative art consisting of wood carving covered with gold leaf, mainly used as rich adornment for church interiors (Convento da Madre de Deus). The Baroque artist Pedro Carvalho Alexandrino made a name for himself with his painting of churches. The Palácio Nacional de Queluz was built to the designs of Mateus Vicente in Rococo style, and both palace and park were clearly influenced by Versailles. Another legacy from the 18th c. in the Lisbon area is the work of Joaquim Machado de Castro, many of whose sculptures are still to be seen here.
Rebuilding of the parts of Lisbon destroyed by the 1755 earthquake was carried out in accordance with the ideas of enlightened absolutism, providing an outstanding example of the European town planning of its day, and some Neo-classical buildings as well, such as Palácio de Ajuda, and Teatro Nacional Dona Maria II. Later in the 19th c. buildings such as the Palácio Nacional da Pena were constructed bearing all the marks of the romantic ecelectism of styles to be found in Historicism.
Monumental structures that made their mark in the 20th c. included the Padrão dos Descrobrimentos and the Monumento Cristo Rei, both epitomising the style of Salazar's "Estado Novo". The most important architect of the 1980s has been Tomás Taveira, the controversial builder of the Amoreiras Shopping Centre.
Portuguese painting in the 19th c. developed in a similar vein to elsewhere in Europe. In 1881 a number of artists came together in Lisbon to form the Grupo do Leão, closely allied to Impressionism. Columbano Bordalo Pinheiro, a painter of frescoes and portraits, was a leading member of this group and also director of the Museu de Arte Contemporânea.
In the 20th c. painting has tended to follow the major European movements, Cubism, Surrealism, Fauvism, etc. Major artists include Almada Negreiros, Amadeu de Souza Cardoso, Costa Pinheiro, Eduardo Viana and João Cutileiro, whose work can be seen in the Gulbenkian Foundation's Centre for Modern Art. Maria-Elena Vieira da Silva is one painter who has won herself an international reputation.

Manueline Style

As discovery and conquest overseas brought Portugal prosperity and its cultural heyday during the reign of Manuel I (see Famous People), a distinctively Portuguese style of architecture emerged. The Manueline style, named after the king, marked the transition from Gothic to Renaissance, but although it included features of late Gothic or early Renaissance the ornamentation largely reflected the events of the day. The constantly recurring themes of the crusader's cross, crowns and M for Manuel represent the sacred and secular moving spirits behind the voyages of discovery, while the equally ubiquitous armillary sphere, much used in those days for navigation, symbolises the seafarer. Stylised stone ropes, nets, shells and corals, also tropical flowers, leaves and fruit serve as reminders of voyaging and contacts with distant lands. Portuguese architects brought back fresh ideas derived from hitherto unknown cultures and incorporated them in their buildings, thus accounting for the Far Eastern and Indian elements of their style. The leading Manueline masters included Diogo de Boytaca (see Famous People), Diogo de Arruda, Francisco de Arruda and João de Castilho, and the Mosteiro dos Jerónimos and the Torre de Belém are examples in Lisbon of their buildings.

Decorative tiles, seen everywhere . . .

. . . and as an advertisement

Mosaic pavements

Artistically composed mosaic pavements, in a great variety of designs and motifs, are a feature of any walk around Lisbon. They often incorporate Lisbon's coat of arms, or a business's address or trademark, and there is the occasional animal or simple geometric pattern. The mosaic of waves on the Rossio commemorates Portugal's traditional importance as a nation of seafarers. For a long while this pattern covered most of the square but it has had to give way almost entirely to the traffic. The 1755 earthquake is supposed to have given the people of Lisbon the idea of making mosaic pieces from the marble rubble and thus reinforce their street paving. This work was taken on by the "calceteiros" and there were in fact about 400 of these workmen still employed in Lisbon in the early decades of the 20th c. but today their numbers have dwindled to barely 30 who are poorly paid. For renovation work or recreation of the traditional patterns they use the old, carefully archived wooden templates.

Azulejos

Visitors to Lisbon cannot fail to be struck by the many churches, chapels and palaces that are decorated with "azulejos" – often whole house fronts are covered with these decorative tiles.

Azulejos – which probably get their name from the Arabic "az-zuleycha", for mosaic pieces, rather than "azul", which is Spanish/Portuguese for blue – are ceramic tiles which were originally imported into Portugal in the early 16th c. from Spain, where they were made by Moorish craftsmen in blue and other ground colours, with geometric patterns in relief.

After the Moors were expelled from Spain towards the end of the 16th c. and Moorish-made tiles were no longer available, numbers of azulejo factories were established in Portugal, particularly in Lisbon, Oporto and Coimbra, producing Portuguese tiles with new decorative motifs. These tiles, however, were no longer made in relief patterns but were flat, in the manner of Italian and Flemish majolica. They were now given a white tin glaze on which the designs were painted in metallic pigments. What is

House façade with azulejos in the Alfama

probably the oldest tile picture in Portugal, dating from 1565, is to be seen in the Quinta de Bacalhoa, to the west of Setúbal.

Characteristic of the 17th c. are the "tile tapestries" (tapetes), with a great variety of patterns in blue, white and yellow. Mass production of azulejos began with the establishment by King José in 1767 of the Royal Factory (Real Fábrica do Rato) at Lisbon. Every conceivable surface – the walls of churches, staircases, fountains, benches, the exterior and interior walls of palaces, churches, etc. – was now covered with tiles.

In the early 19th c., when the court fled to Brazil and the country was convulsed by civil war, the production of azulejos ceased almost completely, but in the middle of the century they enjoyed a revival in popularity. Following the Brazilian model, tiles now began to be used for the decoration, both externally and internally, of ordinary middle-class houses and commercial, municipal and other public buildings throughout the country. There was a final flowering of the art of the azulejo at the turn of the 19th c. Tile-clad buildings have the advantage over stone or plaster surfaces of retaining a fresh, trim appearance – although the more recent azulejos, mass-produced in standard designs, are seldom of high artistic quality. Present-day azulejo factories – notably three large firms in Lisbon – concentrate mainly on reproductions of old designs and export most of their output (mainly to the United States, Holland and Germany).

A good impression of the range and variety of Portuguese azulejos is provided by the Azulejo Museum in the Madre de Deus convent, the cloisters of the old Augustinian house of São Vicente de Fora and the Fronteira Palace, all in Lisbon.

Famous People

The following famous people were all connected in some way with Lisbon, whether as the place of their birth or death, or because they lived or worked there.

Diogo de Boytaca (*c.* 1470–1520)

Although the exact dates of the life of the architect Diogo de Boytaca (or Boytac or Boitaca) are uncertain, he is known to have been working between about 1490 and 1520. Nor is it known for sure whether he was French, Italian or in fact Portuguese – although the fact that there is a village near Batalha with the similar-sounding name of Boutaca may well indicate that he was.

Boytaca is inextricably linked with the Manueline style of architecture, and his buildings are almost without exception characterised by their exuberant decoration. His first major work was the Convent of Jesus at Setúbal, then after 1509 he played a leading role in the building of the abbey at Batalha and, after 1514, the Hieronymite convent at Belém. He also worked on the palace at Sintra, and in Galegã, Caldas da Rainha and Montemor-o-Velho, and was responsible for a large number of fortifications in North Africa.

Luis Vaz de Camões (1524/1525–80)

Lisbon and Coimbra both lay claim to being the birthplace of Luis Vaz de Camões, probably Portugal's most important poet. His date of birth is also uncertain, and may be either 1524 or 1525. He came from a prominent Portuguese family, his father having been appointed by the King to the command of one of his ships.

After studying in Coimbra, Camões went to Lisbon. There he gained entry to the court, writing poetry and plays to order, only soon to be banished from court circles on account of a love affair. In the hope of an earlier return to favour he volunteered to fight in North Africa where he lost his right eye in a skirmish. He was scarcely back in Lisbon again before he was sent to prison in 1552 for taking part in a duel. He was pardoned, but had to leave the country. He was first sent to Goa, where he once again fell from grace and resumed his travels, this time apparently to Macau. His post which involved responsibility for the dead and missing in China left him enough time to devote to his verse. He is supposed to have written his great epic "The Lusiads" (Os Lusiadas, a reference to Lusus, the mythical ancestor of the Portuguese) in the cave that today bears his name.

Camões did not return to Lisbon until 1570, and "The Lusiads" were first published there two years later. Even then, however, fate failed to smile on Camões, nowadays revered as Portugal's national poet, and he lived out his last years in abject poverty. He died of the plague in 1580 on June 10th, now celebrated as a national holiday.

Calouste Sarkis Gulbenkian (1869–1955)

It is difficult for a visitor to Lisbon not to come across the name Gulbenkian. The son of a well-to-do Armenian oil dealer, Calouste Sarkis Gulbenkian was born near Istanbul on March 1st 1869. He studied engineering in London, apparently with such success that as early as 1891 he was appointed oil consultant to the Ottoman court. In the years that followed he became one of the top experts in his field, and in 1911 he founded the Iraq Petroleum Company, incorporating all the biggest oil companies of the day. Gulbenkian's 5% share of the profits won him the nickname "Mr Five Per Cent" and also a huge fortune: at times he was reckoned to be the richest man in the world.

Gulbenkian invested most of his wealth in Britain, having in fact held British nationality since 1902. At the start of the Second World War, however, the British confiscated Gulbenkian's assets as "enemy property". His efforts to leave the country finally met with success when he managed to travel to

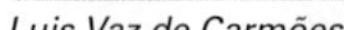

Luis Vaz de Carmões

Calouste Sarkis Gulbenkian

Marquês de Pombal

neutral Portugal in 1942. He settled in Lisbon, living in a suite in the Aviz Hotel (now the Sheraton) and set about rebuilding his fortune.
Calouste Gulbenkian's great love, after the oil business, was art ("I'm head over heels in love with beauty and every form of artistic expression"). Before the war and during his stay in Lisbon he collected fine works of art, buying Egyptian statues and French furniture, Chinese porcelain and Turkish faïence, as well as works by Rembrandt, Rubens, Van Dyck, Frans Hals, Degas and Monet. Over the years he purchased some 5000 items, giving him ownership of one of the greatest private collections in the world.
Gulbenkian lived in Lisbon until his death in 1955, and bequeathed his whole estate, said to be over 66 million dollars, and works of art worth at that time 15 million dollars, to the Fundação Calouste Gulbenkian.
This foundation built a large cultural centre with several theatres, concert halls and cinemas, a library and a museum that has become world-famous since its opening in 1969. A centre for modern art was added to the complex in 1984.

Manuel I
(1469–1521)

Manuel (or Emanuel) I is also known as Manuel "the Great" or "the Fortunate" because it was under him that Portugal experienced its golden age. He was born in 1469, the youngest son of the Infante Fernando. When the Infante Afonso, heir to the throne, died unexpectedly after a riding accident, Manuel was proclaimed King in Alcacer do Sal on October 27th 1495. Manuel used his marriage policy to establish close links with the Spanish royal house. His first marriage, in 1497, was to Isabella of Castile, the widow of the Infante Alfonso. After her death he married her sister, Maria of Castile, who was to provide him with his heir, João III. His third and last wife was Leonor of Spain, who had, in fact, been promised to his son.
Manuel I's rule was aimed at strengthening royal power against the nobility. Administration was centralised, taxation and customs duties were standardised, and the "Fortunate King" was able to keep his country out of any wars. Above all, however, Manuel's reign is associated with the voyages of discovery which he encouraged, primarily because of his trading policy. It was on his orders that Vasco da Gama found the sea route to India and Pedro Alvares Cabral sailed to Brazil. These seafaring feats made Lisbon Europe's paramount trading port, and riches poured into the country, leading to a great flowering in the arts and sciences and, above all, architecture. In their magnificent buildings Belém, Batalha and Tomar still bear impressive witness to the Manueline Style named after the king.
Portugal's "Golden Age" was, however, only short-lived and had already passed its peak when Manuel died of a fever in Lisbon in 1521.

Fernando Pessoa
(1888–1935)

During his lifetime Fernando Pessoa – Fernando António Noguiera Pessoa, to give him his full name – who is considered to be Portugal's greatest poet

after Camões, published nothing but various articles in newspapers and journals and just the one book. Only after his death was the discovery made of two trunks full of manuscripts, primarily fragments.
Fernando Pessoa was born in Lisbon on June 13th 1888. His childhood was sadly clouded by the premature death of his father. On his monther's second marriage, to the Portuguese consul in Durban, the whole family moved to South Africa. Pessoa grew up to be bilingual, enjoyed a good education and composed his first poems in English; until his death he continued to write poetry and stories in both English and Portuguese. Pessoa went back to Portugal at the age of seventeen with the intention of studying at the University of Lisbon, but found it hard to settle down there. He soon abandoned his studies, and made poetic writing the most important thing in his life. He earned his living doing foreign language correspondence for various Lisbon firms, and since this only afforded him a modest income, lived with relatives or in furnished rooms.
To stop himself feeling lonely Fernando Pessoa had already begun as a boy to create companions to talk to in his poetry, and as an adult he lived almost without any human ties, in total isolation. He overcame this by using several different names as a poet, signing his work not only with his own name but also Alberto Caeira, Alvaro de Campos and Ricardo Reis. For Pessoa each of these represented an independent poetic personality complete with his own particular biography, style, and choice of themes.
Pessoa's utter introspection meant that his private life was virtually blameless. Apart from his mother there was only one woman in his life, a colleague called Ophélia. It was, by his own account, consideration for his poetic work that made him decide not to marry her.
Towards the end of his life Pessoa lapsed increasingly into alcoholism, dying of liver failure on November 30th 1935.

Sebastião José de Carvalho e Mello Marquês de Pombal (1699–1782)

The Marquês de Pombal made a decisive impact on the history of his country as the man who paved the way for enlightened despotism. Born into Lisbon's minor aristocracy, his first experiences of the diplomatic service were as envoy to London and Vienna, where he also particularly concerned himself with economic matters. José I appointed him Foreign Secretary in 1750 and Prime Minister in 1756.
Pombal proved adept at filling the offices he held wholly in accordance with his own views; however, he showed little sign of squeamishness in his choice of the means he judged necessary to achieve his long-term ends. He saw his most important tasks as reorganising state finances, reforming education, promoting trade and industry so as to get free of Britain's economic hegemony, and the abolition of slavery.
The part he played in the reconstruction of Lisbon after the devastating earthquake of 1755 was outstanding. He fought passionately with the Jesuits and minor nobility whose inherited privilege stood in the way of his attempts at reform.
The Marquês lost favour after the death of José I and in 1781 the pressure from his many enemies brought about his banishment to Pombal where he died the following year.

José Maria Eça de Queirós (1845–1900)

Eça de Queirós won fame for his epic novels in which he takes a long and quizzical look at Portuguese society in the late 19th c. His portrayals are very much influenced by the works of the French School of Realism. Born in Póvoa de Varzim in 1845, José Maria Eça de Queirós was raised by his grandmother, and was 40 before his parents acknowledged that he was their son, a complex situation that became a recurring theme of his work. He studied Law at Coimbra University, where he was already joining literary circles intent on creating a stir in Portuguese literary life and awakening it with their new ideas. His first works, published in the "Gazeta de Portugal" in 1866, clearly show the influence of Baudelaire and early French Symbolism. In his "Lectures in Lisbon Casino" in 1871, he finally airs his opinions on Realism as a new form of artistic expression. He wrote his first novel "O Crime do Padre Amaro" (Padre Amaro's Crime) under the

influence of life in the provicial town of Leiria, where he was a civil servant for a year. His work in the diplomatic corps took him to Cuba, the North of England, and finally Paris, where he died in 1900.
"The Maias", published in 1888, is just one of the many novels in which he holds a mirror to Lisbon society and its life.

Amália da Piedade Rodriques (born 1920)

Amália Rodrigues, or just Amália as they call her in Portugal, and the most famous fado singer of the 20th c., was born in July 1920 in Lisbon, where she grew up in dire poverty, living with her grandparents in the waterfront quarter of Alcântara. Her extraordinary voice attracted attention quite early on, and she soon realised it was easier to earn money from singing than from selling fruit in the street, which was how she and her sister Celeste had been making a meagre living until then.
At the age of 18, Amália embarked on a storybook rags to riches career, taking her from life on the waterfront to international stardom. Aged 19 she made her first stage appearance at the "Retiro da Severa", then a famous Lisbon fado venue, and a year later had her first success in the musical theatre. At 23 she made her début abroad, in Madrid, and not long after was singing in Paris at the Olympia, in Casablanca, Rio de Janeiro, Rome, and Berlin, later appearing in Sweden, Turkey, Japan, the USSR, Africa and North and South America, performing the Portuguese fado all over the world. Her greatest and best-loved successes were, and still are, "uma casa portuguesa", "nem às paredes confesso" and "barco negro". In the 1940s Amália also appeared in several of the best known Portuguese films as the "fadista", the singer of the fado.
An indication of her enormous popularity was the grand exhibition dedicated to this great fadista, a legend in her own lifetime, which was staged in Lisbon's Theatre Museum to mark her 70th birthday and 50 years on the stage. This coincided with the publication of her biography and five new records of her greatest hits.

António de Oliviera Salazar (1889–1970)

António de Oliveira Salazar was responsible for Portugal living under Europe's longest dictatorship in the 20th c.
Born on 28th April 1889, in the village of Vimieiro in the Dão Valley, Salazar was the son of an agricultural worker who later became farm steward. He grew up in simple circumstances, his childhood very much marked by his family's strong Catholicism. He was educated by the Jesuits at their seminary in Viseu, then in 1910 went to Coimbra to study law and economics, financing his studies by undertaking various teaching duties. In 1916 he became professor of economics at Coimbra, and having acted as finance minister for a short time in 1926, was finally brought to Lisbon by President Carmona in 1928 to bring order into the country's finances. He averted the economic crisis but at the expense of the weak in society while increasing his power base. In 1930 he founded the Fascist Unity Party, "União Nacional", and in 1932 he became Prime Minister. The new constitution that he had adopted by plebiscite in 1933 provided him with the foundations for the "Estado Novo", an elitist, authoritarian state on the Fascist model with only about 16% of the population entitled to vote, and the disenfranchisement of women without secondary school qualifications and anyone not able to read or write. Censorship was introduced, and intellectual and the politically suspect were watched and persecuted by the PIDE, the State secret police, who resorted to Gestapo tactics on anyone arrested. The independence movements in Portugal's overseas possessions were ruthlessly suppressed, leading to the colonial wars of the 1960s. Salazar's private life was lived in seclusion, and unlike other dictators he hated any kind of a personality cult. He had few if any friends, and his only close relationship would appear to have been with his housekeeper. Following an accident in 1968 Salazar suffered a stroke which left him disabled. Marcelo Caetano was appointed Prime Minister, but right until he died on July 27th 1970 Salazar believed that he was still in charge.

Dom Sebastião (c. 1554–78)

Dom Sebastião, Sebastian I, was a Portuguese king who owes his special significance to the myth that has grown up around him, rather than to what he was really like.

Dom Sebastião was born in 1554. His father had died shortly before his birth so, in 1557, on the death of his grandfather João III, he became successor to the throne. A brother of João III acted as regent until Dom Sebastião, or "the longed-for one" as he had been known since birth, assumed the reins of government for himself at the age of 14. He is said to have been arrogant and a religious fanatic, and one of his major concerns was to bring North Africa into the Kingdom of Christ. He led a crusade to Morocco in 1578. The ensuing battle of Alcácer-Kibir was a resounding defeat, and 8000 soldiers lost their lives, the young king among them. The people in Lisbon refused to believe this, and for many a long year they lived in hope that he would return. "The longed-for one" failed to reappear, however, although quite a few "pretenders" did.

Since that time, Sebastião has been idealised as a knightly figure, who, when times are bad, will hopefully ride to the rescue and right all wrongs at a stroke. "Sebastianism" has even been coined as a term to indicate the fatalistic and "something will turn up" approach that supposedly typifies much of Portugal. "Saudade", closely allied with Sebastianism, is also viewed as typical of Portugal since both concepts share the idea of thoughts, dreams and hopes dwelling on the past and also resulting in passive fatalism, both recurring themes in Portuguese art, music and literature.

Gil Vicente (c. 1465–1536)

Little is known in any detail of the life of Gil Vicente, the founder of the Portuguese theatre. Thought to have been born in Guimarães in northern Portugal, he arrived in about 1500 at the royal court in Lisbon where his famous "autos" (plays with music and dancing), comedies and farces were performed. Very probably the playwright was also a goldsmith, and in fact the famous monstrance from the Mosteiro dos Jerónimos (now in the Museo de Arte Antiga) is attributed to him.

A sharp-eyed and critical observer of his times, Gil Vicente's plays give a picture, in down-to-earth language, of Portugal in the early 16th c. when its voyages of discovery were bringing the country growing importance and riches. His knowledge of life at court and his bonds with the people led him to expose social injustice and political abuse. He did not spare the Church, either, and in 1534 was one of the first to be sentenced to two years' imprisonment by the Inquisition. He made a further appearance at the royal court with an autobiographical play, and died in about 1536 in Évora, where he is buried in the church of São Francisco.

His work was not published until after his death, and these were not the complete works, either, since some plays have clearly been lost or bowdlerised. It is considered possible by scholars of literature that his work may well have influenced Goethe and Calderón.

History of the City

From 1200 B.C. Its favourable situation has meant that the area around what is now Lisbon has been settled by various trading peoples since the Stone Age, with the castle hill offering the right conditions for settlement, and the River Tagus, which originally flooded the whole of the Baixa, forming a sheltered bay. It is on this bay, at the foot of the castle hill, that the Phoenicians establish a trading port which they call "Alis Ubbo" (i.e. "still bay"). They are followed by Carthaginians and Greeks who name the port "Olissipo", derived from Odysseus or Ulysses, who, according to legend, is the founder of the city.

205 B.C. Lisbon becomes Roman. Under Julius Caesar it receives the name of "Felicitas Julia" and is the administrative capital of the province of Lusitania. The remains of thermal baths, an amphitheatre and temples found after the 1755 earthquake date from this Roman era.

5th c. A.D. During the great migration of the Germanic peoples, the Alans, Vandals and Visigoths attempt to occupy the site.

585 Lisbon comes under the rule of the Visigoths. King Reccared and the Visigoths convert to Catholicism, and the persecution of the Jews begins soon afterwards.

714 Under Arabic rule the city is named Al Oshbuna or Lishbuna by the Moors, and their townplanning, architecture, farming and fishing skills, and knowledge of navigation leave a lasting mark on Portuguese culture. Many names that today begin with "al" (Alfama, Alcântara, Algarve, etc.) are indicative of Arabic origins.

735–1147 During the Reconquista (the recovery of Arab-occupied territory by the Christians) there are many unsuccessful attempts to expel the Arabs from Lisbon.

1147 During the Second Crusade Afonso Henriques, the first king of Portugal captures Lisbon with the help of English, German and Flemish crusaders. Churches are built in the place of many old mosques, and the Moors are confined to the present-day quarter of "Mouraria", outside the city gates. The city is called Lixboa, later Lisboa.

1179 Pope Alexander III recognises Portugal as a kingdom. Lisbon receives city rights, and gradually extends its area to include the western hills and what is now the lower town.

1241 The Dominicans settle on the Rossio, leading to the growth of this part of the city's activity and importance.

c. 1250 Portugal as the first European state reaches the limits of its territorial expansion which remain unchanged to the present day.

1256 Lisbon becomes the capital of Portugal, displacing Coimbra.

1290 The first Portuguese university is founded in Lisbon (later transferred in 1307/8 to Coimbra).

1337, 1344, 1347 Earthquakes. Sé Patriarcal, the Cathedral, is one of the buildings that are badly damaged.

1348 The first great plague, which flares up intermittently in subsequent decades, claims many lives and leads to the city's temporary decline and the weakening of its economy.

Under Fernando I a 54km/34 mile-long wall is built around the old parts of the city, the lower town and some of the upper town. A population of about 60,000 live in an area of 1.02sq.km/¼sq.mile. Fernando I introduces oil lamps as lighting for the city.	1367–83
João I founds the House of Avis after the extinction of the male line of the House of Burgundy	1383
João's victory over Castile at Aljubarrota consolidates the independence of Portugal. Following the victory João fulfils his vow to establish a Carmelite monastery (Igreja do Carmo) in Lisbon. With the strengthening and expansion of the merchant shipping fleet Lisbon becomes a major centre for trade.	1385
Lisbon becomes an archbishopric.	1393
Start of the African slave trade.	Early 15th c.
Many expeditions are embarked on during the reign of João II. These voyages of discovery and conquest start out from Lisbon, not Lagos. The Portuguese reach the mouth of the Congo, Bartolomeu Dias rounds the Cape of Good Hope, the southern tip of Africa.	1481–95
The first printing press is used in Lisbon.	1487
The "Golden Age" coincides with the reign of Manuel I, the Fortunate. The twofold momentum behind the major voyages of discovery under the flag of the crusaders comes from trade on the one hand and the expansion of Christendom on the other. Manuel I lays the foundation for Portugal's trading empire by establishing trading posts in the East Indies, Eastern Asia, South Africa and Brazil. Lisbon becomes the world's biggest port, and the focal point of world trade, amassing vast wealth in a very short time. It expands beyond the area enclosed by the old city wall, and the Hieronymite convent and Tower of Belém are built in the extravagant style characteristic of the Manueline era, showing the distinctive features of the architects Francisco de Arruda and Diogo de Boytaca.	1495–1521
Many Jews who had fled from Spain not long before to Portugal, where they thought at first they would be safe from persecution, are forced, under Manuel I, to be baptised as Christians. Since the statutory penalty for refusal is immediate deportation, this is to be avoided if at all possible because of the economic consequences.	1496
Vasco da Gama discovers the sea route to India.	1498
Pedro Alvares Cabral reaches Brazil.	1500
Thousands of Jews and "new Christians" are killed in disturbances.	1506
The King moves his official residence from the Castelo de São Jorge into the new Palace on the Terreiro do Paço (now the Praça do Comércio), effectively transferring the city's centre from the castle hill and that part of town, to the riverfront.	1511
The Bairro Alto starts to become part of the city as it is divided up into plots which are sold for building.	1513
Under João III the colonial empire in the Far East disintegrates and economic prosperity starts to wane.	1521–57
Thousands of inhabitants (estimates vary between 1000 and 30,000) lose their lives in a severe earthquake which destroys part of the city, but Lisbon initially manages to retain its importance as a major trading centre.	1531

History of the City

1536 The Inquisition is introduced, with the persecution of Jews, Jewish Christians, atheists, witches and Christians who do not conform to the Inquisitors' views on society, or who stand out because of their lifestyle, philosophy or attitude.

1540 The Inquisition holds its first auto da fé in Lisbon, when sentences on heretics are publicly pronounced and executed, usually by burning alive. The inquisitors install themselves in the Palácio dos Estaus, later the site of the Teatro Nacional Dona Maria II. The auto da fé is mainly staged on the Rossio or the Terreiro do Paço, later to become the Praça do Comércio. Censorship is introduced, and an index of banned books is published in 1547. The arrival of the Jesuits lends added momentum to the Portuguese Counter Reformation. In 1553 the Jesuits found the Colégio de Santo Antão, and two years later the Igreja de São Roque.

1558 Fernão Mendes Pinto returns to Lisbon from 20 years of travels in the Far East and gives a critical account of the great voyages of discovery and their less pleasant side-effects in "Peregrinação", originally a banned book.

1569 The plague claims about 60,000 lives.

1572 Publication of "The Lusiads" by Luis Vaz de Camões in which he mainly glorifies the voyages of discovery and conquest as a heroic epic.

1578 Sebastian I, the legendary Dom Sebastião (see Famous People), embarks on a crusade against Morocco, and loses his life in the disastrous battle of Alcácer-Kibir.

1580–1640 Portugal is forcibly occupied and brought under Spanish rule. In 1581 Philip II of Spain is recognised as Filipe I of Portugal. He brings with him the Italian architect Filippo Terzi, who draws up plans for the reconstruction of the church of São Vicente de Fora and for other buildings, and has a marked influence on the architectural style of the age. During this period Portugal loses part of its colonial empire through defeats at sea by the Spanish.

1640 On December 1st, several Portuguese nobles rise up successfully against the Spanish Government and restore Portugal's independence. The Duke of Bragança becomes King João IV of Portugal and founder of the House of Bragança. Spain does not recognise Portugal's independence until 1688 and the Treaty of Lisbon.

1641 Appearance of "Gazeta", the first Portuguese newspaper, initially to report events in the war of the Spanish Succession.

1706–50 Under its spendthrift King João V, Portugal becomes totally impoverished despite its vast holdings in Brazilian gold and diamond mines, and grows financially dependent on Great Britain. João V uses Brazilian gold to finance grandiose church and state buildings, while leaving essential public amenities, such as the aqueduct, to be paid for from taxes.

1724 A disastrous storm sinks sixty-two ships on the Tagus at Lisbon.

1750–77 The reign of King José I is the great age of enlightened absolutism in Portugal. His controversial chief minister, the Marquês de Pombal, carries through a series of reforms based on the principles of the Enlightenment and Mercantilism, chiefly concerned with education, trade and industry, state finances and the organisation of the army.

1755 On All Saints' Day, November 1st, Lisbon and its outlying districts are rocked by a devastating earthquake: thousands of citizens lose their lives, and a large part of the city is utterly destroyed, together with major treasures of its cultural heritage. This disaster, which shocks the world, signifies a decisive break in Lisbon's development.

Assent to the plans for reconstruction is given as early as January. Pombal 1756
makes a name for himself by the speed with which he reacts, and the rapid rate at which the ruined parts of the city are rebuilt. By 1760 people are moving into the newly built streets of the lower town.

Expulsion of the Jesuits from Portugal and the Portuguese colonies and 1759
confiscation of their property.

Abolition of the slave trade. 1761

After the death of José I the authoritarian Pombal is compelled to go into 1777
exile. During the reign of Maria I, clerical reaction triumphs with the return of the Jesuits. Most of Pombal's reforms are reversed and the ideas of the Enlightenment are combated with the help of the Inquisition.

The very first order is placed for a steam engine, to be bought from London. 1778

The Royal Academy of Sciences is founded in Lisbon 1779

Introduction of more widespread street lighting, still with oil lamps. 1780

Last Inquisition auto da fé in Lisbon. 1794

Introduction of paper money. 1797

Opening of Lisbon's first post office. 1800

Introduction of public cemeteries. 1805

Napoleon's troops, under General Junot, march into Portugal. The royal 1807
family flees to Brazil.

Appearance of "Diário Lisbonense", the first daily paper. 1809

A liberal revolution starts in Oporto and spreads to Lisbon. The Inquisition 1820
is abolished.

On his return from Brazil João VI is forced to confirm the liberal constitution 1821
proclaimed by the Cortes.
Foundation of "Banco de Lisboa", the Portuguese bank that is later to become the "Banco de Portugal". The first steamer joins the shipping on the Tagus.

Brazil gains independence. Deprived of its gold supply, Portugal plunges 1822
into a serious economic crisis.

With British help, João VI defeats a conspiracy, directed against the new 1824
liberal measures, which is supported by his wife Carlotta and their younger son Dom Miguel. Miguel is banished from Portugal.

On the death of João VI, his elder son Pedro, now King Pedro I of Brazil, 1826
abdicates the Portuguese crown in favour of his seven-year-old daughter Maria da Glória (Maria II), promulgating a moderate constitution and appointing his brother Miguel as Regent.

Miguel has himself made king, revokes the constitution and harshly perse- 1828
cutes the liberals.

Civil wars between the supporters of Miguel's reactionary regime and the 1832–34
liberals under Pedro, now returned from Brazil. The Liberals succeed in overcoming the Miguelists, and Miguel is exiled.

On her father's death Maria da Glória becomes queen as Maria II. Religious 1834
orders are dissolved, and their land and property sold to nobles and wealthy burghers.

Rulers of Portugal

House of Burgundy

Henrique (Henry of Burgundy) Count of Portucalia	1093–1112
After Henry's death his widow Teresa acts as Regent during the minority of her son Afonso	
Afonso I Henriques, the Conqueror King of Portugal	1139–85
Sancho I, the Populator	1185–1211
Afonso II	1211–23
Sancho II (deposed 1245, d. 1248)	1223–45
Afonso III, the Restorer (brother of Sancho II)	1245–79
Dinis I, the Farmer	1279–1325
Afonso IV, the Brave	1325–57
Pedro I, the Cruel or the Inexorable	1357–67
Fernando I	1367–83

House of Avis

João I, Defender of the Kingdom (illegitimate son of Pedro I; Grand Master of the Order of Avis) Regent	1383–85
King of Portugal	1385–1433
Duarte (Eduard) I	1433–38
His brothers are Pedro (Duke of Coimbra), Henrique (Henry the Navigator), Fernão (d. in Moorish captivity) and João (Grand Master of the Order of Santiago)	
Afonso V, the African	1438–81
João II, the Perfect Prince	1481–95
Manuel I, the Great, the Fortunate	1495–1521
João III	1521–57
Sebastião (grandson of João III)	1557–78
Henrique II (brother of João III; Cardinal Archbishop of Lisbon)	1578–80

Spanish Kings of the House of Hapsburg

Filipe I (Philip II of Spain) King of Portugal	1580–98
Filipe II (Philip III of Spain)	1598–1621
Filipe III (Philip IV of Spain)	1621–40

House of Bragança

João IV (Duke of Bragança) King of Portugal	1640–56
Afonso VI	1656–67
Pedro II (brother of Afonso VI) Regent	1667–83
King	1683–1706
João V, the Magnanimous	1706–50
José I	1750–77
Maria I (wife of Pedro III, who d. 1786)	1777–92
João VI Prince Regent	1792–1816
King	1816–26
Pedro IV (Emperor Pedro I of Brazil)	1826–28
Miguel I (brother of Pedro IV)	1828–34
Maria II da Glória (daughter of Pedro IV; m. Duke Ferdinand of Saxe-Coburg-Koháry 1836)	1834–53
Duke Ferdinand rules as Regent during the minority of his son Pedro	1853–55
Pedro V	1855–61
Luis I	1861–89
Carlos I (assassinated in Lisbon in 1908 with his heir Luis Filipe)	1889–1908
Manuel II (second son of Carlos I; leaves Portugal 1910, d. in exile 1932)	1908–10

Reintroduction of the liberal constitution of 1821, to be replaced only two years later by a more moderate constitution. Founding of the Conservatoire and Academy of Arts. 1836

First Portuguese industrial exhibition. Founding of first trade union. 1838

The first use of steam power in industry. Portugal's industrial revolution is relatively late in starting and only makes slow progress. In Lisbon factories are built along the Tagus between the inner city and Belém. Industry does not settle on the riverbank east of the city until later, when worker districts are also built there. 1840

Gas street lighting. 1848

Portugal's first railway line is built. The Lisbon–Carregado line follows three years later. 1853

Portugal's first telegraph lines. 1855

The first edition of the Lisbon daily newspaper "Diário de Noticias" appears in December. 1864

Opening of Santa Apolónia station. 1865

The Civil Code enters into force. Abolition of the death penalty. 1867

"O Americano", the horse tram, enters the public transport system. 1873

Founding of the Portuguese Socialist Party 1875

Electric streetlights go up on the Chiado. 1878

The building of the grand Avenida da Liberdade starts off rapid expansion of the city towards the north. 1879

The "Elevador da Lavra" becomes Lisbon's first funicular; the "Elevador de Glória" follows in 1885. 1884

Electric streetlighting on the Avenida da Liberdade. Opening of the railway tunnel going north-west out of the city from the Rossio Station, which is itself officially opened in 1890. 1889

Lisbon's population virtually doubles between 1864 and 1890 to about 300,000, and the city extends over more than 80sq.km/30sq.miles. 1890

Lisbon's first public film show. 1896

Opening of the electric tramline by the Tagus along the Praça do Comércio towards Belém. 1901

First telephone connection between Lisbon and Oporto. 1904

Growing dissatisfaction among the population and the rising wave of republicanism lead to a crisis of the monarchy. Carlos I attempts to rule without Parliament, with his minister João Franco exercising dictatorial powers. 1906–08

Carlos is assassinated in the Praça do Comércio together with the heir to the throne, Luis Filipe. 1908

Manuel II, Carlos's younger son, is unable to save the monarchy. The revolution in Lisbon forces him to abdicate and flee to Britain. A republic is 1908–10 declared on October 5th 1910, and Teófilo Braga, the acting president, forms an anti-clerical government.

1911 Separation of State and Church (April 20th). Republic constitution comes into force (September 11th); Manoel d'Arriaga becomes President (1911–15). Reforms are carried through, but not the urgently needed land reform. Party strife among the Republicans, who are divided among themselves, and such problems as political corruption and the continuing financial crisis prevent the formation of a stable government. Between 1911 and 1926 under eight presidents there are no fewer than 44 governments. Re-establishment of Lisbon University.

1917/1918 Sidónio Pais starts the attempts to form a dictatorial government. He is assassinated on Rossio station in 1918.

1919/20 Dissatisfaction with the ineffectiveness and lack of credibility of the constantly changing governments increasingly leads to strikes and disturbances.

1926 General Manuel de Olveira Gomes da Costa instigates a military coup. He dissolves Parliament, forms a military dictatorship and suspends the constitution. The Communist Party is banned.

1927 Gomes da Costa is displaced by General António Oscar de Fragosa Carmona, who represses uprisings in Oporto and Lisbon aimed at returning to a parliamentary regime.

1928 Carmona becomes President and puts down several revolts against the military dictatorship. All worker organisations are banned. The economist António de Oliveira Salazar (see Famous People) becomes Minister of Finance. His drastic economy measures, at the expense of the socially weak, quickly resolve the financial crisis. He becomes Portugal's leading political personality.

1930 Salazar founds União Nacional, his Fascist national unity party. The political secret police, "PIDE" (Policia Internacional e de Defesa do Estado), also start their work.

1932 Salazar becomes prime minister.

1933 The constitution of the fascist "Estado Novo" (New State), which has close links with the Catholic church, is ratified by a plebiscite. Illiterates (in 1960 still 38% of the population) and women with no secondary school qualification are disenfranchised. The constitution also affirms the colonial policy in Portugal's African possessions, bans strikes and abolishes trade unions.

1939–45 Portugal's neutrality in the Second World War enables many Germans to flee overseas via Lisbon.

1940 Portugal marks the 800th anniversary of its nationhood and the 300th anniversary of regaining its independence from Spain by staging a grand International Exhibition in Belém as a celebration of the nation's great past.

1959 Opening of the first section of the Lisbon Underground.

1964 Fire destroys the interior of the Teatro Nacional Dona Maria II.

1966 The opening of the bridge over the Tagus improves communications by linking the capital with the south of Portugal, and helps extend Lisbon's commuter area to the south bank of the river.

Salazar suffers a stroke after falling out of a deck chair. He dies in 1970, and 1968
is succeeded by his longtime colleague, the lawyer Marcelo Caetano.

Pressure from abroad directed at the harsh methods of the PIDE causes 1969
them to change their name to the Directorate General of Security (DGS), but their methods stay the same.

The dictatorship is overthrown in the "Carnation Revolution", a military 1974
coup d'état by the MFA (Movimento das Forças Armadas) on April 25th. The signal for the revolution is given over Radio Renascença by José Afonso's forbidden song "Grandola, Vila Morena", and is named after the carnations placed in rifle barrels to signify a bloodless coup. Tomás and Caetano are removed from office, and General Spinola (whose book "Portugal and its Future" prepared the ground for the military putsch) becomes acting president, to be succeeded on September 30th by General Francisco da Costa Gomes. Mário Soares is foreign minister. Formation of a left-wing democratic government, nationalisation of banking, insurance and large companies, expropriation of the big estates aiming for comprehensive land reform. Amnesty for all political prisoners, abolition of censorship, a right of assembly, new media laws.

Adoption of a socialist constitution. The Socialist PSP is victorious in 1976
parliamentary elections, but without an absolute majority. General António Ramalho Eanes becomes president, and Mário Soares prime minister.

The decade after the revolution has frequent changes of government, 1977–87
many of the coalitions formed showing a great variety of strange groupings, although a common pro-Western, pro-European stance starts to emerge from what seemed at first to be very much a hard left regime. The economic situation deteriorates as Portugal has to absorb thousands of refugees from its former colonies; serious problems are created by unemployment, inflation and an acute housing shortage. Vast unofficial shanty towns of the homeless spring up around Lisbon.

Portugal becomes a full member of the European Community; its low 1986
wages attract many foreign companies to set up in and around Lisbon. Former prime minister Mário Soares becomes president.

Anibal Cavaco Silva's minority government is toppled by a vote of no 1987
confidence. In the fresh elections Silva's liberal-conservative social-democratic party, the PSD, scores a convincing victory, and he is re-elected prime minister, having been a member of various coalition governments for a number of years. His policy is aimed at reducing State influence on the Portuguese economy, and amending the constitution to eliminate its basic socialist principles.

Cavaco Silva's measures meet with some stubborn resistance from the 1988
people and March sees a wave of strikes protesting against planned new labour laws to facilitate dismissals and fixed-term working.

A fire on August 25th destroys about 20 old buildings in Lisbon's inner city Chiado district.

Portugal has an economic growth rate of almost 5%, exports in 1989 are up 1989
by 26%, and the unemployment figure, at just on 5%, is the lowest in Europe. The standard of living is still only half that of Spain. There are clear signs of the boom's impact in the capital.

The local government elections on December 17th make Jorge Sampaio (PS) Mayor of Lisbon in place of Nuno Abecasis.

Plans to build a conference centre above the Parque Eduardo VII and a big cultural centre next to the Hieronymite convent in Belém provoke heated discussion among the people and the politicians concerned.

1990 Cavaco Silva's privatisation legislation is ratified by the Constitutional Court.
Siza Vieira, an Oporto architect, is put in charge of the rebuilding of the parts of the Chiado district destroyed by fire.

1991 Mário Soares is re-elected president for a further five years.

Lisbon in Quotations

Christopher Columbus (1451–1506)

After sunrise we saw that we really were close to land. Was it the cliffs of Cintra? On to Lisbon, then? Really there was no other choice.
At midday we were already close to the shore. I tried to put in at Cassaes, but the gale drove me away from the coast time and again. Perhaps it will be possible to sail up the Tagus.
I succeeded in anchoring off Rastello. We are saved. Saved? Whether we are or not will appear by and by. Immediately after coming ashore I sent a messenger to Juan II with a detailed letter informing him of my arrival and asking for help – and also for leave to continue on my way to Lisbon. I did not let the opportunity pass of remarking that I had not been to Guinea but to India. The best way of protecting yourself against an ox is to grasp it by the horns! Perhaps he will be so surprised that he will forget to gore me.

The log book of Christopher Columbus, March 5th 1492.

Samuel Pepys 1633–1703

Dined with Captain Lambert and his father-in-law and had much talk of Portugall from whence he is lately come, and he tells me that it is a very poor, dirty place – I mean the City and Court of Lisbone. That the King is a very rude and simple fellow; and for reviling of somebody a little while ago and calling of him cuckold, was run into the cods with a sword, and had been killed had he not told them that he was their king. That there is no glass windows, nor will have any; which makes sport among our merchants there, to talk of an English factor that being newly come thither, he writ unto England that glasse would be good commodity to send thither, &c. That the King hath his meat sent up by a dozen of lazy guards and in pipkins; sometimes to his own table – and sometimes nothing but fruits, and now and then half a hen. And now that the Infanta is become our Queene, she is come to have a whole hen or goose to her table – which is not ordinary.

Diary, October 17th 1661.

Henry Fielding (1707–64)

Lisbon, before which we now lay at anchor, is said to be built on the same number of hills with old Rome; but these do not all appear to the water; on the contrary, one sees from thence one vast high hill and rock, with buildings arising above one another, and that in so steep and almost perpendicular a manner, that they all seem to have but one foundation.
As the houses, convents, churches, etc., are large, and all built with white stone, they look very beautiful at a distance; but as you approach nearer, and find them to want every kind of ornament, all ideas of beauty vanishes at once. While I was surveying the prospect of this city, which bears so little resemblance to any other that I have ever seen, a reflection occurred to me, that is a man were suddenly to be removed from Palmyra hither, and should take a view of no other city, in how glorious a light would the ancient architecture appear to him! and what desolation of arts and sciences would he conclude had happened between the several eras of these cities! . . .
About seven in the evening I got into a chaise on shore, and was driven through the nastiest city in the world, though at the same time one of the most populous, to a kind of coffee-house, which is very pleasantly situated on the brow of a hill about a mile from the city and hath a very fine prospect of the river Tajo from Lisbon to the sea. Here we regaled ourselves with a good supper.

Journal of a Voyage to Lisbon, 1754.

Lisbon in Quotations

John Moore
1729–1802

I expressed surprise to one person that they should have ventured to raise houses to such a height in a town so lately overthrown by an earthquake. "It is because it has been so lately overthrown," he replied, "that we venture: for as other capitals in Europe deserve an earthquake as much as Lisbon, and none of them have been alarmed with more than the first symptoms hitherto, it is reasonable to believe that they will all have their turn, according to their deserts; and, of course, it will be a long time before it comes round to Lisbon again."

Mourdaunt, 1800

Lord Byron
(1788–1824)

We sailed from Falmouth on July 2nd, reached Lisbon after a very favourable passage of four days and a half, and took up our abode in that city. It has often been described without being worthy of description; for except for the view from the Tagus, which is beautiful, and some fine churches and convents, it contains little but filthy streets, and more filthy inhabitants. To make amends for this, the village of Cintra, about fifteen miles from the capital, is, perhaps in every respect, the most delightful in Europe; it contains beauties of every description, natural and artificial. Palaces and gardens rising in the midst of rocks, cataracts, and precipices; convents on stupendous heights – a distant view of the sea and the Tagus . . . It unites in itself all the wildness of the western highlands, with the verdure of France.

Letter to his mother, 11th August 1809.

Sir William
Wraxall
(1751–1831)

In the year 1772 the Court of Lisbon offered scarcely any sources of amusements to the foreigner. Neither levees nor drawing-rooms were ever held except on birth-days, and on a few particular festivals. The King, Queen, his brother Don Pedro, his three daughters and the young Prince of Beyre, lived all under the same roof and inhabited a long wooden range of apartments at Belem, lower down the bank of the Tagus than Lisbon. The terrors and recollections of the earthquake of 1755 were so deeply impressed on their minds that they preferred residing in a wooden building, however mean or inconvenient, rather than encounter the perils annexed to a stone edifice. Joseph had never slept under a house, properly so denominated, during near sixteen years. Wherever he moved, either wooden barracks or tents were provided for his accommodation. I have seen tents pitched for his reception in the fields adjoining the palace of Maffra, while that immense and costly edifice was totally abandoned, neglected and unfurnished. These precautions, however singular and almost pusillanimous they may at first sight seem, were nevertheless necessary. Evidence had fully domonstrated that the most solid, massy and well-constructed buildings of stone only exposed the inhabitant to greater and more inevitable destruction, in the event of an earthquake, because the resistance made by such materials to the undulation or shock produced their overthrow. On the contrary, any structure composed of wood, supported like the barracks inhabited by the Royal Family, on pillars of the same materials, yielding to the concussion of the earth, rocked and waved with the convulsion, thus excaping its worst effects.

Historical Memoirs of My Own Time, first published 1815.

Baedeker's Spain
and Portugal
1908 edition

On the authority of British travellers, most of whom, like Byron, have approached by sea, Lisbon has been called the most beautiful city in Europe after Constantinople and Naples, and as an old saying asserts "quem não tem visto Lisboa, não tem visto cousa bona" (he who has not seen Lisbon does not know what beauty is). However this may be, everyone will willingly allow that nature and man have here co-operated to great advantage, and that the city, in spite of the absence of a mountain background or distinguished buildings, possesses a beauty of its own in the picturesque disposition of its terraces, its view of the wide expanses of the Tagus and the luxuriant vegetation of its public gardens and parks.

Karl Baedeker's Spain and Portugal, third edition 1906.

Museu Gulbenkian, Jardim Zoo
Campo Grande, Museu da

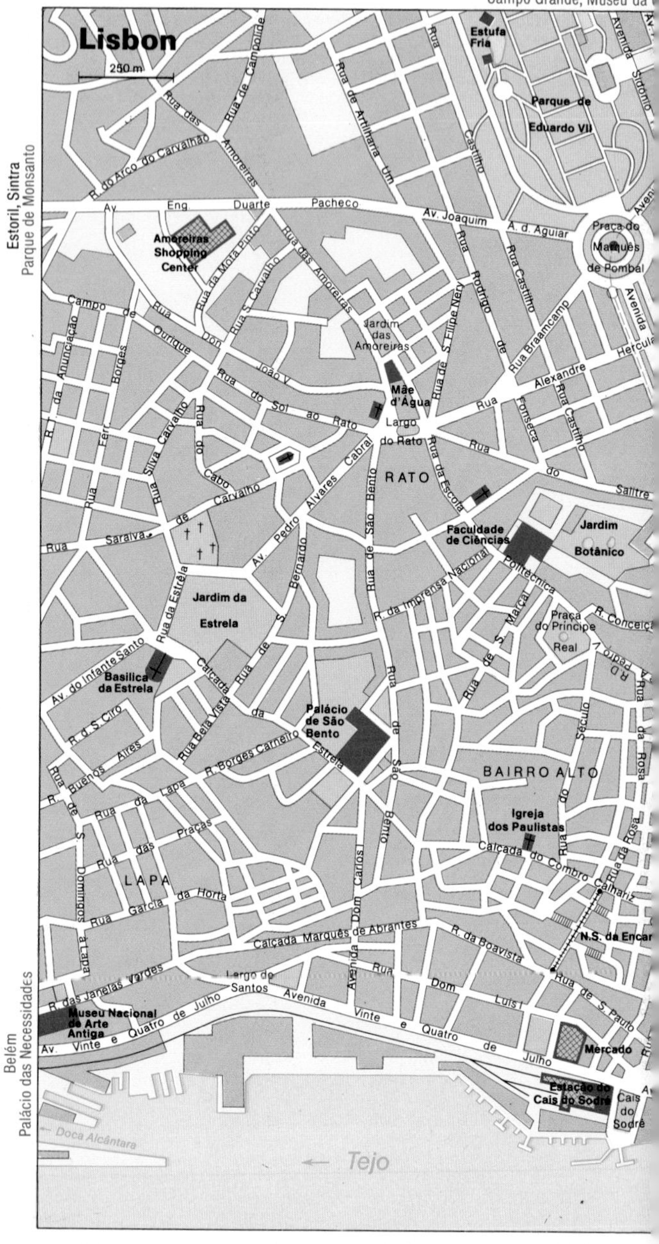

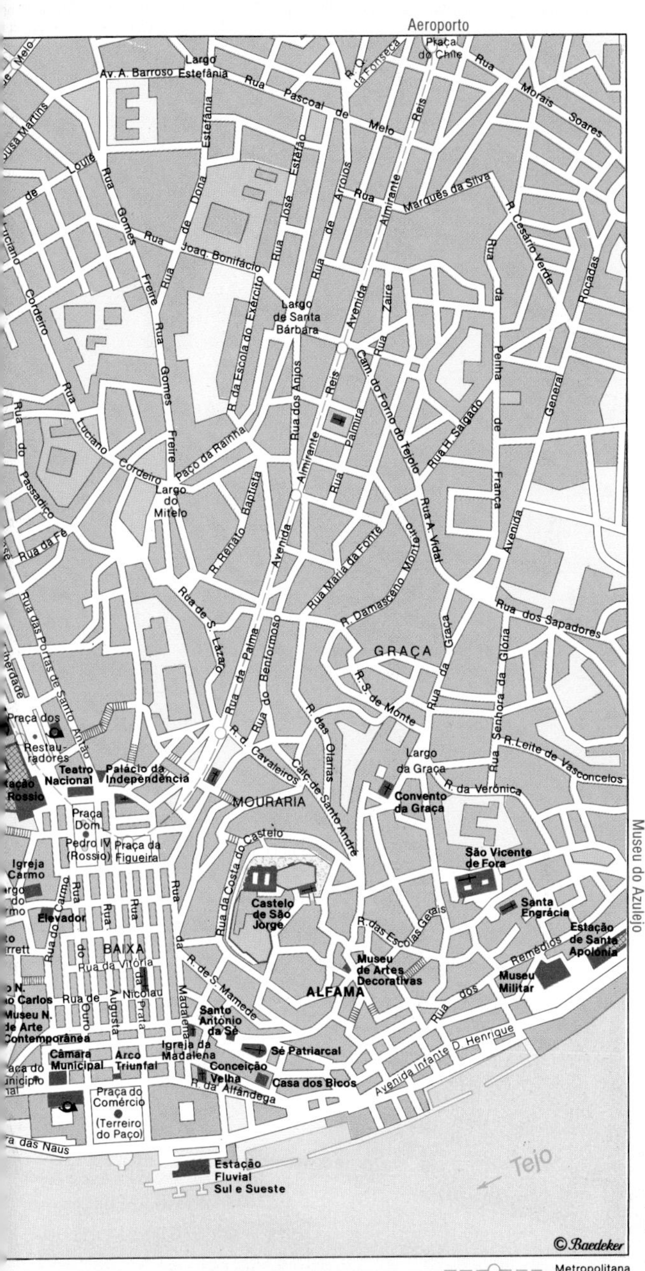
Aeroporto
Praça do Chile
Largo Estefânia
Av. A. Barroso
Rua Pascoal de Melo
Rua Morais Soares
Rua Marquês da Silva
Largo de Santa Bárbara
Rua Joaq. Bonifácio
GRAÇA
MOURARIA
Largo da Graça
Convento da Graça
São Vicente de Fora
Santa Engrácia
Estação de Santa Apolónia
Museu Militar
Castelo de São Jorge
Museu de Artes Decorativas
ALFAMA
Santo António da Sé
Sé Patriarcal
Casa dos Bicos
Avenida Infante D. Henrique
BAIXA
Praça Dom Pedro IV (Rossio)
Praça da Figueira
Teatro Nacional
Palácio da Independência
Praça dos Restauradores
Câmara Municipal
Arco Triunfal
Praça do Comércio (Terreiro do Paço)
Estação Fluvial Sul e Sueste
Tejo
Museu do Azulejo
Metropolitana
© Baedeker

Lisbon from A to Z

For suggestions on how to organise a short stay in Lisbon see Sightseeing Programme in the Practical Information Section.

Advice

**Alfama (Old Quarter) J/K 2/3

Location
South-east inner city

Trams
3, 16, 24, 28, 28B

Buses
9, 13A, 17, 25, 25A, 28, 35, 37, 39, 46, 59, 81, 82, 90

Located on the south-eastern slope of the hill crowned by Castelo de São Jorge is Alfama, Lisbon's oldest quarter, which suffered only slight damage in the 1775 earthquake. Visitors will find the unique atmosphere prevailing in the streets and alleyways of far greater interest than individual buildings. Some houses in this quarter still stand on foundations dating from the times of the West Goths, but the whole structure of the area was essentially shaped by the Arabs. Although no houses remain from this era, the confused arrangement of its maze of streets and alleyways does. The name Alfama is also derived from Arabian origins and probably evolved from the word *al-Hama*, the name of the thermal spring which once bubbled here.

Moors, Christians and Jews lived in the old quarter. Rua da Judiaria recalls one of its three former Jewish ghettos. Today it seems almost inconceivable that during the Middle Ages Alfama was once a respected, rich quarter where prosperous members of the bourgeoisie and aristocrats lived. From the 16th c. mainly fishermen, craftsmen, workers and sailors settled here, while in the 18th c. the area was temporarily regarded as a centre of prostitution. Regarding higgledy-piggledy Alfama the rational planning minister Pombal is supposed to have said that Lisbon could really do with a second earthquake.

Travel guides of the 19th c. paint a picture of an extremely gloomy, dirty and depressing area. Reference is made to the many cases of tuberculosis and the ever-present danger of epidemics which arose as a result of unhealthy living conditions.

Today the poorer classes continue to live here, mainly in houses in need of renovation. Insufficient heating, or a complete lack of it, and draughty walls in the small, closely-built flats, where little sunlight penetrates, ensure poor living conditions, especially in winter. At present some of the houses in the inner city are being renovated as part of a redevelopment scheme. To maintain the structure of the population that has evolved within the quarter, drastic rent increases are being avoided as much as possible. Even the inhabitants themselves pay attention to whoever becomes the next tenant of a flat which has become available.

This old quarter appears very picturesque to visitors in the summer. As the city of Lisbon is fully aware of Alfama's attraction to visitors, it gives financial support to the maintenance and improvement of the quarter's façades. Wandering through the labyrinth of winding alleyways, small archways and little flights of steps, many idyllic and picturesque corners are encountered. Bright washing flaps in front of colourful house fronts, canaries sing from their cages hanging from windows and doors, numerous flower pots compensate for the lack of greenery in the streets. On warm days the shade offered by the densely-built houses explains the reasoning behind this style of construction.

Alfama's structure is such that few cars can enter there, emphasising the feeling of having been transported to a different time. Correspondingly, the atmosphere in the quarter is considerably defined by the different noises and smells. Life is lived for the most part on the street. The many tourists

◀ *Sé Patriarchal, one of the oldest buildings in Lisbon*

who stream through Alfama in the summer are tolerated in a serene and friendly manner. In the evenings fado, the kind of music which was particularly popular in the 19th c., can be listened to in bars provided specially for tourists.

Tour

The route into Alfama leads via Rua Augusto Rosa/Rua do Limoeiro past the Sé Patriarchal (see entry) and the Igreja de Santo António da Sé to the Santa Luzia viewpoint. One of the "entrances" to the quarter, via the steps of Rua Norberto Araújo next to the Igreja de Santa Luzia, is located here. From the Tagus a tour around the Largo do Terreiro do Trigo can be begun through the Arco do Rosário.

Miradouro de Santa Luzia

On Alfama's north-western edge on Rua do Limoeiro lies the Miradouro de Santa Luzia, one of the city's finest view points. From here a marvellous view across Alfama's roof-tops to the Tagus, the Igreja de Santo Estêvão and the white dome of Santa Engrâcio (see entry) can be enjoyed. The viewpoint is in the form of a small park situated on part of the old city wall, which King Ferdinand I had laid out between 1373 and 1375. The original wall contained 34 doors and 77 towers, although only a few relics remain today.

Igreja de Santa Luzia

A tile on the south side of the now closed Igrja de Santa Luzia (18th c.), built directly by the viewpoint, depicts the Praça do Comércio (see entry) below on the Tagus in a view dating from before the earthquake and then still called Terreiro do Paço. A second tile shows the Portuguese conquest of the castle in 1147.

Igreja de São Tiago

The Igreja de São Tiago, located on the opposite side of the road, dates from the 12th c. It was rebuilt after the earthquake. Of interest are the ceiling paintings and some painted tiles in the interior.

Largo das Portos do Sol

The square immediately to the north of Santa Luzia viewpoint offers a comprehensive view of Alfama. Rising in the background are the white

The Alfama, a huddle of houses and a special atmosphere

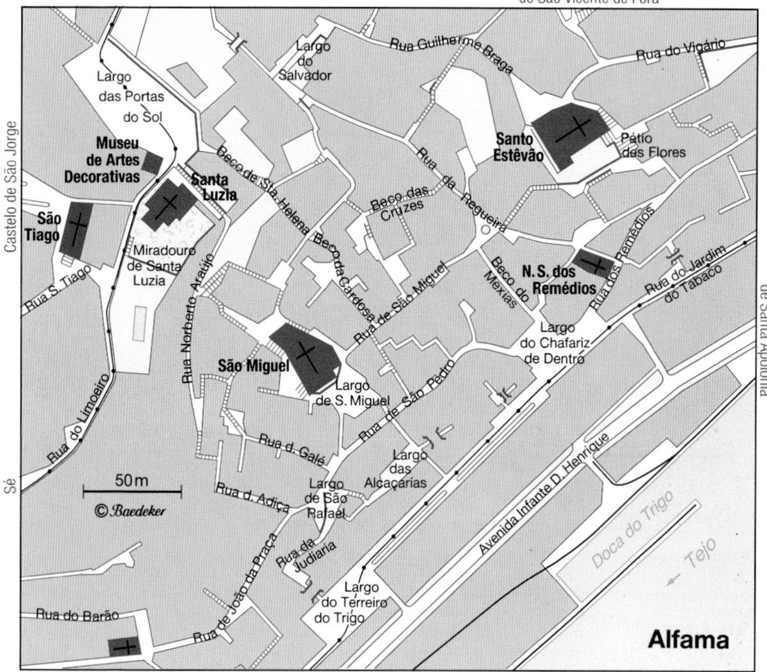

dome of the Igreja de Santa Engrácia (see entry) and the tall form of the Igreja de São Vincente de Fora (see entry) with its twin towers.
The modern statue on the Largo das Portos do Sol is dedicated to St Vincent, after whom the monastery is named and whose life is perpetuated on Lisbon's coat of arms.
On the southern side of the square the former city palace of the Visconde de Azurara houses the Museum of Decorative Arts (see Museu-Escola de Artes Decorativas).

Igreja de São Miguel

Steps lead from the Largo das Portos do Sol (immediately behind the Igreja de Santa Luzia) down to the Igreja de São Miguel on the square named after it. The original church was built in 1150 and was renovated several times in the 13th c. and 17th c. After the earthquake it had to be almost completely rebuilt, although old parts of the building were incorporated, such as the valuable carving. The ceiling is of Brazilian jacaranda wood.

Igreja de Santo Estêvão

Follow the Rua de São Miguel to reach the Igreja de Santo Estêvão on the raised Largo de Santo Estêvão. The church was founded in the 13th c. by Dinos I. It originally consisted of five aisles, a unique feature in Lisbon. The earthquake almost completely destroyed it and it was rebuilt in 1773 to an octagonal plan. The ceiling paintings in the chancel and the sacristy come from the original church.

The small square in front of the church offers a fine view across the quarter to the Tagus. Steps lead down from here to the Pátio das Flores, which is surrounded by decorated houses.

The Largo das Portas do Sol

Ermida de Nossa Senhora dos Remédios

The inconspicuous, mid-16th c. Ermida de Nossa Senhora dos Remédios, which stands somewhat below the Igreja de Santo Estêvão in the Rua dos Remédios, still has the Manueline entrance portal dating from before the earthquake. Some fine plates are on view in the interior.

Chafariz de Dentro

On the Largo do Chafariz de Dentro is located the unobtrusive fountain of the same name. It was called Chafariz de Dentro (inner fountain) as it was unusually positioned, i.e. within the old city walls. Originating from the 14th c., it once also bore the name "Horses' Fountain", as the gargoyles portrayed two bronze horses heads. These were stolen in 1373 by Spanish troops. The fountain was built in its current form in 1622.

Rua de São Pedro

The Rua de São Pedro ends at the north-western boundary of the Largo do Chafarizde Dentro. This narrow street is very lively; an open-air fish market takes place here every morning. Building number 6–10 is representative of the houses in this quarter.

Chafariz d'El Rei

The Rua de São Pedro leads into the Largo de São Rafael, from where Lisbon's oldest fountain, the Chafariz d'El Rei (King's Fountain), can be reached via the Rua da Judiaria, the centre of the former Jewish quarter, and through the Arco do Rosário to the Largo do Terreiro do Trigo. It originates from the 13th c., although a fountain possibly stood on this site in Moorish times. The current fountain dates from the 18th c. The King's Fountain is built right by a piece of the old city wall. Not only did Lisbon's inhabitants come here to fetch water, ships anchored in the harbour were also supplied with water from this fountain. The high demand for water must have led to fights amongst the users as an official decree passed in 1551 regulated exactly the withdrawal of water according to sex, race and position.

A street in the Alfama

Chafariz d'El Rei

Feira da Ladra

Flea market

Lisbon's best-known flea market, the Feira da Ladra (Thieves' Market), has taken place every Tuesday and Saturday since 1881 on the edge of Alfama on the Campo de Santa Clara near the Igreja de São Vicente de Fora (see entry). The origin of the market is considerably older, with a market thought to have been held in the 12th c. In 1610 the name "Feira da Ladra" first appeared in a municipal decree. Before the market occupied its permanent site here it had been located on the Praça da Alegria, on the Rossio (see entry), on the Campo de Santaria and near the castle.
Most of the professional traders on the flea market have meanwhile adapted themselves and their wares primarily to tourists, so a lucky bargain is unlikely to be found. Amateur traders can only be found in a small area of the market.

*Amoreiras Shopping Center E5

Location
Av. Eng. Duarte Pacheco/Rua Carlos Alberto da Mota Pinto

Trams
10, 24, 25, 26, 29

Buses
11, 15, 23, 48, 53, 58

Since the mid 1980s, Lisbon's north-western skyline has been characterised by a high-rise building complex designed by the architect Tómas Taveira. The building style of the twelve-storey block is striking and has been designated by the architect himself as "Neo-Modern". The whole building project was hotly disputed as soon as it was unveiled – namely because the unusual style and colouring of the architecture clashes with the predominantly older constructions of the city. In the meantime, buildings in this unmistakable style can continually be found within Lisbon; Tómas Taveira has meanwhile become one of the Portuguese capital's leading architects.
The Amoreiras quarter owes its name to the mulberry trees which Minister Pombal had planted in the 18th c. at the Praça das Amoreiras next to the

Open: daily 10am–midnight

Mãe d'Água (see entry), a castle surrounded by water. Silkworms were then released here and a silk factory established.

Shopping centre

The three tower blocks and the neighbouring lower building complex accommodate offices, luxury flats and cinemas. Today the name Amoreiras signifies first of all the spacious, fully air-conditioned shopping centre located on the two bottom floors. With about 350 shops covering 86,000sq.m/102,856sq.yds and parking spaces for 1200 cars, it constitutes Europe's sixth largest centre of this type. When it opened in 1985, it covered almost twelve times the area of the Centro Comercial Alvalade, until then the largest centre. Some of the shops are very luxurious, prices are very high for Portugal and typical Portuguese goods cannot be found anywhere in the complex. All in all the interior could be mistaken for any shopping centre in other Western capital cities. This becomes more striking when the centre is compared with the many small, dark shops in Lisbon's old quarters such as Alfama and Bairro Alto. It is a delight to experience the variety of choice to be found here within one city but at the same time it is possible to sense what the Portuguese capital stands to lose through the Western tendency to standardisation. The people of Lisbon love their shopping centre; it represents a real contrast to the traditional shopping areas in Baixa and Chiado (see entries). Its integrated cinemas and restaurants have made it a well-frequented meeting place until midnight.

*Aqueduto das Águas Livres (Aqueduct) D 7

Location
Alcântara valley, North-west city
(Entrance via the Calçada da Quintinha)

Trams: 10, 27

Earlier visitors to Portugal considered the Aqueduto das Águas Livres to be the city's loveliest construction. By this they meant the most impressive section of Lisbon's water supply system which spans the Alcântara valley to the north-west of the city. Water passes above the valley for 941m/3088ft. The aqueduct is supported by 35 arches (14 pointed arches in the centre and 21 rounded arches at the sides), the tallest of which measures 62m/203ft high and 33.7m/111ft wide. Footpaths 1.4m/5ft wide run along both sides of the aqueduct at a height of 65.3m/214ft. The section of the

Amoreiras Shopping Center: exterior . . .

. . . and the interior

aqueduct spanning the Alcântara valley is visible from afar but actually forms only a small part of the 18.6km/11½ mile long pipeline; the full length of the aqueduct, including its tributaries, totals 58km/36 miles and 127 arches had to be built. Around Lisbon and within the city itself parts of the Aqueduto das Águas Livres continually appear. In some places the pipeline is supported by pillars, in others, where the water flows underground, only the little ventilation shafts can be seen.

Buses
2, 12, 13, 15, 18
42, 51, 58

Open
July–Oct.:
Sat.,Sun.
10am–5pm

History of construction

The construction of a water pipeline had been under discussion since the time of Manuel I. It was supposed to solve the city's yearly summer water shortage and the ensuing hygiene problems. For some time the idea of transporting fresh water into the centre from the springs (known as "Águas Livres") at Canecas to the north of Lisbon had been considered. During the reign of João V, who had a love of anything grandiose, the project was finally tackled. Although sufficient funds were available at that time from Brazilian goldmines, the construction had to be financed through public taxes, as João's priorities were for prestigious and sacred buildings.
Work on the aqueduct took place over several decades. Building started in 1731 under the direction of the Italian Antonio Canevari, although shortly afterwards Custódio José Vieira and Manuel da Maia, both Portuguese, took charge. The latter was heavily involved in the reconstruction of Lisbon after the earthquake; he first made his name through the building of the aqueduct, which survived the earthquake undamaged. The crossing of the Alcántara valley was completed in 1748, immediately guaranteeing the city's water supply. The complete water pipeline continued to be worked on until the 19th c.

Construction

The construction is based on the principle of gravity. Water flows for kilometres into the city at a constant rate, partly underground, partly at ground level or – as at Alcántara valley – at a height of approximately 65m/213ft. The gently sloping style of the aqueduct – at its beginning it

A huge aqueduct spans the Alcântara Valley

measures 178m/584ft high and at its end 94.3/309ft – meant that water could be transported to Lisbon and collected there at Mãe d'Água, a castle surrounded by water at the Jardim das Amoreiras. Until 1880 Lisbon's water demands were mostly met by the aqueduct, but then the increasing needs of the growing city rendered its capacity insufficient and a new main was constructed. Although the whole extent of the Aqueduto das Águas Livres could be used in principle today, it was finally closed down.

Viewing

The Aqueduto das Águas Livres was open to the public until 1853. It served the inhabitants of the suburbs as a short cut across the Alcántara valley. Attacks by the then famous/infamous robber Diogo Alves, who lay in wait for his victims up on the other side, robbed them and pushed them over the edge into the valley below, together with the increasing number of suicides led to the crossing being closed off.

For some years the aqueduct has been opened at weekends in the summer for visits and for walking across. At the same time the water pipeline can be viewed directly. From the aqueduct an interesting view across the Alcán-tara valley with its network of roads to the Tagus can be enjoyed. The northern view includes the railway line to Sintra, as it leaves the 2.6km/2 mile tunnel which passes under the city.

Advice

To be sure of finding the aqueduct open (times are frequently altered) it is wise to check before visiting.

Arco do Cego (Quarter) J 6/7

Location
North-east of the city centre

The Bairro Social do Arco do Cego is one of the first planned residential areas of Lisbon.

After the founding of the republic work began on establishing housing

settlements in what were then still the suburbs of the city. These were supposed to develop as standardised living areas within the framework of a social house building programme. A decree of April 5th 1918 sought a remedy to the housing difficulties of the poor and the gradual solution of the problems acknowledged in the old quarters by constructing new living areas for the working classes.
Under the leadership of the architects Edmundo Tavares and Frederico Machado small semi-detached houses fronted by little gardens began to be built in the Arco-do-Cego quarter in 1919. Political change caused considerable building delays during the following years so that the new settlement was not officially opened until 1935 under the Salazar regime. In the meantime the general shortage of accommodation had increased, and in addition the political line had clearly altered. The result was that – allegedly because of mistakes made in planning the project – rents were set so high that people on low incomes could not afford them. Instead of the people they were intended for, tenants from the lower levels of the bourgeoisie such as civil servants and members of the national unions were preferred. Today the quarter lies on the edge of newer tower block complexes; in contrast to these it appears an almost idyllically peaceful area.

Buses
7, 20, 22, 33, 40

The Igreja de São de Deus, built in 1949 to the design of the architect António Lino, stands at the entrance to the Arco-do-Cego quarter right on the Praça de Londres

Igreja de São João de Deus

Arquivo Nacional da Torre do Tombo

See Cidade Universitária

Avenida da Liberdade G/H 3–5

One of the most important arterial roads in Lisbon is the Avenida da Liberdade. The 90m/295ft wide road gradually climbs over a distance of about 1.5km/1 mile from the Praça dos Restauradores (see entry) to the Praça Marquês de Pombal (see entry) at the southern end of the Parque Eduardo VII (see entry). The boulevard, built in 1879, forms a connecting axis between the old 18th c. quarters of the Baixa (see entry) and the northern parts of the city which developed in the 19th and the 20th centuries. The construction of the Avenida da Liberdade took interest away from the Tagus which, until then, had been the focus of attention as Lisbon's "main artery of life", and led to the opening up and general orientation of the city to the north. The course of the Avenida da Liberdade corresponds approximately to that of one of the Tagus' earlier branches, which flowed here in pre-Christian times and combined with another branch at Rossio. As the two main metro lines run along the Avenida da Liberdade and the Avenida Almirante Reis they follow in principle the former courses of the river beds.
A forerunner of this boulevard was the Passeio Público, initiated in 1764 by Pombal after the earthquake, an extensive park laid out in this fertile former river valley. The park was used as a "promenade" where people strolled about in public in order to be seen.
With the idea of building a prestigious and elegant street Lisbon turned its gaze, as was often the case, to Paris: a counterpart to the Champs Elysées was planned for Portugal's capital city. Despite numerous protests directed, amongst other things, at the felling of old trees, construction began in 1879 under the initiative of the then mayor Rosa Aráuja. The boulevard was officially opened in 1882. The Avenida da Liberdade was then used, particularly on Sundays, as a promenade for Lisbon's society and became a scene of parades, march pasts and demonstrations.
During the century the character of the Avenida da Liberdade became increasingly shaped by the growing amount of traffic. The small areas of

Location
Extends from the lower city to the Parque Eduardo VII

Metro
Restauradores, Avenida, Rotunda

Trams
20, 25, 26

Buses
1, 2, 6, 9, 11, 12, 20, 21, 22, 23, 27, 31, 32, 36, 38, 39, 41, 44, 45, 46, 48, 49, 53, 88, 90

parkland and the ten rows of trees have lost their effect in competition with a total of seven lanes of thunderous traffic. Some imposing town houses dating from the time when the avenue was first developed can still be found, but on the whole the frontage has been interspersed completely thoughtlessly with plain, ill-suited new buildings, more of which are planned. During the last few decades mainly administrative and business offices, hotels, banks and shopping centres have become established here. A number of street cafés have been opened on the grassed areas, complete with pools and fountains, tempting passers-by – although not during rush-hours!

Strolling along the Avenida da Liberdade several buildings and places of interest on and around the boulevard are worthy of attention. The numbering of the houses begins at the Praça dos Restauradores, even numbers on the western side, odd on the east. The following list specifies places of interest in the order in which they would be encountered if walking up the left-hand side of the Avenida da Liberdade to the Praça Marquês de Pombal and then down the opposite side to the Praça dos Restauradores.

Café Palladium

The building immediately next to the Elevador da Glória (see Praça dos Restauradores), which forms the beginning of the Avenida da Liberdade, bears the name "Café Palladium". Nowadays, a shopping centre is to be found behind its highly-decorated exterior.

Fountain figures "Tejo" and "Douro"

Shortly before the junction of the Praça da Alegria and the Rua das Pretas two water courses border the length of the road between lush greenery. A figure sits at the end of each fountain, pouring water from a jug. The two figures symbolise Portugal's most important rivers. The Tagus is represented on the eastern side opposite the Douro on the west, which enters the Atlantic at Oporto. The allegories were created by the sculptor Alexandre Gomes for the old Passeio Público and are the only relics along the Avenida da Liberdade dating from this time. A similar representation of Tejo and Douro can be found on the triumphal arch leading to the Rua Augusta on the Praça do Comércio (see entry).

Praça da Alegria

A circular park, dedicated to the artist Alfredo Keil (1850–1907), has been laid out on the small Praça da Alegria, which is located behind the row of houses on the Avenida da Liberdade. The bronze bust, placed there in 1957, was created by Teixeira Lopes, a sculptor famous in Portugal.
Alfredo Keil was a painter, writer and, above all, a composer. His opera "A Serrana" ("The Girl from the Mountains") is generally considered to be Portugal's national opera and his song "A Portuguesa" ("The Girl from Portugal") was declared the national anthem of the Portuguese Republic in 1911.

"Mortos da Grande Guerra" memorial

The most impressive monument on the Avenida da Liberdade is the war memorial, erected to honour the Portuguese soldiers (Mortos da Grande Guerra) who died in the First World War.

Parque Mayer

In the Travessa do Salitre – a short way from the Avenida – can be found an entrance to the so-called Parque Mayer. This "pleasure park" has existed here since 1922 on land once belonging to the Lima Mayer family, whose city palace still remains in the neighbouring Rua do Salitre (no. 1). The Parque Mayer contains four theatres, constructed in the 1920s and 1930s: Maria Vitória, Variedades, Capitólio and ABC. Particularly in the 1940s and 1950s the extraordinarily well-loved revistas were performed here. These were a special form of lively musical theatre, peculiar to Lisbon, with shades of satire and even veiled criticism of the times of dictatorship. The first Portuguese films, produced in the 1930s, took on substantial elements of the revistas.

Cinema S. Jorge

The Cinema S. Jorge (no. 175) was built at the end of the 1940s by Fernando Silva and underwent fundamental alterations in 1980. The original, very spaciously-designed cinema was then divided into three smaller cinemas.

The "Mortos da Grande Guerra" monument on the Avenida da Liberdade

Rosa Araúja memorial

On the Rua Rosa Araúja a memorial was erected in 1936, dedicated to the initiator of the Avenida da Liberdade: Rosa Araúja held the office of mayor, when it was decided to build this boulevard. The figure of a woman wearing a crown shaped like a small tower is meant to embody the city of Lisbon. She is presenting the mayor with a bunch of flowers as thanks for the avenue that enhances the city.

On the eastern side of the Avenida da Liberdade can be seen some fine old buildings, most of which were designed by well-known Lisbon architects.

Diário de Noticias

The editorial offices of the Diário de Noticias (no. 266) were built in 1936 by the architect Pardal Monteiro and were awarded the Valmor Prize in 1940, a prize regularly presented since the turn of the century to newly-erected buildings. The offices of the old-established daily paper were formerly in the Bairro Alto (see entry) in the present-day Rua do Diário de Noticias. In the entrance hall can be seen a painting by Almada Negreiros, one of Portugal's most famous 20th c. artists.

Aero Clube de Portugal

One of the oldest houses on the Avenida is the building housing the Aero Clube de Portugal (no. 226–228). It was built in 1888 according to plans drawn up by the Frenchman Henri Lusseau.

No. 206–218

During the first decade of this century many of the houses in Lisbon were designed by the architect Norte Júnior and many were awarded the Valmor Prize, including building no. 206–218, which received it in 1916.

Tivoli

One of the most striking buildings is the Neo-Classical no. 188, the former Tivoli cinema, built in 1924 by the architect Raul Lino. Today films are no longer shown, instead various larger functions (concerts, etc.) take place here.

The kiosk, which stood in front of the Tivoli cinema, was installed here in 1925 by the directorship of the Diário de Noticias. It has been maintained as the last of several of its type which once stood in the Avenida da Liberdade.

Avenida da Liberdade: Nos 206–218 . . . *. . . and Casa Lambertini*

Hotel Vitória

The main seat of the Communist PCP is located today in the Hotel Vitória (no. 170), designed by Cassiano Branco in 1936. During the 1930s the architect built many houses and some large cinemas.

Casa Lambertini

Casa Lambertini (no. 166), built by Nicola Bagaglia, dates from 1901. Unique on the Avenida da Liberdade is the mosaic on its exterior composed of small stones and depicting stylised flowers on a gold ground.

Palácio Nunes Correia Almedina

In 1895 the Palácia Nunes Correia Almedina (no. 22–26) was constructed according to the plans of Luis Cinatti. Today it accommodates the EPAL (City Waterworks).

Elevador da Lavra

A short distance from the Avenida da Liberdade, where there is an exit from the Rua das Portas de Santo Antão/Rua S. José, is the Lavra lift. It was opened in 1884 as the city's first funicular railway and thus constitutes the oldest of the four elevadores still in existence in Lisbon.
From the upper station the following can easily be reached: the Jardim de Torel viewpoint on the Rua de Júlio de Andrade, the Campo dos Mártires da Pátria with its charming park and the memorial to Dr Sousa Martins (see Practical Information, Monuments and Sculpture).

*Bairro Alto (upper city) G 3/4

Location
North-west upper area of Baixa

Bairro Alto ("high-lying quarter") is located above Baixa and developed in the 16th c. in the course of an extension of the city centre towards the west and the north-west. The quarter only suffered relatively little damage during the earthquake of 1755. The real Bairro Alto is considered to consist of the streets between Rua do Século, Rua de D. Pedro V, Rua de S. Pedro de Alcântara/Rua da Misericórdia and Rua do Loreto/Calçada do Combro. The rather unusual geometric design used at that time for the construction of the city originates from a period when previously rural land was divided up for sale into rectangular and trapeziform parcels. The construction of the Jesuit church (see Igreja de São Roque) in the middle of the 16th c. played no insignificant part in attracting settlers to the area, the original name of this residential district being Bairro Alto de São Roque.

Trams
10, 20, 24, 28, 28B, 29, 30

Buses
15

Lift
Elevador do Carmo, Elevador da Glória

In its beginnings Bairro Alto was temporarily the quarter where richer citizens and the nobility settled. When Alfama (see entry) increasingly changed its character and fell into disrepair, some of Lisbon's prosperous inhabitants moved here and had houses and palaces built for themselves. Despite this Bairro Alto is predominantly regarded as a residential and working quarter for craftsmen and small shopkeepers.
At times the area was strongly influenced by the newspaper industry with many small printing works and editorial offices setting up business here. "Journalist Quarter" was until recently an unofficial nickname for Bairro Alto. The roads Rua do Diário de Noticias and Rua do Século still bear witness to the offices of two of the larger daily newspapers which were once produced here and the Rua Eduardo Coelho commemorates the founder of the Portuguese newspaper industry and the daily paper "Diário de Noticias".
Drug trafficking and prostitution have given this quarter a bad reputation for a long time. Recently Bairro Alto has become fashionable with younger people and is popular as an evening meeting place. Many small restaurants, bars and pubs as well as some unusual, expensive shops make the change very clear.
It is interesting that Bairro Alto presents a fundamentally different face during the day than from night-time. Throughout the day the busy hustle and bustle of the inhabitants, who mostly know one another, predominates – Bairro Alto is one of the few unanonymous quarters in this city of two million inhabitants. The many small retail outlets serve not only as places to shop but at the same time to exchange the latest gossip. In the evenings the narrow streets are equally as lively, but then it is the frequenters of restaurants and inns who throng through the quarter. Many tourists also come here; a number of fado bars have openend and compete for customers. There are also differences within the quarter – the eastern part appears the most lively, while the western half is comparatively quiet and self-contained.

Elevador da Glória

Two unusual means of transport link Baixa with Bairro Alto: the Elevador do Carmo (see entry) and the Elevador da Glória. This funicular railway dates from 1885. It starts from the Praça dos Restauradores (see entry) next to the Palácio Foz and it climbs to above the Calçada da Glória. The upper station is located on the Rua de São Pedro de Alcântara immediately next to the Miradouro of the same name.

Miradouro São Pedro de Alcântara

The Miradouro São Pedro de Alcântara vantage point is a two-tiered small park, of which only the upper level is open to the public today. From here a marvellous view of the northern part of the city can be enjoyed, as well as views to the east of the Graça (see entry) hill, the Igreja de São Vicente de Fora (see entry) and the Castelo de São Jorge. A tile clarifies the places of interest and helps with orientation.
A memorial was erected in the garden in 1904, dedicated to the first chief of the famous "Diário de Noticias", Eduardo Coelho. Eduardo Coelho (1835–1889) founded the daily paper in 1863 and led it for its first 25 years.
The small bronze in the foreground portrays an ardina, a newspaper boy who sold the daily paper in the streets. João Baptista Borges, depicted here, was the first to promote the "Diário de Noticias", at a time when its sales were poor.

Palácio Ludovice/ Solar do Vinho do Porto

Directly opposite the upper station of the Elevador da Glória stands the Palácio Ludovice (Rua de São Pedro de Alcántara 39/49). The building bears the name of its first owner and creator, the architect Johann Friedrich

A street in the Bairro Alto

View from São Pedro de Alcântara

Ludwig (1673–1752). The German, who had been educated in Italy (hence the Italian name Ludovice), built the famous monumental monastery at Mafra. He constructed the city palace in 1747.

The Port Wine Institute, "Solar do Vinho do Porto", is housed on the ground floor (entrance no. 45). Here the famous wine from the Douro valley can be tasted in luxurious surroundings and a quiet atmosphere. For port wine lovers and connoisseurs the wide choice of samples – some even from quite old vintages – is of particular interest.

Igreja de São Roque

A few hundred metres to the south of the São Pedro de Alcântara, the Igreja de São Roque (see entry) is well worth visiting.

Praça do Principe Real

Follow the Rua D. Pedro V in a northerly direction to reach the Praça do Principe Real. This square was laid out in 1860 as an extremely fine, small park (Jardim França Borges) with greenery from distant lands. An old cedar has grown above a supporting trellis to form an imposing "roof" offering shade and has become a favourite meeting place for card players.

Palácio Ribeiro da Cunha

The houses on the square were built at the same time. Some magnificent palaces were built here, including the Neo-Arabic-looking Palácio Ribeiro da Cunha (no. 26), in which a department of the Universidade Nova de Lisboa is currently accommodated.

Jardim Botânico

Not far to the north of the Praça do Principe Real lies the Jardim Botânico on the edge of Bairro Alto (entrance via the Rua da Escola Politécnica).

Convento da Conceição dos Cardais

The Rua do Século can be reached from the south-east corner of the Praça do Principe Real. The long building, which once housed the Carmelite monastery Convento da Conceição dos Cardais (no. 123), makes a very spartan impression here. The two decorated entrance doors stand out strikingly from the plain façade. Constructed around 1700, the building survived the earthquake undamaged. The wall decoration in the interior (carving and blue and white tiling) is the work of the Dutchman Jan Van Dort. The whole complex was very run-down and dilapidated; it is now being restored.

Palácio Pombal

The Palácio Pombal (Rua do Século no. 93), also called the Palácio dos Carvalhos, was for a long time the home of the Pombal family. Sebastião José de Carvalho e Melo, later Minister Pombal (see Famous People), was born here in 1699. The building remained undamaged by the earthquake; however, after the disaster, Pombal had it altered by Carlos Mardel, who was one of the main architects to assist with the city's reconstruction. In accordance with the taste of the forerunner of rational enlightenment in Portugal, the long building is relatively plain and unadorned. The small bridge, which crosses the adjoining Rua da Academia das Ciências, used to link the palace with its garden.
The fountain area opposite the palace, which is no longer in working order, is said to be the work of Carlos Mardel. The small square is lined by high, partly overgrown walls, which form the border to the higher plain of Bairro Alto.

Former editorial offices of the "O Século"

Also located in the Rua do Século are the former editorial offices – built 1913 – of the "O Século" newspaper (no. 41–63), after which this street, the former Rua Formosa, was renamed in the second decade of the 20th c.

Conservatório Nacional de Músicae Teatro

By following the Travessa dos Inglesinhos uphill to the left, we reach the former S. Caetano de Thiene monastery (Rua dos Caetanos no. 29). Since 1837 the city conservatoire has been housed here. Initially only for drama, it was later combined with the music conservatoire, which was founded in 1833 and whose first head, João Domingos Bontempo, was one of the most famous Portuguese composers. The establishment of the conservatoire contributed substantially to an independent development of music in Portugal, where otherwise music had been adopted almost exclusively from Italy.

Rua da Rosa

A legend has grown up around the house standing not far away to the north-east on the corner of Rua da Ruaora/Cunhal das Bolas. The building, striking for its border of half tiles, is said to have been built by a rich shopkeeper. The half tiles are supposed to represent a counterpart to the "diamond points" of the Casa dos Bicos (see entry) – they were apparently originally made of gold. Both the tile decoration and the diamond pattern have been taken up and used in the mixture of styles of the Palácio de Pena at Sintra (see entry).

Igreja dos Paulistas

On the southern edge of Bairro Alto, on the Calçada do Combro (no. 82), stands the Baroque Igreja dos Paulistas (also known as the Igreja de Santa Caterina). The church was founded as the Igreja de S. Paulo da Serra de Ossa in 1647 and originally belonged to a monastery of the same name. In the middle of the 19th c. and once again in the 1920s the church was renovated and reformed into its current style.
The façade, which has since been somewhat destroyed, stands out because of its harmonious articulation. In contrast with other Portuguese churches the interior is unusually bright. The ceiling is richly decorated with stucco and structured through having been painted in different colours. The Baroque organ, with its gold-painted wood carving and figures, and the carving on the main altar and in the eight side chapels give a somewhat over-ornate impression.

Baixa (Lower City) — H 2/3

Location
City centre

Baixa is regarded as the real centre of Lisbon. It lies in a hollow between Bairro Alto (see entry) and Chiado (see entry) in the west and the opposite quarter which rises up to Castelo de São Jorge (see entry). During the time

Baixa

Metro
Rossio

Trams
3, 15, 16, 17, 18, 19, 24, 25, 26, 28, 28B

when the Lisbon area was first settled the whole of Baixa remained flooded with water from the Tagus; up at Rossio two tributaries of the Tagus converged.

Present-day Baixa is particularly noteworthy as an urban development area. This part of Lisbon was completely destroyed by the earthquake of 1755. Afterwards town planners were faced with alternatives typical of such a situation; either to reconstruct the quarter exactly as it was before or to create a completely new structure. Moving the centre of the city towards Belém was also discussed at this time.

Minister Josés I, the Marqûes de Pombal (see Famous People), assumed leadership of the reconstruction. Pombal is considered the forerunner of Benevolent Despotism in Portugal; rational and functional planning were essential parts of his political thought. The controversial minister decided on a completely new remodelling based on a plan which would give the new quarter a strongly geometric, easily comprehensible structure, corresponding to his understanding of the world. This concept was ahead of its time and foresaw a "chess board layout" of the streets as they had been constructed in Greek cities in the 5th c. B.C. The Praça do Comércio on the river bank was linked to the more northerly Rossio and the Praça da Figueira by means of right-angled streets dissecting a long field. The grid-like area of Baixa thus stands in stark contrast to the neighbouring quarters of the old city with their twisting and confused streets and alleyways. In the main three architects were involved in the construction of the so-called Pombal lower city; Manuel de Maia, who had made a name for himself through the building of the aqueduct (see Aqueduto das Aguas Livres), Eugénio dos Santos and the Hungerian Carlos Mardel. One criterion was of prime importance: houses were to be built that would stand less danger of collapse during an earthquake. For this reason buildings were to be no more than two storeys high. This was economically unrealistic for future owners of properties in such a central position. Finally a half-timbered construction was developed, whose stability and elasticity permitted buildings of up to a maximum of five storeys.

Characteristic of the construction of the lower part of the city was the standardised uniformity in its appearance. Height, roof shape and size of windows of the new houses were originally the same. Many new buildings have since been constructed in a divergent form so that the Pombal concept no longer appears so obvious. Recently attempts have been made during renovation to preserve at least the façades of the many extremely dilapidated buildings.

The quarter between Rossio and the Praça do Comércio is today above all a quarter of shops and banks. The roads running from north to south were each originally assigned to a specific craft guild or profession. Road names such as Rua dos Douradores (Gilders' Street), Rua dos Sapateiros (Shoemakers' Street) or Rua Aurea (also known as Rua do Ouro) and Rua da Prata (gold and silversmiths) provide continuing evidence of this. In the wider main streets, Rua Aurea and Rua da Prata, and in the now pedestrianised Rua Augusta (whose mosaic design was resurfaced in 1989) mostly larger, very elegant shops prevail today. In the narrow side streets, however, simpler shops and workshops are still to be found. During the day Baixa is very lively but after the shops have closed it appears deserted and dead; few restaurants or cafés remain open at this time of day.

Places of interest

Amongst the most important places of interest in Baixa are Rossio (see entry) with the Estação Rossio (see entry) and the Teatro Nacional Dona Maria II (see entry), the Praça dos Restauradores (see entry) on the northern border, the Praça do Comércio (see entry) as well as the somewhat remote town hall (see Praça do Conselho). The most striking and at the same time most curious construction in this quarter is the Elevador do Carmo (see entry), which links the lower and upper parts of the city.

Termas Romanus

After the disaster of the earthquake excavations were made under the foundations of the houses that had been destroyed and underground

Baixa: *Rua Augusta . . .*

. . . and the Igreja de São Nicolau

springs dating from Roman times were discovered. Today they are occasionally opened to the public and can be reached through an entrance in the Rua da Prata (between the Rua da Conceição and the Rua da São Julião).

Ermida de Nossa Senhora da Vitória

Located inconspicuously in the most westerly corner of the Rua da Vitória is the Nossa Senhora da Vitória chapel. An earlier church dating from 1556 was destroyed by the earthquake. It was rebuilt in 1765 and restored in 1940. The uniform and sparsely-decorated interior radiates a unique atmosphere, which emanates mainly from the poor candle lighting. Natural light only penetrates through a small window and a few fanlights. The small interior, with just one aisle, has a barrel-vaulted ceiling, which is continued at a lower level above the chancel. On the side walls two small altars and tiling attract the visitor's attention.

Igreja de São Nicolau

The Igreja de São Nicolau on the Rua da Vitória was founded in the 13th c. The construction of the present church was begun in 1780 and completed in 1850. It is noteworthy on the one hand because of its location – the uniformity of the buildings is somewhat less monotonous here – and on the other because of the tiling on the exterior walls. The painting in the interior is the work of Pedro Alexandrino.

Animatógrapho

The Animatógrapho do Rossio in the Rua dos Sapateiros was one of Lisbon's first cinemas. It was opened in December 1907 by the Cardoso Correia brothers. They placed particular emphasis on decorating the Art Nouveau façade (which has since been slightly altered) in a typically Portuguese style; tiles hand-painted by Jorge Pinto and Baroque-style wood carving adorn its front. The Animatógrapho remains a cinema today – though not showing particularly high-quality films.

Igreja de Madalena

On the eastern edge of Baixa the portal of the Igreja de Madalena on the small Largo da Madalena stands out, having been integrated into an 18th c.

façade with a single tower. The church was built in 1783, the substantially older portal comes from a small 12th c. church. The height of the single-aisled interior and the bright light entering through the high window above the eight side altars comes as a surprise. The ceiling is decorated with fifteen symmetrically arranged medallion paintings. The painting on the high altar is by Pedro Alexandrino.

*Basilica da Estrela E 4

Location
Praçada Estrela

Trams
25, 26, 28, 29, 30

Buses
9, 20, 22, 38

Open
Daily 7.30am–1pm
3–8pm

To the north-west of the city centre, on one of Lisbon's many hills, stands the Basilica da Estrela ("Star Basilica"). Its striking position and gleaming white dome make it resemble the National pantheon (see Igreja de Santa Ingrácia), which is situated considerably further to the east but whose dome causes them to be easily confused, and which is a prominent point of reference in a panoramic overview of Lisbon. The church is regarded as the most important sacred building in the Portuguese capital dating from the second half of the 18th c.

Queen Maria I ordered the construction of the church. She had taken a vow to have a church built if she bore a son and thus a successor. Her son José was born but died, however, two years before the church was completed. The construction of the Basilica da Estrela began in 1779 under the direction of the architect Mateus Vicente de Oliveira. He had already been consulted by Maria I and her husband Pedro III about the palace at Queluz. The Late-Baroque style of the church originates from his blueprint. Mateus Vicente died in 1786 and Reinaldo Manuel took charge of further work. To him are ascribed the classical elements, which dominate the exterior in particular. Architects and sculptors predominantly from the school belonging to the huge monastery at Mafra (see entry) worked on the church, which was completed in 1790. Mateus Vicente himself studied under Ludovice

Igreja da Madalena

Basilica da Estrela

who built the monastery palace at Mafra. The orientation of the basilica there is clearly recognisable, that of the Basilica da Estrela was conceived to be substantially more restrained.

Exterior

The church, which can be seen from a long way away, radiates an overall impression of friendliness and elegance, due not least to the use of white limestone and to the delicately slender cupola over the crossing. The classical exterior is flanked by two bell towers. The three portals, framed by four Corinthian columns, are reached via a wide, flat flight of steps. Four marble statues, representing Belief, Honour, Freedom and Thankfulness, rise above the columns. The statues in the niches represent four saints.

Interior

The singled-aisled, harmoniously-proportioned interior also appears light and bright. The church is completely lined with pink, white and grey marble. The ceiling is barrel-vaulted, this continuing into the chancel where it changes into a semi-cupola. The high cupola spans the barrel-roof creating a pleasant expanse. It is divided by large, bright windows and fluted pilasters. The conspicuous high altar was created by Pompeu Batoni in Rome. The grave of Maria I, the only member of the Bragança family not to be buried in the family pantheon in the Igreja de São Vicente de Fora (see entry), can be seen in the right transept. The tomb of her father confessor (the archbishop of Évora, Inácio de São Caetano) is located in the sacristy. It is even more richly decorated than that of the queen.
The buildings surrounding the church and the cloisters are used today for administration and are not open to the public.

Marble statues
Christmas crib

Of note are the various marble statues both inside and outside the basilica, which come from the famous sculpting school at Mafra. The work of its leader, Machado de Castro, includes the figures of Mary and Joseph standing to the left and the right of the entrance hall and a Christmas crib with more than 500 figures (it is located in a sideroom which will be opened to interested visitors). Machedo de Castro also decorated the sacristy.

Jardim da Estrela

The Jardim da Estrela (see entry), opposite the church, is regarded as one of Lisbon's finest parks.

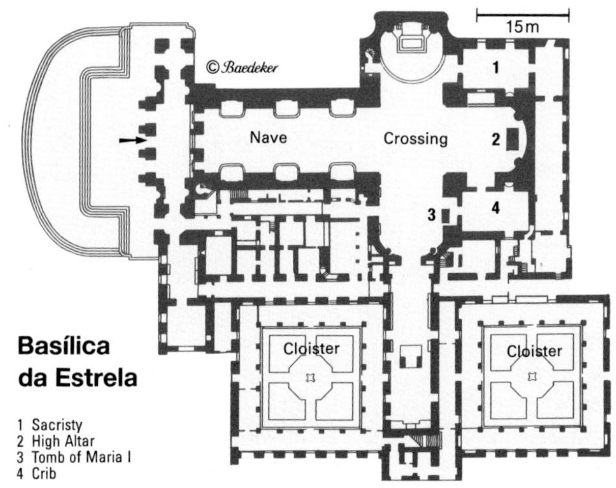

* Belém (suburb)

Location
5km/3 miles west of Lisbon

Trams
15, 16, 17

Buses
14, 27, 28, 29
43, 49, 51

Train
from Estação Cais do Sodré, Station Belém

Belém lies on the bank of the Tagus on the western edge of Lisbon. Its historically important buildings document the most important epoch of Portuguese history. The name "Belém" is a typically Portuguese shortening of "Bethelehem". The village, which was independent until 1885, suffered very little from the effects of the earthquake of 1775; thus its historic buildings are amongst the oldest in the Portuguese capital.

The origins of Belém's importance lie in the earlier harbour of Restelo. The harbour served as the departure point for the voyages of discovery undertaken by Portuguese sailors. They also returned here after their voyages with their booty from far-off lands.

The direct combination of political and religious interests in large-scale ocean navigation is clearly recognisable in Belém. A former small hospice chapel standing on the site of the current Mosteiro dos Jerónimos (see entry) was used as a place to pray before the Christian journeys of discovery and conquest. The fortress-like Torre de Belém, a more secular symbol, stands at the place where the mouth of the Tagus opens to the Atlantic. Both the monastery and the old tower of Belém were commissioned by King Manuel "the Happy", during whose reign Vasco de Gama discovered the sea route to India and Pedro Alvares Cabrals journeyed to Brazil. During this time many members of the nobility as well as prosperous business people moved to Belém. After the devastating damage caused by the earthquake in Lisbon had temporarily paralysed the life of the city, brief thought was given to beginning reconstruction not in present-day Baixa but to creating a new city centre in Belém.

The Praça do Império with the façade of the Mosteiro dos Jerónimos

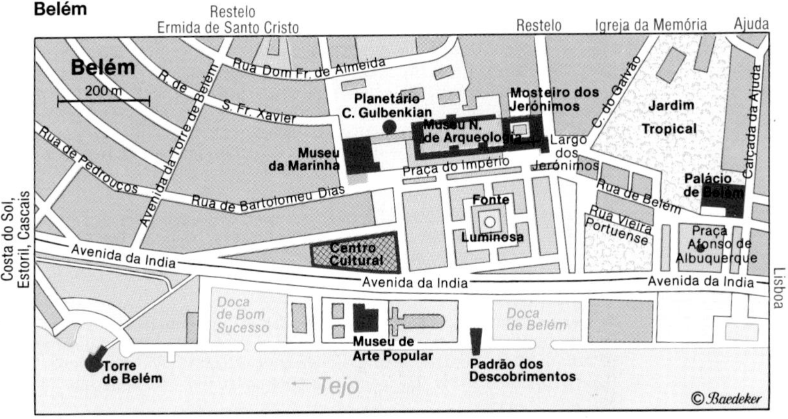

During the time of the *estado novo* under the dictator Salazar, Belém was given the role of reviving the resurgence of awareness of Portuguese history and the former greatness of the nation. On the occasion of the 300th anniversary of independence from Spain (December 1st 1640) a pompous "Exhibition of the Portuguese World" was staged on the land between the Hieronymite monastery and the bank of the Tagus. The area was laid out in a completely new way, with architectural direction assumed by Cottinelli Telmo, whose work also includes the glorified Padrão dos Descobrimentos (Memorial to Discovery) (see entry).

Round trip

The Praça do Império, in front of the Mosteiro dos Jerónimos (see entry), is suitable as a setting-off point for a round trip through Belém. After visiting the world-famous monastery continue in a south-westerly direction to one of Lisbon's symbols, the Torre de Belém. From here follow the bank of the Tagus in an easterly direction passing the Museu de Arte Popular to the Padrão dos Descobrimentos (see entry). The Praça Afonso de Albuquerque, whose north side is flanked by the Palácio de Belém, lies a short way to the north-east. The Museu Nacional dos Coches (National Coach Museum) (see entry) is housed in the palace's former riding school. The Rua Vieira Portuense leads back to the Praça do Império.

Having thus seen the most important places of interest in Belém, and if time remains, it is worth including a visit to the Jardim Tropical or to three chapels located further to the north.

Praça do Império

The Praça do Império (Imperial Square), which was created on account of the world exhibition, consists in the main of a small park with accurately cut hedges depicting Portugal's different municipal coats of arms. The over-sized fountain basin in the centre also has coats of arms around it; on special occasions the imposing, colourfully lit fountain is turned on.

Centro Cultural

Against some fierce opposition from the public a new cultural centre has been built to the west of the Praça do Império. The new cultural centre, complete with hotels, conference rooms and concert halls, was officially opened in 1992.

Rua Vieira Portuense

It is worth viewing the row of houses along the one side of the Rua Vieira Portuense on the edge of a large expanse of grass between the Praça do Impéio and the Praça Afonso de Albuquerque. The narrow houses date from the 16th c. and 17th c. Compared with the many large-scale and historically famous places of interest in the near vicinity, these small dwellings with their brightly painted exteriors appear cheerful and restrained. They give an impression of a life lived on the edge of great events, in which little would be gained from the heroic deeds and wealth of those days.

Praça Afonso de Albuquerque

The Praça Afonso de Albuquerque has been laid out as a geometric park. A neo-Manueline pillar has been placed in the centre, bearing a 4m/13ft tall bronze statue of Afonso de Albuquerque. Scenes from his life are depicted on the plinth.

Afonso de Albuquerque (1453–1515) took part in the conquest of important trading centres for Portugal and was named as the first Portuguese viceroy of India in 1509. There he bore the significant nickname "Leão dom Mares" (Lion of the Sea). In his "Lucíados", Camões called him "Albuquerque the Terrible".

Palácio de Belém

The Palácio de Belém, the current seat of office of the president, extends along the north side of the Praça Afonso de Albuquerque. Mário Soares, the current president, gave up his flat in the city for the dwelling in Belém. The palace – often called the Palácio Cor de Rosa because of its pink exterior – was founded in 1559. It was renovated several times during the 17th c. and 18th c. Joáo V, who had purchased the palace in 1726 from the Count of Aveiro, had considerable alterations made and planted a large garden behind the palace. The present building is the result of renovation carried out in 1886.

Praça Afonso de Albuquerque

Igreja de S. José da Memória

During the earthquake on November 1st 1755, José I and his family stayed in the Palácio de Belém and not in the royal palace at Terreiro do Paço (see Praça do Comércio), which was completely destroyed.
The palace's previous riding school now accommodates the Museu Nacional des Coches (National Coach Museum) (see entry).

Jardim Tropical

Behind the Palácio de Belém (entrance on the Largo dos Jerónimos) stretches a grassed area covering about 7ha/17 acres. Once belonging to the palace, it was laid out in 1912 as a tropical garden (open: Tues.–Sun., 10am–5pm). About 400 different plant species flourish in the peaceful park, which is worth visiting, and in some hothouses. The museum is normally closed and can only be visited by appointment.

Igreja de S. José da Memória

Halfway between the botanical garden of Ajuda (see Palácio Nacional da Ajuda) and the Jardim Tropical, the small Igreja de S. José da Memória stands on the Calçada da Memória. After an unsuccessful attempt on the life of José I, the king had the well-proportioned cupola church (designed by the well-known architect Mateus Vicente) built in 1760. Vicente also contributed to the construction of the Basilica da Estrela (see entry) and the Palace of Queluz (see entry). The grave of José's Minister Pombal was transferred to the church in 1923.

Ermida de Santo Cristo

Of three small chapels which once belonged to the Hieronymite monastery only the Ermida de Santo Cristo and the Ermida de São Jerónimo remain. A third, the Santa Maria Madalena, was completely destroyed.
The inconspicuous little Ermida de Santo Cristo stands not far from Restelo stadium on the Rua de Alcolena. The Manueline church, now closed, was built in 1517 by João de Castilho and was originally integrated into the wall surrounding the grounds of the Hieronymite monastery.

Ermida de São Jerónimo

By climbing up a grassed area on the Rua de Alcolena we reach the Ermida de São Jerónimo, which was built in 1514 according to the plans of the famous Manueline architect Diogo de Boytaca.
The chapel, which looks almost like a monolith, stands out from the other remaining constructions of this epoch through its simple harmonious proportions and, above all, its restrained Manueline upper ornamentation. The building, in an exposed location, represents in principle simply a rectangular cube, whose heaviness is only tempered by the sparse decoration on the four corners and on the upper edge.
The true features of Manueline design appear particularly clearly in its simplicity. The corner pillars adorned with Gothic gargoyles jut out beyond the building and taper into finely pointed turrets. The upper edges resemble nautical cabling. A slender cross rises above the Manueline portal.
The impressive little chapel is generally closed; however it is worthwhile climbing up to it because of the unusual view of the Torre de Belém (see entry) and the Atlantic, which appears very close from here.

Benfica (suburb) A/B 11

Location
North-west edge of the city

Metro
Sete Rios-Colégio Militar

Buses
16, 46, 58

The suburb of Benfica lies on the north-west edge of Lisbon. In the past Benfica was known for its villas and the spacious quintas (country houses) belonging to rich citizens of Lisbon who spent their weekends here. Since then tower block complexes, shopping centres and light industry have come to dominate this part of the city. The rapid development of the area has been accelerated through the extension of the metro to the north-west. Beyond Portugal's borders the name of this part of the city is known above all for its old-established football team Benfica Lisboa; in 1944 a stadium for 120,000 spectators was built here.

Benfica: Igreja de São Domingos

Trains
from Estação Rossio, Stations Cruz da Pedra and Benfica

A zoological garden (see Jardim Zoológico), about 100 hundred years old, is situated between the city centre and Benfica. A little of the earlier country-like atmosphere of this region can be detected on the southern edge as far as the Parque Florestal de Monsanto (see entry). Here it is worth visiting the Palácio dos Marqueses de Fronteira with its unique garden.

Igreja de São Domingos de Benfica

The Igreja de São Domingos de Benfica stands on the Largo de São Domingos very close to the palace. It forms part of a Dominican monastery, founded in 1399, which has been renovated several times – most recently in the 19th c. The small church, which is generally kept closed, was so badly damaged in the earthquake that most of it had to be rebuilt. The walls are decorated with azulejos by António de Oliveira dating from the 18th c. Of note is the 17th c. right side chapel, S. Gonçalo de Amarante, inside which stand several statues carved from carrara and arrábida marble. The graves of many members of the Fronteira family, to whom the neighbouring palace belonged, are to be found in the main chapel.

Biblioteca Nacional

See Cidade Universitária

Bica (Quarter) G 2/3

Location
Between Bairro Alto and the Tagus

Buses: 13

This simple little quarter, which runs down from the Calçada do Combro/Rua do Loreto to the Tagus, exudes considerably more peacefulness than neighbouring Bairro Alto (see entry). Only a few cars journey here due to its sloping site and its dense construction. Narrow streets and flights of steps dissect the old quarter, which appears extremely self-contained and unspoilt. Here, as in Alfama and Mouraria (see entries), there are simple pubs, which serve the inhabitants of Bica, almost exclusively, as meeting places.

Trams
16, 18, 19, 25, 26
28, 28B

Elevador da Bica

The Elevador da Bica rises above the steep Rua da Bica de Duarte Belo and forms the connection between the Calçada do Combro/Rua do Loreto and the Rua de S. Paulo. The lower station of this funicular railway is almost hidden behind a façade on the Rua de S. Paulo with the inscription "Ascensor da Bica" (no. 234). It was constructed by Raoul Mesnier de Ponsard and opened to the public in 1892.

Alto de Santa Catarina

Not far from the Elevador da Bica lies the lovely viewpoint Alto de Santa Catarina. From here there is an extensive panorama of the Tagus, the Ponte 25 de Abril (see entry) and the opposite bank. A stone colossus was placed in the small park in 1927, representing an allegorical figure, well-known in Portugal, from Camões Lusiaden and thus symbolises Portugal's "Golden Age". According to Camões' fantasy the *Adamastor* surfaced at the Cape of Good Hope and warned the Portuguese explorers of storms and danger. The Adamastor is a work by the artist Júlio Vaz Júnior.

Mercado da Ribeira Nova

The Mercado da Ribeiro Nova, Lisbon's largest market hall, stands on the Tagus below Bica, in the Avenida 24 de Julho, near to the Estação Cais do Sodré. The building was constructed in 1902 by João A. Piloto; its current appearance, with the gleaming white cupola, has existed since renovation in 1930. A previous 1882 construction was destroyed by fire.
Those who enjoy markets can visit the Mercado da Ribeira Nova on weekdays between 6am and 2pm.

Câmara Municipal

See Paços do Conselho

Campo Grande — H 9–11

Location
north of the city centre

Metro
Entrecampos

Buses
1, 7, 7A, 17B, 21
27, 32, 36, 38
44, 45, 46A, 47
49, 83, 90

The 1.2km/¾ mile long and 200m/656ft wide Campo Grande park stretches from the Entrecampos roundabout to the motorway in the north. This area was already used by the public in the 16th c. The legendary Dom Sebastião allowed his troops to practise here before he set off on a crusade to Morocco. The park began to be planted with selected species of trees and shrubs in the late 18th c.
For a long time the park was used mostly by aristocratic citizens for weekend excursions and today many city dwellers continue to spend their Sunday afternoons here. Visitors can hire a rowing boat on the small lake or sit at the attractive café. However, the peace which used to prevail here in earlier decades cannot be found today; several carriageways flank the length of the park to left and right, and, in addition, the Campo Grande lies directly below the last few metres of the approach path of Portela airport.

Guerra Peninsular

The "Guerra Peninsular" monument, a reminder of the battles against the Napoleonic invasion at the beginning of the 19th c., stands in the middle of the Entrecampos roundabout. Scenes of resistance are depicted on the plinth, with the victorious Portuguese nation portrayed above. Some soldiers are driving off the eagle of the Napoleonic empire. The memorial, whose design exhibits a variety of neo-Manueline features, was erected here in 1933.

Further places of interest

Two museums worth visiting, the Museu da Cidade (see entry) and the Museu Rafael Bordalo Pinheiro (see entry), are located at the northern end of the Campo Grande. To the west of the Campo Grande lie the buildings of the university (see Cidade Universitária).

*Casa dos Bicos (House of Facets) J 2

Location
Rua dos Bacalhoeiros 10

Trams
3, 16, 24

Buses
9, 13A, 17, 25
25A, 28, 35, 39
46, 59, 81, 82, 90

A typical Renaissance palace stands in the square-like eastern part of the Rua dos Bacalhoeiros. The then chairman of the senate, Brás de Albuquerque, son of Afonso de Albuquerque, the first viceroy of India, had the "House of Facets" built in 1523 according to plans drawn up by the architects Santa-Rita Fernandes and Manuel Vicente.

The extravagant façade requested by Brás de Albuquerque was built in accordance with European taste of that day – similar buildings dating from this epoch are to be found in Spanish, Italian and French towns. The striking frontage gave the palace its name. It is faced in a geometric pattern with pyramid-shaped, pointed stones. Association with polished diamonds gave rise to the nickname "House of Diamonds". Wilhelm von Eschwege, the architect of the Palácio da Pena at Sintra (see entry), used this diamond motif in the architecturally mixed style of the Pena palace.

The palace was built on four floors, but the two upper storeys were destroyed during the earthquake of 1755. For over 200 years the House of Facets remained in its two-storey state and was used by fishmongers for storage. Not until 1982 were the two top floors replaced to look like the originals. (In the cloister of the Convento de Madre de Deus (see entry) the original Casa dos Bicos can be seen on a tile depicting a panoramic view of Lisbon.) However, during the rebuilding of the two top storeys some modern materials were used (e.g. in the windows) so that the new section can be recognised as a reconstruction. The low flight of steps in front of the Casa dos Bicos has been constructed in the shape of a Manueline arch.

After an arcitecturally-interesting renovation of the palace interior, the ground floor of the House of Facets is now being used for small exhibitions while offices are accommodated on the upper floors.

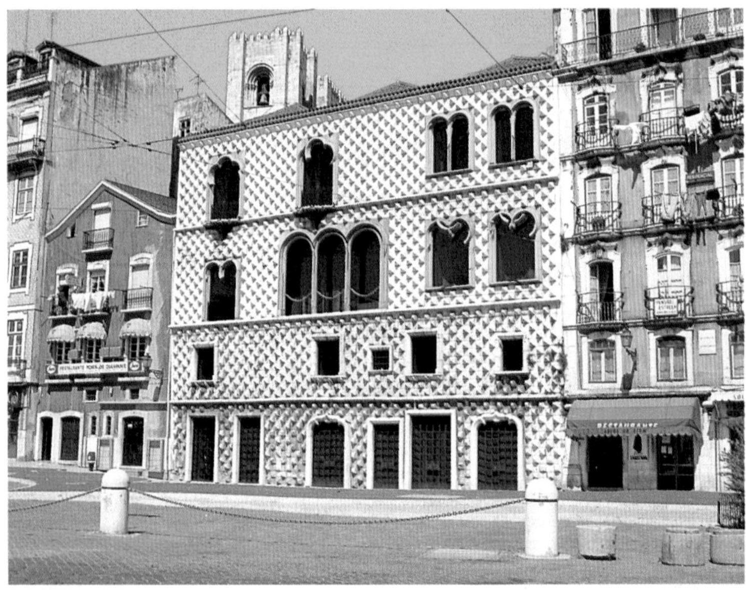

Casa dos Bicos

Cascais (excursion)

A popular seaside resort and, at the same time, a fishing port, Cascais lies on the Costa do Estoril (see entry) and is easily reached from Lisbon. The area around Cascais was settled as early as Roman times and since the 14th c. the coastal resort has held a town charter. A historical event is often referred to in connection with Cascais: in 1580 the town was the last place that the Spanish general, General Alba, needed to pass through on his way to Lisbon. Yet another defensive battle took place here before Spain assumed control of Portugal for the next 80 years.

Location
25km/15½ miles west of Lisbon

Trains
From Estação Cais do Sodré

Since 1871 the citadel in Cascais has served as a royal summer residence. At the end of the 19th c. the small fishing port began to develop into a bathing resort. Cascais has also become increasingly popular with foreign holidaymakers mainly on account of its pleasant climate – cold winds are tempered by the Sintra mountains to the north.

During the last decade almost the whole coastal region to the west of Lisbon has been developed, and Cascais and the neighbouring resort of Estoril (see entry) are merging into one another. At the beginning of the 20th c. the town had about 6000 inhabitants, today there are over 30,000.
Cascais presents a very varied face. On the edge of the town many high rise developments have been built, yet extensive areas filled with villas can also be found in Cascais, where rich Portuguese as well as English, French and Germans live. Fortunately a lovely old centre has been retained and in some rather isolated, quiet alleyways a little of the character of the old fishing village can be detected. The origin of the town can also be seen in the many brightly-painted fishing boats tied up in the harbour, which still set sail to sea daily. Many restaurants, cafés and stalls selling tourist souvenirs fill the centre.

The citadel, built in 1681, stands above the south-west side of the harbour. Today it is used by the military and remains closed to the public.

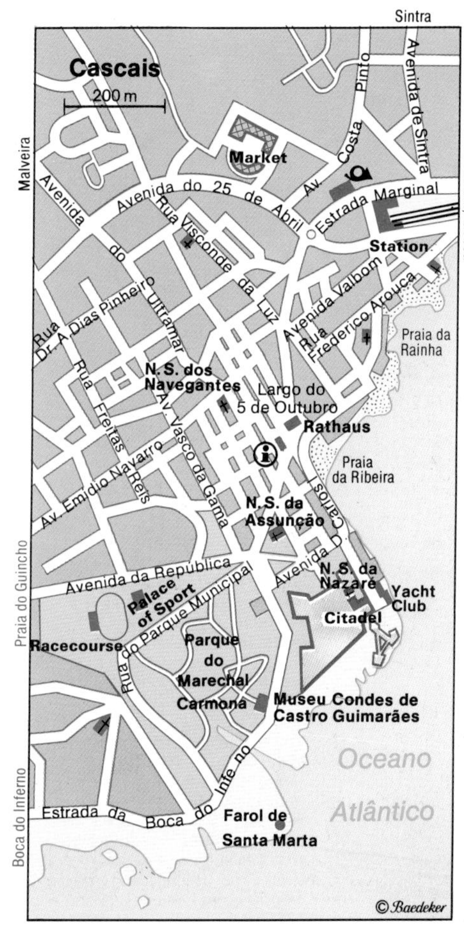

Parque do Marechal Carmona

The Parque do Marechal Carmona extends to the left of the citadel. At the beginning of the 20th c. the Conde de Castro Guimarães had a country seat built in its southern section, within which a library and a small museum were opened by Cascais town council during the 1920s. Exhibits in the museum include prehistoric finds from the area, porcelain, gold and silver work and Portuguese furniture.

N. S. da Assunção

In a small square opposite the entrance to the citadel stands the Igreja de Nossa Senhora da Assunção. In 1745 the walls of this single-aisled church were clad with blue and white tiles, depicting scenes from the Apocalypse. The ceiling painting is the work of the artist José Malhoa, who has become very well-known in Portugal.

Nossa Senhora dos Navegantes

The Baroque Igreja de Nossa Senhora dos Navegantes, located further north, was built to an octagonal ground plan. The azuléjos of the interior are worth viewing.

Town hall

The town hall, with its tile-clad façade, stands between the popular Largo do 5 de Outubro and the Praia da Ribeira.

Beaches

The promenade Avenida de D. Carlos I follows a north-easterly direction from the citadel and makes it possible to walk to Estoril (see entry) along a made-up path on the water's edge. On the way there is a fine view of the bay stretching from Cascais towards Estoril can be enjoyed, and also of the mass of houses on the shore. In comparison the sandy bays of Praia da Ribeira and Praia da Rainha in Cascais appear very picturesque; further towards Estoril lies the Praia da Duchesa, with its good bathing facilities. During the summer months all of these beaches are overcrowded.

Along the coast to the north-west of Cascais there are several larger beaches and some very lovely smaller resorts. Also worth seeing are the Cabo de Roca – the most westerly point of the European mainland – and the Boca do Inferno (see Costa do Estoril).

*Castelo de São Jorge (St George's Castle) J 2/3

Location
east, above Baixa

Trams
28, 28B

Buses
37

Open
Daily 9am–7pm (Apr.–Sept. until 9pm)

The Castelo de São Jorge stands above the centre of Lisbon to the east and is clearly visible from a long way off.

The origins of this former fortress date back to an Iron Age settlement on this site, which was occupied by the Romans in about 205 B.C. The 110m/361ft high hill on which the castle stands also constitutes the central starting point of Lisbon's development. Later the castle was used as a fortress by both the West Goths and then finally by the Arabs. After its capture by Portugal's first king, Afonso Henriques, in 1147 it was renovated and extended several times.

It gained its present name in honour of the dragon-killing St George, Portugal's patron saint.

Part of the complex was converted into a royal palace in about 1300 and the kings of Portugal resided here until 1511. Until this time the castle and the area surrounding it had for centuries been the centre of all events owing to the location. At the beginning of the 16th c. Gil Vicente, goldsmith and poet, staged his "Monologue of a Cowherd" here and thus laid the basis of Portuguese theatre. After his voyage to India, Vasco de Gama was received at the castle by King Manuel I. In 1511 Manuel I moved into his newly-built residence on the present-day Praça do Comércio, then named after the royal palace Terreiro do Paço, and from then on events shifted themselves increasingly directly to the bank of the Tagus. Thus the Castelo de São Jorge lost its former importance; only Dom Sebastião, the "longed for", who has been well nigh forgotten until now, resided here once more for a short time before he set off for Alcácer Quibir in 1578. After 1640 the complex was used as a prison and an ordnance depot. The earthquake of 1755 almost completely destroyed the walls of the buildings.

Site plan

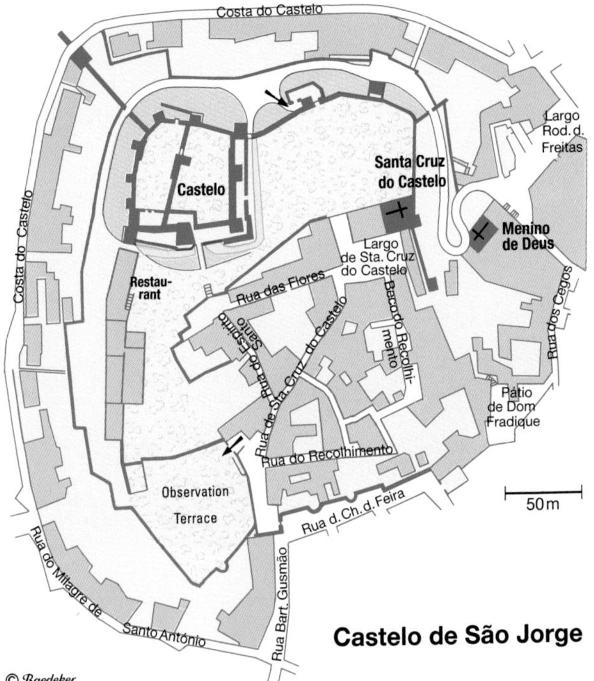

Castle complex

It was not until the 20th c. that the castle was rebuilt as present-day visitors see it. Early photographs of the town show a completely different picture of the castle. Between 1938 and 1944, under Salazar's rule, the whole castle complex was restored. In doing this more attention was paid to historical authenticity than to the resurrection of national history. Thus a very fine and varied reconstruction has arisen. The heart of the complex is a wall with ten massive towers, which can be climbed and which offer a fine view of the city. Within the inner courtyard of the castle ruins a small park with water courses and with some animal enclosures has been laid out. Peacocks sit in the old trees or walk along the paths, here and there there are quiet corners in which little fountains babble. A restaurant has been opened in one part of the former royal residence and in addition a Gothic hall has been reconstructed. On the north side of the castle is the Martim Moniz Gate, named after a knight who, in 1147 at the risk of his own life, kept it open to facilitate access for the troops of Afonso Henriques.

Viewing terrace

The ascent to the Castelo de São Jorge is worthwhile purely for the view it affords over the city. A fine prospect of the whole of the inner city can be enjoyed from the large tree-filled square at the entrance. To the south-west we look across the Tagus to the Monumento Cristo Rei (see entry) on the opposite bank. The Atlantic can be seen behind the Ponte 25 de Abril and on clear days the Padrão dos Descombrimentos and the Torre de Belém (see entries) are visible in the distance. A tile picture shows the exact locations and helps with orientation.

A fine view from the Castelo de São Jorge

Igreja de Santa Cruz do Castelo

By making a tour of the streets within the castle walls, the little Largo Santa Cruz do Castelo, on which stands the church of the same name, is automatically reached. It dates from the 12th c. and has been renovated and restored several times owing to damage. It is supposed that a mosque stood on this site during the time of the Arabs. Within the church stands a statue of St George, which used to be carried in Corpus Christi processions.

Cemitério dos Prazeres (Prazeres Cemetery) C/D 4

Location
Praça São João Bosco

Trams
28

Buses
9, 13, 18

Open
Daily, 9am–5pm (May–Sept. until 6pm)

Laid out in 1833, the Cemitério dos Prazeres, the "Cemetery of Pleasure" (the name derives from a previous property on this site) lies above the Alcântara valley. The white graves stretch for more than 110,000sq.m/ 131,560sq.yds in the shade of old cypress trees. The cemetery resembles a miniature town: along a total of 73 systematically arranged streets house-like graves and mausoleums lie to the left and the right. The graves have "front doors" at whose windows hang crocheted curtains, with little tables and sometimes chairs standing inside – diverse accessories are supposed to give a homely atmosphere. Some truly monumental, historically interesting graves are worth visiting (nos 2060, 2086, 4090, 5250, 5284, 5411, 6301).

Graves of well-known Portuguese families as well as some famous personalities can be found in the Prazeres cemetery. One of the most famous, Fernando Pessoa, whose literary greatness was only recognised some time after his death, was first buried here and then moved in 1985 to the cloisters of the Mosteiro dos Jerónimos (see entry) in Belém, where he now rests very close to the most important people of Portuguese history.

From the western edge of the cemetery a marvellous view can be enjoyed over the Alcântara valley, the Parque Florestal de Monsanto (see entry) and the Tagus with the Ponte 25 de Abril (see entry).

Centro de Arte Moderna

See Fundação Calouste Gulbenkian

*Chiado (Quarter) G/H 2/3

Location
West of Baixa

Trams
10, 20, 24, 28
28B, 29, 30

Buses
15

Lift
Elevador do Carmo

Chiado is the name given to the quarter west of the Baixa (see entry), located on the slope that forms the link between the lower and the upper parts of the city. The name is often also used to denote only the elegant shopping street, Rua Garrett, situated in the centre of the quarter. The poet and playwright António Ribeiro (*c.* 1520–91) gave the area its name. A contemporary of Luis Vaz de Camões, he was originally a Franciscan monk but left his order and went to Lisbon where he became known as "Chiado". For a long time the Chiado quarter was considered to be the most elegant shopping area in Lisbon. Now shopping takes place mostly in streets such as the Avenida de Roma and the Rua Braancamp, and principally in the Amoreiras Shopping Center (see entry) and the Baixa (see entry). However, some exclusive fashion shops with ranges reminiscent of Paris can be found in Chiado.

At the turn of the century and during the first decade of the 20th c. Chiado was the meeting place for writers and artists. Political and cultural exchanges constantly took place in the cafés here.

A short while ago Chiado hit the world headlines when an enormous fire destroyed part of the quarter on August 25th 1988. The effects of the fire were less by far than the media first reported but nevertheless the destruction seriously spoilt the character of the district. In the main it was the Rua do Carmo, a pedestrianised street, which was affected by the catastrophe. Together with homes and offices two old department stores burnt down, as well as the famous Pastelaria Ferrari and the valuable archives of the music shop Valentim do Carvalho containing unique documents relating to the history of Portuguese music. After the fire the city council was mainly held to blame for allowing the construction of a pedestrianised street without access for fire engines, together with the totally inadequate safety precautions taken in the buildings. In 1989 a pedestrian bridge was constructed above the burnt-out part of the Rua do Carmo from which the ruins, illuminated at night, can be partially viewed. In a long-winded discussion about the reconstruction of the destroyed quarter the main alternatives put forward were either to rebuild the area as close to the original as possible by using the remaining façades or to replace completely the remains with new, modern buildings. The project was finally awarded to Siza Vieira, an architect from Porto. A reconstruction was decided on (which by 1991 had not progressed very far) based on the original character of the quarter; provided that they still exist, the façades of the earlier buildings will be incorporated into the new construction. In particular, sufficient flats are to be built to combat domination by offices and shops, thus saving Chiado from becoming "lifeless". It had already been noticed in the years leading up to the fire that after the shops closed there was a tendency for the quarter to appear uninhabited. In addition there are plans for the construction of a shopping centre and a hotel on the site of one of the former department stores.

Rua Garrett

The name of the Rua Garrett in the centre of Chiado commemorates the writer Almeida Garrett (1799–1854), who was also temporarily active as a liberal politician. Several old-established shops are to be found in the street, some with very splendid interiors worth seeing. The famous "Livraria Bertrand" (no. 106) was founded by a Frenchman more than 200 years ago. The café and restaurant "Bénard" (no. 106) also has French origins and it is quite clear what the fashion shop "Paris em Lisboa" models its name on.

Igreja dos Mártires

Lying a little apart near to the blue-tiled corner house Livraria Bertrand on the Rua Garrett stands the Igreja dos Mártires, which was constructed in 1769 as part of new building work carried out after the earthquake. The builder was Reinaldo Manuel. The interior with its bright marble walls appears very balanced and harmonious. The painting of the barrel-vaulted ceiling is the work of Pedro Alexandrino.
Before the earthquake a small church of the same name stood in a different part of Chiado. It was founded by Portugal's first king, Afonso Henriques, on the occasion of the conquest of Lisbon in 1147. A representation of this can be seen above the main portal of the new church.

Largo do Chiado

The Largo do Chiado forms the upper western end of the Rua Garrett. The alternative name of the square, Largo das Duas Igrejas, refers to the two churches which face each other here. Originally a gate forming part of the city wall built by Fernando I in the 14th c. was located here.
A bronze memorial to the poet and playwright "Chiado" has been placed here. It depicts him as a derisive orator who does not completely believe in authority.

Igreja do Loreto

The Igreja do Loreto (1517), striking on account of its double flight of entrance steps, forms the north-western corner of the square leading to the Rua Misericórdia. It was destroyed by fire in 1651 and 100 years later destroyed again by the earthquake. The architect of the opera house (see Teatro Nacional de São Carlos), J. da Costa e Silva, was responsible for the renovation and the rebuilding in 1784, when the original Mannerist façade was retained. The ceiling painting in the single-aisled interior portraying the Santa do Loreto, the work of Pedro Alexandrino, is most striking.
A further name, Igreja dos Italianos, dates from the time when an apparently large Italian colony used the church as the centre of their community. At the beginning of the 20th c. Sunday Mass here served as a meeting point for the upper classes.

Igreja dos Mártires

Igreja do Loreto

Largo do Chiado

Igreja da Encarnação

Also single-aisled, the Igreja da Encarnação on the opposite corner was newly built in 1784 by M. Caetano de Sousa after its complete destruction by the earthquake. Most impressive of all is the tiled western façade on the Rua do Alecrim, which appears huge in the relatively narrow street.
The interior appears very dark. On the barrel-vaulted ceiling, also painted by Pedro Alexandrino, preaching scenes are portrayed.

Café "A Brasileira"

In 1922 the Café "A Brasileira" (The Brazilian Woman) established itself on the Largo do Chiado. The café developed from a shop selling coffee founded in 1905. A Brasileira became a famous meeting place for intellectual writers, journalists and artists. A peculiarity of that time was that the owner allowed paintings to be hung in the café; these were portraits by the young Almada Negreiros, who thus achieved a much-visited exhibition. In the meantime they have become museum pieces, have been replaced by the present pictures and now hang in the Centro de Arte Moderna (see Fundação Calouste Gulbenkian).
The course of time has altered the style of the café. In order to be able to cope with and take advantage of the summer influx of tourists the café has extended on to a platform on the pavement. On the occasion of the 100th birthday of Fernando Pessoa a bronze memorial to the poet was placed outside the café; his regular café was, however, the Martinho da Arcada on the Praça do Comércio (see entry).

Praça Luis de Camões

In 1867 a memorial to the well-known Portuguese poet Luis de Camões (see Famous People) was erected on the tree-lined Praça de Luis de Camões which borders the Largo do Chiado to the west. Camões was the creator of the "Lusiadas", a heroic epic which glorifies the Portuguese voyages of discovery and conquest. (A contrasting portrayal of these events is given in "Peregrinação", written by the author Fernão Mendes Pinto, which was censored for a long time.)
Camões, the date of whose death has become a Portuguese national

holiday, is depicted with a sword and books – certainly a somewhat too bombastic portrayal of the poet, who reported for duty in the civil service because of personal difficulties and who died in poverty. The 4m/13ft high bronze statue stands on an octagonal pedestal, around which are grouped eight important Portuguese scientists and authors.

Eça de Queiròs monument

From the Largo do Chiado the Rua de Alecrim leads down to the Tagus. On the Largo do Barão de Quintela, which opens onto the street immediately to its west, a monument of questionable beauty was erected in memory of the poet Eça de Queiròs (1846–1900) three years after his death. The author of the famous social novels "Os Maias" and "Primo Basilio" looks into the eyes of the naked figure of a woman, which is apparently supposed to personify the "naked truth". The work is that of the then very fashionable sculptor Teixeira Lopes.

Teatro de São Luis

The Teatro de São Luis in the Rua António Maria Cardosa (no. 54), a parallel road to the Rua do Alecrim, was built in 1916. A previous building dating from 1894 burnt down in 1914; the present building is a true reconstruction of the original.
The interior of the theatre is impressive because of its old-fashioned charm; the artistic past of the house is impressively presented by way of the name boards and pictures on the walls of the staircase. Apart from theatrical productions, the theatre also presents films, concerts, lectures and dance displays.

PIDE building

In the same street (nos. 18–26) can be seen a building which was used as the headquarters of the secret police under the dictator Salazar and his successor Caetano. The PIDE (Policia Internacional da Defesa do Estado) collected all possible putative evidence to use against inconvenient opponents of the regime of dictatorship. The arrangement of the building with individual cells for those arrested, bugging devices, instruments of torture, etc., was the result of discussions with the Gestapo.
Growing foreign criticism of the rigorous methods of the state police led to the PIDE later being renamed as the DGS (Direcção Geral de Segurança) without any changes to its methods. On the day of the revolution, April 25th 1974, members of the DGS barricaded themselves into the building after Marcelo Caetano and the regime had already given up. They shot blindly into the crowd which had collected around the building; four people were killed and 45 injured. A memorial to the event and to the four who were shot dead was placed here four years after the event.

Largo de São Carlos

The Lisbon Opera House (see Teatro Nacional de São Carlos) is situated in the Largo de São Carlos nearby to the west.
On the fourth floor of the house opposite (no. 4) Fernando Pessoa, the most famous 20th c. Portuguese author, was born. Some wall paintings recall Pessoa, of which drawings by the artist Almada Negreiros served as patterns – similar to those at the entrance to the university (see Cidade Universitária). To be seen is a portrait of Pessoa as well as the poet in his regular café Martinho da Arcada (see Praça do Comércio).

Academia das Belas Artes

The Lisbon Academy of Art is situated on the Largo da Academia das Belas Artes. The Academy of Art, like the Museu Nacional de Arte Contemporânea, is housed in the rooms of a former Franciscan monastery.
Until 1969 the national library could be found on this square, then called Largo da Biblioteca Pública. A lift, which was constructed before Raoul Mesnier de Ponsard's Elevador do Carmo (see entry), once terminated here.

Chiado Trinidade

Further to the north, on the other side of the Rua Garrett, lies a small quarter known as Trinidade (Trinity). The name commemorates the Trinidade monastery which used to be here. Of this monastery the former refectory

survives and today houses the restaurant "Cervejaria da Trinidade", worth visiting for its tiled walls dating from 1863.
Also remaining from this time are the later renovated Teatro da Trinidade (Rua Nova da Trinidade 9) and a house opposite the theatre (Rua da Trinidade 32), impressive on account of its azulejo tiles. The interior of the Teatro Gymnásio, founded in 1864, is currently being completely rebuilt (Rua Nove da Trinidade 5).

Cidade Universitária (University) G/H 9/10

Location
Alameda da Universidade

Metro
Cidade Universitária

Buses
1, 7, 7A, 17B, 31, 32, 36, 38, 45, 46A, 47, 83

The university buildings lie in the north of Lisbon, to the west of the Campo Grande (see entry) parkland. A university was first founded in Lisbon in the 13th c. After Lisbon succeeded Coimbra as the capital city in the middle of the 13th c. Coimbra gained a university at the beginning of the 14th c. as "recompense" and this remained Portugal's only university until 1911, when Lisbon was once again given its own university. Plans for a university to be built on its present site arose in the 1930s, but the buildings, designed by Pardel Monteiri, were only constructed between 1955 and 1960. Until 1962 Marcelo Caetano, Salazar's successor, was rector of the university.
The rector's office stands in the centre of a wide lawn, with the Faculty of Law located to its south and the Faculty of Arts to its north. At the entrance to the Faculty of Arts, Fernando Pessoa's heteronyms designed by the artist Almada Negreiros are depicted.

Arquivo Nacional da Torre do Tombo

Since 1990 a new building complex has stood next to the Faculty of Arts. This is the seat of the Torre do Tombo National Archive, which had been

"Torre do Tombo" National Archive

"provisionally" housed in the Palácio de São Bento since the earthquake of 1755. Transfer of the archive materials took place over several months. An area of 60,400sq.m/72,238sq.yds is available here and the archive's books and documents can be accommodated on 135.4km/84 miles of shelving.
The National Archive was founded in 883, during the time of Moorish rule in Lisbon. The oldest document dates from that year. In 1375 Fernando I ordered that the collection of documents should be housed in a tower of the then royal seat, the Castelo de São Jorge (see entry), in the so-called Torre do Tombo. Thanks to this fortunate move the archive was accommodated there at the time of the earthquake in 1755 and not at the new royal residence down by the Tagus, and thus many old documents and important manuscipts relating to Portuguese history have survived. Manuel da Maia, architect of the aqueduct who was heavily involved in the reconstruction of the city, brought the materials to safety from the ruins of the destroyed castle.
Amongst the archive's possessions is the first document written in the Portuguese language, the testament of Afonso II from the early 13th c., a Hieronymite bible, which Manuel the "Happy" had ordered, as well as 36,000 records from the trials of the Inquisition.

Biblioteca Nacional

Since 1969 the buildings of the National Library have been on the Campo Grande to the south of Cidade Universitaria. The National Library was founded in 1798 and was then housed on the newly-built Praço do Comércio. Later it moved to Chiado. Parts of the library's collection originate from closed monasteries, religious foundations and institutes. The National Library now owns more than two million volumes, accommodated on approximately 45km/28 miles of shelving – during the 20th c. its stock has increased almost five-fold.
On the upper floors of the building can be found the so-called Museu do Livro (Book Museum) and the Museu Instrumental do Conservatório Nacional (Museum of Musical Instruments; see Practical Information, Museums).

Convento do Carmo

See Igreja do Carmo

**Convento da Madre de Deus · Museu do Azulejo M 4

Location
Rua da Madre de Deus 4

Trams
3, 16, 27

Buses
13A, 18, 39, 42
59

Open
Tues.–Sun.
10am–12.30pm,
2–5pm

The Convento da Madre de Deus is located at some distance from the city centre – about 500m/547 yards from the Estação de Santa Apolonia (see entry) – but is well worth visiting. Today the National Tile Museum (Museu Nacional do Azulejo) is housed in some of the rooms of the convent.
The former Convent of St Clare was founded in 1509 by Queen Leonor, the sister of Manuel I, on whose initiative the Igreja da Conceição Velha (see entry) was also built. Leonor herself lived as a widow here. Until 1871 the building complex of Madre de Deus served as a convent.
The Convento da Madre de Deus was originally built in the Manueline style and was renovated several times by succeeding rulers. The earthquake of 1755 caused great damage to the complex and it was rebuilt during the reign of José I. From the Manueline era there remains one of the two cloisters as well as the small side portal to the left of the main entrance on the long frontage.

Main portal

In contrast the main portal is a reconstruction from 1872. In creating this authentic replacement a panel which can be seen in the Museu Nacional da

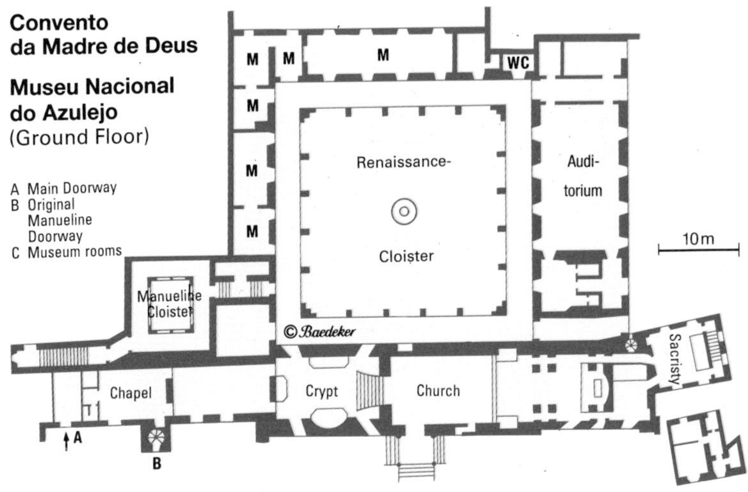

Arte Antiga (see entry) was relied on. The panel dates from the 16th c. and shows how a relic acquired in Cologne was brought to Lisbon. The scene depicted is in front of the then new Madre de Deus convent, with the original portal clearly recognisable.
Apart from the particularly Manueline elements – plant decorations and the two stone side columns fashioned like ropes – a fishing net and a pelican can be seen below the crown next to the Portuguese coat of arms. These emblems of Leonor and her husband João II were also used in the articulation of the upper ends of the façade. Leonor's son, Afonso, died in 1491 as the result of a riding accident at Tejo near to Santarém and his body was carried by fishermen in a net to the royal palace – hence the reason for the queen's choice of her personal coat of arms.

Church interior

The Baroque decoration of the interior is worth seeing. The internal decoration is not particularly in the usual Baroque style but it nevertheless contains typically Portuguese elements of this period. The warm gold colouring of the over-rich Talha Dourada contrasts with the cool blue-white of the tiles, both combine to present a striking impression. The altars and the lavish pulpit have been fashioned in pure Talha woodwork.
The one-aisled building is spanned by a barrel-vaulted coffered ceiling, on which 20 paintings illustrate events in the life of Mary. Large tile decorations depicting biblical and country scenes fill the lower halves of the walls, while above them can be seen pictures of St Francis. A semi-circular painting above the archway leading to the chancel shows the Coronation of the Virgin Mary. Old pictures dating from the 16th c. hang in the altar room itself. Immediately to the left of the entrance, the Madre de Deus convent and a fishing net are depicted on tiling. A stone net is noticeable in the small sacristy – another reminder of the emblem of the founder.
Steps at the far end of the church lead to the part of the original building that has been retained. This is faced with Spanish tiles dating from the 16th c.; the green colour and the geometric pattern of the azulejos are characteristic of the Spanish style of that time.

Renaissance cloister

Two cloisters remain from the former convent – both two storeys high. The Renaissance cloister used to be the resting place of the convent's founder, Leonor, with a tombstone set into the floor bearing witness to this. The

Convento da Madre Deus: the church

National Tile Museum (see below) is today housed in the rooms of the Renaissance cloister.

Manueline cloister

The cloister dating from the Manueline era is built on a considerably smaller area. This causes the two storeys to appear relatively taller. The cloister radiates unity and peace. Archways and columns are sparingly decorated in a Middle Eastern style.

Chapter House

The former chapter house in the high chancel is reached through the cloisters. The choir stalls date from the 16th c. From the chapter house there is a view down into the church; there once was a grille positioned in the wall which is now open. The nuns of the Order of St Clare used to leave from here to attend services unseen.

Representation room

Opposite the high chancel lies the representation room of the Madre de Deus. For a time it served the sculptor Machado de Castro as a studio. Today a small collection of paintings can be seen here. These include a portrait of the founder of the convent; in a historical painting Francis of Assissi hands the first abbess of the Madre de Deus the statutes of the Order of St Clare in the presence of the pope and Queen Leonor who is kneeling on the left and holding a crown.

Museu Nacional do Azulejo

The Renaissance cloister and other rooms accommodate the Museu Nacional do Azulejo (National Tile Museum). With funding from the Fundação Calouste Gulbenkian a collection has been assembled here which gives an informative insight into the history of azulejos dating from the 15th c. Supplemented in parts by photographs, it provides a complete documentation of how tiles developed from Moorish influences and came via

Convent: Manueline side doorway . . .

. . . and the Cloister

Spain to Portugal, spread here and developed an independent style. Materials and photographs explain the procedure behind the manufacture and decoration of azulejos.

Cityscape

Particularly striking is a long wall picture composed of tiles showing a panoramic view of Lisbon from before the earthquake. Places that can be recognised include the Praça do Comércio, then still called the Terreiro do Paço, with the royal palace and the Casa dos Bicos. They appear in their original form and have since been reconstructed in accordance with this. The Sé Patriarchal (then with a differently shaped tower), the Igreja da Conceição Velha, São Vicente de Fora and, further to the west, the chapel of Santo Amaro, the Mosteiro dos Jerónimos and the Torre de Belém can also be seen.

Costa Azul

Location
South of Lisbon

Buses
From Cacilhas, Areeiro, Praça de Espanha to the Costa da Caparica

By the Costa Azul ("Blue Coast") is meant the coastline lying offshore to the south of Lisbon, which surrounds the peninsula formed by the Serra da Arrábilda and its northern foothills between the mouths of the rivers Tagus and Sado. Although this area remains mainly undisturbed by international tourism, many of the people of Lisbon spend their free time here in the summer months. The delightful scenery and excellent beaches make up the especial charm of this coastal region. Particularly in the southern part of the Costa Azul are to be found appealing and, for the most part, undeveloped villages and relatively empty beaches. Accommodation is, however, limited.

Costa da Caparica, Praia do Sol, Sesimbra, Setúbal and Palmela can all be reached by bus directly from Lisbon. Connections to any other places here

Setubal

A bay on the Costa de Lisboa

may prove difficult, i.e. buses may not run daily. Information is available from tourist offices.

Costa da Caparica

Costa da Caparica, once a small fishing town, some 15km/9 miles south of Lisbon, has developed during the last few years into a not particularly attractive resort with dismal tower blocks and snack bars. Immigrants from former Portuguese colonies live in the shanties on the outskirts of the town. The Convento dos Capuchos, which stands above the town, was completely restored in 1960; today summer concerts take place in the former Capucin monastery.

*Praia do Sol

The Praia do Sol extends for more than 20km/12½ miles to the south of Costa da Caparica. The wide sandy beach is lined by wooded dunes and rocks. A narrow-gauge railway leads from the Costa da Caparica to the remote stretches of beach (as far as the Fonte da Telha Station), which are, however, crowded in summer.

*Cabo de Espichel

Cabo de Espichel is the western point of the peninsula formed by the western foothills of the Serra da Arrábida (bus from Sesimbra). The scenery is stark, the view of cliffs falling steeply into the sea is impressive. Not far to the north of a lighthouse stands the Baroque pilgrimage church Nossa Senhora do Cabo. The church is flanked by long two-storey buildings, which were used as accommodation for pilgrims. The traditional fishing festival, which takes place every year on the last Sunday in September, attracts many visitors.

Sesimbra

The fishing town of Sesimbra (population 8000; bus from Cacilhas and Praça de Espanha) lies about 13km/8 miles from the cape on the southern slopes of the Serra da Arrábida. The charming hillside location of the seaside resort, which the Portuguese themselves particularly enjoy visiting, has suffered over the last few years from widespread development.

The busy town earns its living chiefly from tourism and fishing. Fishermen can be watched at work in the harbour on the western edge of the town. In the centre of the town, almost on the beach, stands the Fortaleza de Santiago, a fortress built in the 17th c., which was used for a time as a prison. A short way to the north archaeological finds are on view in the museum, as well as a collection of coins and sacred exhibits.
A castle originally built during the 12th c. and 13th c. stands high above the town. At the beginning of the 17th c. it was almost completely rebuilt by Flemish Jesuits and the master builder Cosmander for King João IV.

Portinho da Arrábidas

Portinho da Arrábida, a small fishing village between Sesimbra and Setúbal, lies in a sandy bay at the foot of the Serra da Arrábida, which here falls away steeply into the sea (bus from Sesimbra, Setúbal). The Convento Novo da Arrábida was built by Franciscans in 1542 on the slopes above the village. The complex, enclosed by walls, is in private ownership.

Setúbal

The industrial and district capital of Setúbal lies on the wide estuary of the Rio Sado. With 98,000 inhabitants it is Portugal's fourth largest town and third largest port, with important fish processing factories, car assembly plants, shipyards and salt-works (bus from Cacilhas, Praça de Espanha). It apparently developed in the 5th c. in place of the Roman town of *Cetobriga*, which lay further to the south-east on the Tróia peninsula and which was destroyed by a catastrophic flood. In the 15th c. Setúbal was temporarily a royal seat and is the birthplace of the satirist and writer Manuel Maria Barbosa du Bocage (1765–1805); a small museum has been set up in the house in which he was born in the Rua do São Domingo.
For an industrial town Setúbal enjoys a very appealing appearance. The freight, yacht and fishing harbour extends along the Rio Sado, which becomes very lively every morning after the fishing boats have landed their catch and the fish auction takes place. To the north of this, one of the main traffic routes, the Avenida de Luisa Todi, named after the celebrated singer, runs from east to west. On the other side of the Avenida huddles the attractive old town, in which the few places of interest remaining from the earthquake of 1755 are to be found. The centre comprises the Praça do Bocage with a statue of the poet.
The Igreja de Jesús, the first church built in the Manueline style in Portugal, stands in the west of the old town. Work was begun on this sacred building between 1490 and 1491 under the direction of Diogo de Boytaca, who later gained fame through the building of the monastery at Batalha and the Museu dos Jerónimos (see entry). The exterior of the three-aisled hall church appears relatively plain; in the interior the early-Manueline columns, the stellar vault in the choir and the azulejo depictions of the life of Mary are especially impressive.
The rooms of the former Jesus monastery, which neighbours the church, and the 17th c. cloister built of Arrábida marble now house the town museum (Museu de Setúbal). Its exhibits include works by Portuguese, Flemish and Catalan masters as well as archaeological finds from the area around Setúbal.
Also worth visiting are the Igreja de São Julião on the Praça do Bocage with its two Manueline portals, the 16th c. Igreja de Santa Maria da Graça in the east of the old town and two museums on the Avenida de Luisa Todi: the Museu Oceanográfico de Arqueologia (Oceanographic and Fishing Museum) and the Museu de Arqueologia e Etnologia (Archaeological and Folklore Museum). To the west above Setúbal stands the Castelo de São Filipe, which today has been partly redesigned as a Pousada (see Practical Information, Pousadas). It was built in the 16th c. to the plans of the Italian Filippo Terzi, who also designed the Igreja de São Roque and the São Vicente de Fora in Lisbon.

*Tróia

The children's holiday camp of Tróia, whose tower blocks make it visible from afar, lies on the northern point of one of the offshore spits of the estuary lagoon, the Peninsula de Tróia, south-west of Setúbal (ferry and speed boat connections from Setúbal). The Tróia peninsula has many sand dunes and is partly wooded, it is barely accessible to modern traffic, possesses Portugal's longest sandy beach (30km/18½ miles) and also proves an ideal area for walking.

*Palmela

The small hill town of Palmela (population 6000), 10km/6 miles north of Setúbal in the Serra de São Luis, is principally known for the wine produced in its vicinity (ferry from Estação Sul e Sueste to Barreiro, bus from Barreiro).
Standing above Palmela and visible from afar is a castle, in the western part of which – the former 15th c. São Tiago monastery – a pousada (see Practical Information, Pousadas) has been established. In Moorish times the castle was considered the strongest fortress in southern Portugal. After Afonso Henriques had first occupied it in 1147 and after reconquest by the Moors, he finally reoccupied it in 1166 and gave it to the São Tiago order of knights. Within the area of the fortress are to be found the remains of the Igreja de Santa Maria do Castelo, a Renaissance church, which was built on the site of a Moorish mosque and which collapsed in the earthquake of 1755. The whole fortress site can be viewed from the keep, built at the end of the 14th c., from which, in good visibility, the estuary of the Tagus and Lisbon can be seen in the distance.

Serra da Arrábida

Excursions into the quiet Serra da Arrábida, whose lush vegetation contains a variety of rare plants, are well worth undertaking (bus from Setúbal, Sesimbra). The highest point is the Alto do Formosinho (501m/1644ft above sea level). The road (N 379,1) that crosses the mountain offers a whole series of fantastic views of the sea and the coastal stretch.

Costa do Estoril

Location
West of Lisbon

The Costa do Estoril, the coast west of Lisbon, also quite rightly called the Portuguese Riviera, is scenically one of the most beautiful parts of the Portuguese west coast. Its attractive scenery, good beaches as well as its pleasant climate, which encourages lush vegetation, combine to make its towns and seaside resorts very popular, particularly to the Portuguese. During the high season beaches and approach roads are very busy.
The places between Caxias and Cascais are easy to reach by suburban trains from Cais do Sodré. Travelling by public transport to any remaining places is somewhat more difficult. It is almost impossible to reach Boca do Inferno, Cabo do Roca and Cabo Raso without a car. However, organised bus excursions often visit them (see Practical Information, excursions).

Caxias

After leaving Lisbon in a westerly direction and passing through the suburbs of Belém (see entry), Algés and Dafundo, Caxias is reached – although the station is a good 10km/6 miles from the town centre. Under the Salazar dictatorship, the fortress in the little town served as one of the most notorious prisons for political detainees; a youth hostel is now housed in another fort.

Oerias

Oerias (population 14,000), 4km/2½ miles west of Caxias, is a lively and attractive little town in which the Marquês de Pombal (see Famous People) had his country seat. The 18th c. villa, attributed to the architect Carlos Mardel, is surrounded by lovely parkland. The estate, which is not open to the public, is currently owned by the Fundação Calouste Gulbenkian (see entry). Before this cultural foundation built its own museum, Gulbenkian's collection was displayed here. The small pelourinho near to the summer palace dates from the 17th c.

Fort São Julião da Barra

The road leading to Fort São Julião da Barra ascends steeply to the left about 2km/1¼ miles beyond Oerias. The fortress site was built in 1580 and served as a defence for the entrance to the Tagus.

Estoril, Cascais

A well-built four-lane highway (Marginal) ends shortly before the resorts of Estoril and Cascais (see entries), which have merged into one large town. The suburban railway also ends at Cascais.

*Boca do Inferno

Leaving Cascais we pass by the viewing platform at the Boca do Inferno, the "Mouth of Hell". From a safe position here visitors can experience the great power of the Atlantic Ocean and view the cliff formations which have arisen through thousands of years of sea erosion. Below the powerful waves break against a 15–20m/49–66ft high series of cliffs, partly hollowed by the sea.

In summer, souvenir stalls for tourists line the side of the road here.

Cabo Raso

Cabo Raso (lighthouse) stands about 5km/3 miles beyond Cascais. From here a marvellous view of the Cabo da Roca can be enjoyed.

Praia do Guincho

Praia do Guincho, lying 3km/1¾ miles from Cabo Raso (bus from Cascais), is a really lovely beach but overcrowded in the high season. Its hinterland is composed of dunes and pinewoods but the overall impression is spoilt by a relatively new hotel complex.

*Cabo da Roca

A small road turns left off the main road 7km/4 miles beyond the Praia do Guincho and leads Cabo da Roca, 144m/472ft above sea level and Europe's most westerly point. Called by the Romans *Promontorium Magnum*, this is a foothill of the Serra de Sintra (see Sintra).

Azenhas do Mar

Further north we pass through a few smaller resorts of which the fishing village Azenhas do Mar stands out owing to its fine position on the cliffs and its peaceful charm. At the beginning of the century its beauty attracted many artists.

Azenhas do Mar on the Costa do Estoril

Ericeira

The fishing village of Ericeira (population 3000), which lies about 10km/6 miles west of Mafra on the coast (bus via Mafra from the Praça de Marquês de Pombal), belongs to the Costa de Prata. Compared with Azenhas do Mar it is considerably more lively.
Ericeira enjoyed a long tradition as a small trading and fishing town with crayfish being the main catch. However, at the beginning of the 20th c. the harbour lost its importance and since then the lovely beaches nearby have enabled Ericeira to live mainly from tourism.

*Elevador do Carmo (Carmo Lift) H 3

Location
Rua de Santa Justa

Metro
Rossio

Buses
1, 2, 9, 11, 32, 39, 44, 45, 46, 80, 83, 90

Open
Daily 7am–11pm (Sun. from 9am)

At the western end of the Rua de Santa Justa stands Lisbon's most striking and novel means of public transport. The Carmo Lift (also called the Santa Justa Lift) links the lower town (see Baixa) with Chiado (see entry) in the upper town. The lift is a typical iron construction from the turn of the century and its design is often wrongly attributed to Alexandre Gustav Eiffel. In fact Raoul Mesnier de Ponsard was commissioned to design a lift which would overcome the approximately 32m/105ft height difference at this point. A few years earlier the same inventor had constructed another lift (no longer in existence) further south on the Largo do Municipio.
The Carmo Lift was built between 1898 and 1901 and was officially opened on August 31st 1901. Two cabins travel up and down the tower with room for 25 people in each. The elaborate exterior is in a neo-Gothic style with touches of filigree.
From the upper exit there is a marvellous view of the Rossio (see entry) and the grid-like street layout of the Baixa, as well as the Castelo de São Jorge (see entry) opposite. There is also an interesting view from the bridge which crosses the Rua do Carmo at a great height and links the lift with the Largo do Carmo. The streets below, which were destroyed in August 1988 by a great fire are, now gradually being rebuilt (see Chiado). The fire was only put out a short way from the lift.

Ermida da Nossa Senhora do Monte

See Graça

Ermida de Santo Amaro B 2

Location
Calçada de Santo Amaro

Trams
15, 16, 17

Buses
14, 27, 28, 32, 43, 49, 51, 56

The Renaissance chapel Santo Amaro, which is unfortunately usually kept closed, lies between Belém (see entry) and Lisbon city centre. The ground plan, over which the chapel was built in 1549, is of interest. The round main body of the chapel is joined to the circular, somewhat lower, choir. A wide, semi-circular hall lies off the the interior and is decorated with valuable tiles dating from the first third of the 17th c.

The azulejos inside the chapel come from the famous tile factory at Rato. They depict scenes from the lives of the saints.

Estação do Rossio (Rossio Station) G/H 3

Location
Praça Dom João da Cámara

Metro
Restauradores

The original façade of Rossio Station, located on the north-west corner of the Rossio (actually on the Praça Dom João da Cámara), is most striking. The building is one of the few remaining typical examples of neo-Manueline architecture. Public buildings in this style are very rare in Portugal, it is more often seen in romanticised villas and palaces in private

optica
santa
justa
Tatiana
CAFÉS

Rossio Rail Station

Buses
1, 2, 9, 11, 21, 31, 32, 36, 39, 41, 44, 45, 46, 80, 83, 90

ownership. The station was built to the plans of the architect J. Luis Monteiro in 1887, at a time therefore when imitation of past building styles was customary and when the architecture of the "Golden Age" was being recalled. Moorish and Gothic decorations are included as typical elements of the Manueline style. The stone cabling used as a dividing line and the window embellishments are particularly characteristic of this epoch.

A shopping centre can be found behind the façade, with escalators leading to the station's booking hall and to the actual station concourse on the third floor. Trains on the popular suburban line to Sintra (see entry) leave from here, first running through a 2.6km/1½ mile long tunnel passing under Bairro Alto and Amoreiras and only emerging into daylight at Campolide to the north-east of the aqueduct.

In his novel "Felix Krull" Thomas Mann had the confidence trickster Krull, travelling from Paris, alight from a train at Rossio station – in fact this was the original station for international train connections.

Estação de Santa Apolónia (Santa Apolónia Station) K/L 2/3

Location
Largo dos Caminhos de Ferro

Trams
3, 16, 24

Buses
9, 13A, 17, 25, 25A, 28, 35, 39, 46, 59, 81, 82, 90

The Santa Apolónia Station (Estação de Santa Apolónia) is situated on the eastern side of the Largo dos Caminhos de Ferro. The building dates from 1886, although 30 years previously the first train ran along this stretch from the station which was then provisionally located in a former monastery. Trains for the north of Portugal as well as for France and Madrid use this terminus.

In 1981, following an initiative by the newspaper "Tempo", a memorial was erected commemorating the many Portuguese who emigrated in search of work and better living conditions.

Estoril (Excursion)

Location
About 20km/ 12½ miles west of Lisbon

Trains
From Estação Cais do Sodré

During the course of the 20th c. this former fishing village on the Costa do Estoril (see entry) has developed into a chic seaside resort with a golf course, casino, well laid-out parks and extensive areas of villas. The Sintra mountains lying to the north afford Estoril an unusually mild climate and sub-tropical vegetation. In addition, the carbonated and radioactive spas located here contribute to Estoril's reputation as an elegant resort and today it has become an internationally famous meeting place – there is little evidence of its earlier role as a fishing village.

With a current population of 25,000, Estoril's new buildings have caused it to expand so much that it has merged into neighbouring Cascais (see entry). A promenade for pedestrians leads along the water's edge from Estoril to Cascais.

In the resort itself there is little of interest to see, and it is definitely its atmosphere that can make a stay in Estoril attractive. The casino, standing on the edge of a park filled with lush tropical and exotic plants, offers a comprehensive entertainment programme of films, shows, concerts and theatrical performances.

Good travel connections between Lisbon and Estoril mean that in the high season the resort's beaches are filled with day trippers from the Portuguese capital.

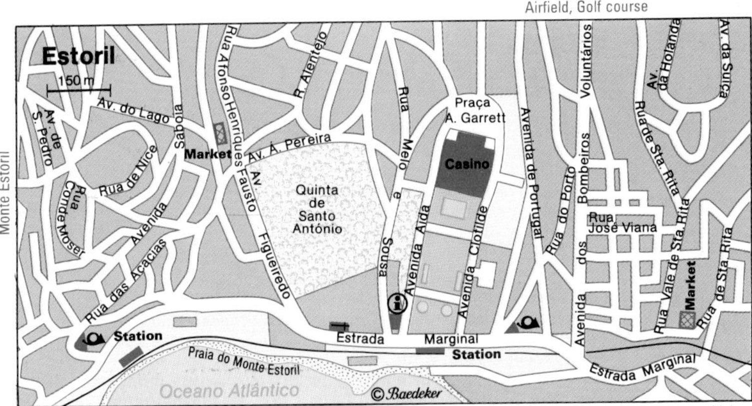

Fundação Calouste Gulbenkian (Gulbenkian Foundation) G 7

Location
Avenida de Berna

Metro
Palhavã, S. Sebastião

Buses
16, 26, 30, 31, 46, 56

Portugal's decision to allow the Armenian oil magnate Calouste Sarkis Gulbenkian (see Famous People) to enter the country in 1942 has certainly paid off handsomely for the cultural life of this small country on the south-western edge of Europe. When Gulbenkian died in 1955 he bequeathed his estate to the Portuguese people and left written testimony that his fortune and his immense art collection should be used to equip a cultural foundation bearing his name.

Following the terms of this endowment an extensive cultural centre was built in Lisbon with several theatre, concert and conference halls, a library and, not least, a museum which has since become world famous. In addition to all this individual grants are awarded and money is given to support

Estoril: a favourite excursion venue for the people of Lisbon (see p. 87)

Open
Museum:
June–Sept.:
Tues., Thur., Fri., Sun. 10am–5pm, Wed., Sat. 2–7.30pm;
Oct.–May: Tues.–Sun. 10am–5pm

Admission free on Sundays

cultural, social and scientific projects throughout the country. Thus Portugal is provided with a network of 230 libraries, of which 59 are set up as travelling libraries. The fact that the Gulbenkian Foundation has almost a monopoly on Portugal's cultural sector has not been without its problems. However, the opportunities gained by the country through this financial support can hardly be overestimated.

The building of the foundation occurred during the time of the Salazar dictatorship. The government's fear of criticism from the cultural sector, which led, particularly in the literary sphere, to censorship, persecution and suppression (the then director of the Lisbon branch of the Goethe Institute, Curt Meyer-Clason, wrote about this in his "Portuguese Diaries") meant that at first only a "safe" area, namely music, was promoted. Thus a separate orchestra, choir and ballet corps developed during the 1960s. Since 1977 a concert featuring contemporary music has taken place each year, with another featuring old music since 1980. In the early 1970s a main focus of the foundation was on the production of Portuguese films with film retrospectives and festivals being mounted.

The Museu Calouste Gulbenkian was opened in 1969 on the occasion of the Armenian's 100th anniversary. This fulfilled one of Gulbenkian's wishes, that all his approximately 6000 exhibits from all over the world should be accommodated under one roof – until then they had only been exhibited in parts in the Pombal palace in Oeiras (see Costa do Sol). Since 1984 the Centre of Modern Art has belonged to the Gulbenkian Foundation. Its collection of 20th c. Portuguese art is continually increased and adds to Gulbenkian's own collection, which goes up to Impressionism. An educational museum was set up in the park belonging to the foundation for further exhibits. Many, often international, exchange exhibitions are brought each year to Portugal by the Gulbenkian Foundation.

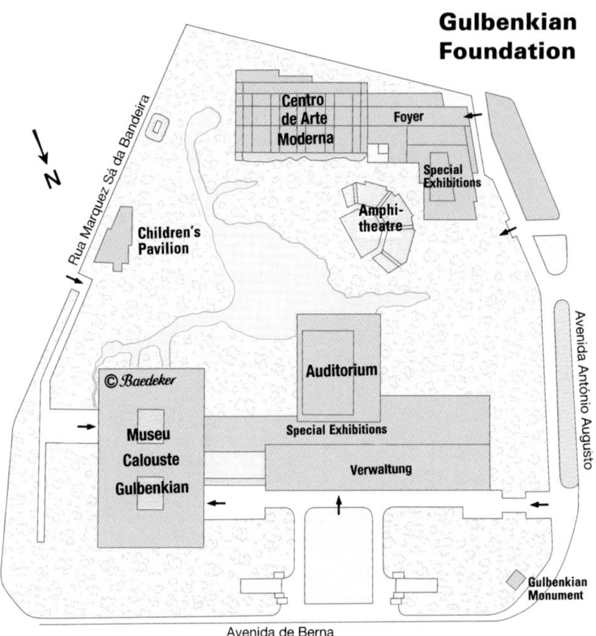

**Museu Calouste Gulbenkian

The 25,000sq.m/89,700sq.ft complex housing the Gulbenkian Museum was built between 1964 and 1969 according to the plans of the architects Alberto Pessoa, Pedro Cid and Ruy Athouguia. In accordance with Gulbenkian's variety of art interests the collection exhibited encompasses an extraordinarily wide spectrum of artwork from every era.

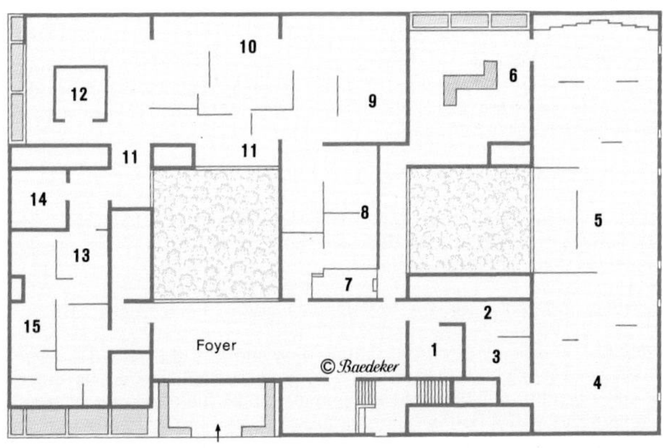

Fundação Calouste Gulbenkian

Room 1	Ancient Egyptian art: sculptures, reliefs, skeletons (2,700–1 B.C.).
Room 2	Greek-Roman art: Greek faience, marble sculptures (5th c. B.C.), Roman glassware (3rd and 4th c. A.D.).
Room 3	Greek, Roman and Mesopotamian art; jewellery from the Hellenistic era (4th–2nd c. B.C.), faience from the Mesopotamian area (3rd or 2nd c. B.C.), a collection of Greek gold coins (561–305 B.C.); coins found during excavations made in 1901 at Abukir (Egypt). As the coins obviously come from a series that refer to Alexander the Great it is assumed that the coins were struck on the occasion of the Olympic Games of 242/243 dedicated to Alexander the Great.
Room 4	Oriental-Islamic art: Persian and Turkish faience (13th c. to 16th c.), Persian carpets (13th c. to 18th c.).
Room 5	Oriental-Islamic art, Armenian art: Persian book illustrations (16th c.), Turkish carpets, faience, tiles (16/17th c.), Syrian glass lamps (14th c.), Armenian book decoration (16th c. to 18th c.).
Room 6	Art from the Far East: Chinese porcelain from the T'sing Dynasty (17th c.) and the Ming Dynasty (1368–1644), Japanese lacquer work, medicine containers (13th/14th c.), pictures and illustrative drawings by the Japanese artist Sugakudo (19th c.).
Room 7	European art (11–15th c.): book illustrations from France, Flanders, Italy, Holland, England (12–15th c.), ivory carvings from France (11–14th c.).
Room 8	Paintings and sculptures (14–17th c.): exhibits include works by the German artists Tilman Riemenschneider, with two wooden statuettes, and Stefan Lochner, with the painting "Presentation in the Temple"; the Flemish painter Peter Paul Rubens ("Flight into Egypt", "Portrait of Hélène Fourment", "Centaurs"), Anton Van Dyck ("Portrait of a Man"), Jan Gossaert ("Virgin and Child") and Thierry Bouts; the Dutchman Rembrandt ("Pallas Athene", "Portrait of an Old Man"), Frans Hals with a portrait and Jacob Ruysdael with landscapes; the Italian artist Domenico Ghirlandaio and Guiliano Bugiardini with portrait paintings.
Room 9	Italian and French art from the Renaissance: wall hangings, wallcoverings, sculptures, garments, medallions.
Room 10	French decorative art (18th c.): paintings and interiors, clocks, porcelain, furniture.
Room 11	Paintings and sculptures from France (18th c.): including Houdon's "Diana"; this figure was owned by Catherine of Russia but was removed as it was considered too obscene: Gulbenkian finally bought it at an auction of the collection of the hermitage.
Room 12	French silverwork (18th c.): utensils.
Room 13	Paintings from England (18th and 19th c.): portraits and landscapes by Thomas Gainsborough, John Hoppner, George Romney, Sir Thomas Lawrence and Joseph Turner.
Room 14	Paintings from Italy (18th c.): 19 Venetian views by Francesco Guardi.
Room 15	Paintings and sculpures from France, England and the USA (19th c.): landscapes by Charles-François Daubigny, Jean-Baptiste Camille Corot, Stanilas Lepine; still-lifes by Henri Fantin-Latour; paintings by Edouard Manet ("Boy with Cherries", "Soap-bubbles") and by the Impressionists Claude Monet, Edgar Degas, Auguste Renoir; sculptures by Auguste

Exhibition room in the Gulbenkian Museum

Gulbenkian Museum: "Burgher of Calais" . . . . . . and a Chinese vase

Rodin, Jean-Baptiste Carpeaux and Antoine-Louis Barye; paintings by the American artists Mary Cassatt and John Singer Sargent and the English artist Edward Burne-Jones ("Mirror of Venus").

Inner Courtyard

A bronze figure – one of the "Burghers of Calais" by Auguste Rodin – stands in the small inner courtyard, which can be seen from the foyer.

Basement

Displayed in the basement, in rooms fitted out especially for it, is the marvellous collection of Art Nouveau pieces by the French artist René Lalique. Presented extremely attractively here, thanks to modern museum techniques, lovely glassware and, above all, many pieces of jewellery can be seen, some of which were created purely as commissions for Gulbenkian and were never meant to fulfil their real role as jewellery. Gulbenkian and Lalique enjoyed a long friendship.
Also located in the basement is a much-visited public library which concentrates on the field of art and art history.

*Centro de Arte Moderna

Open:
Same hours as Museu Calouste Gulbenkian

Admission free on Sundays

The Centre for Modern Art (Centro de Arte Moderna; CAM), located in the south-west corner of the Gulbenkian Park, was officially opened in 1984. The architecturally interesting building with its terraced, planted roof fits in marvellously with its parkland surroundings. Apart from an administrative wing, archives and function rooms, a large presentation area has been developed for 20th c. art. Temporary exhibitions, and some international touring exhibitions, are frequently mounted here.

Permanent Exhibition

Work of this century by Portuguese artists can be seen in a permanent exhibition. Limited by Portugal's museum system, CAM's collection is not

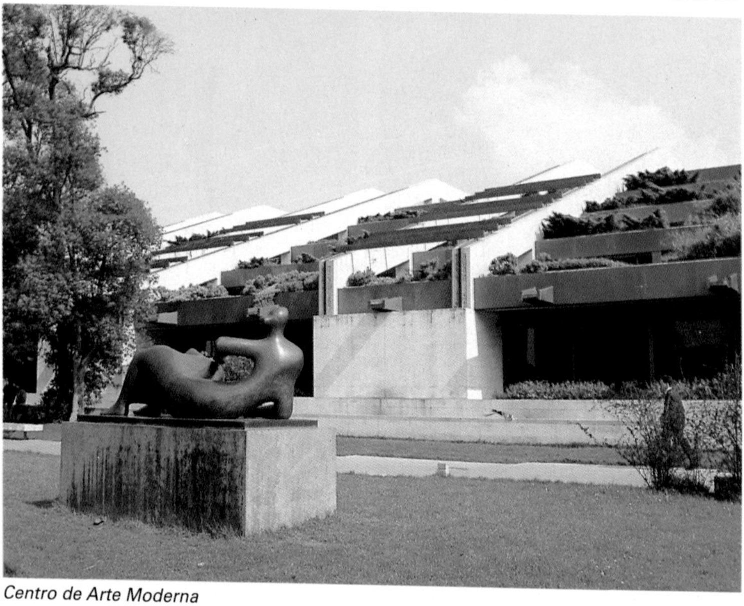

Centro de Arte Moderna

always representative, as small museums, usually well worth visiting, have often been set up in the town where an artist was born, or where he lived or worked for most of his life, and exclusively exhibit the work of that artist. Exhibits in the Centre for Modern Art include many works by José Almada Negreiros (1893–1970), one of Portugal's most famous "all round" artists of the 20th c. Included in the exhibits are the paintings that were hung in the café "A Brasileira" (see Chiado), and a very well-known portrait of Fernando Pessoa, variations of which have entered into everyday art. A depiction of Pessoa with his three most famous heteronyms was painted by António Costa-Pinheiro (born in 1937). Of interest are the works of Eduardo Viana (1881–1967), Armadeo de Souza-Cardosa (1887–1918), Marcelino Vespeira (born in 1925) and the poet and artist Júlio (1902–83), in which both a leaning towards and a clash with pictures by famous European artists and art trends, such as cubism, fauvism and surrealism, are seen. The artist Maria Vieira da Silva (born in 1908), whose works can also be seen in Lisbon's metro stations, has become famous beyond Portugal. The paintings of Mário Eloy (1900–51) demonstrate a unique style influenced by Portuguese themes; famous and well-loved are the views of Lisbon by Carlos Botelho (1899–1982). Amongst sculptors, João Cutileiro (born in 1937) has made a name for himself. Of the newer artists, Paula Rego, Teresa Magalhães, Graça Morais, Rui Sanches and José Pedro Croft stand out.

Parque Gulbenkian

The park, into which the buildings of the Gulbenkian Foundation are integrated, covers an area of about 7ha/17 acres. A very great variety of native and tropical plants is to be found here, among which little streams and ponds with water-lilies have been landscaped. Above all, however, the park serves as an open-air museum for modern sculptures by artists from various countries, such as Henry Moore, Hein Semke, John van Alstine, Irene Vilar and Pierre Szekely. In addition, works by the Portuguese artists António Duarte, Jopao Cutileiro, Vasco Pereira da Conceição and Amaral da Cunha are on view.
Those with children will be pleased to know that in the park is a Centro Artistico Infantil, well stocked with toys and offering free 90-minute child-care sessions for 4–12 year olds between 9am and 5pm.

Bronze bust of Calouste Gulbenkian

On the Praça de Espanha, in front of the building complex, a 3m/10ft high seated bronze has been erected; it portrays Calouste Gulbenkian in front of a stone Horus falcon. The memorial is the work of Leopoldo de Almeida, who also created the statue of José I on horseback which stands on the Praça da Figueira (see entry).

Graça (Quarter) J 3

Location
North-east of Baixa

Trams
28, 28B

Buses
12, 17, 26, 30, 35

The Graça quarter, which lies on a hill north-east of the Castelo de São Jorge, is a very interesting and lively part of the city. At the turn of the century many houses were built here for the families of workers. The façades, some extremely narrow, give an indication of the cramped living conditions to be found inside. An example of these workers' houses can be seen in the Largo da Graça; through an entranceway (no. 82), the "Villa Sousa" is found in a courtyard. Built in 1890 on the site of an earlier palace.

Igreja e Convento da Graça

Location
Largo da Graça

Graça's church and monastery was built here in 1271 by the Augustinians, who until then had had their seat on the neighbouring hill to the north. The monastery, which was once the wealthiest in Lisbon and in which up to 1500 people could be accommodated, serves today as barracks, therefore

only the interior of the church can be viewed. The whole complex was rebuilt after the earthquake in the 18th c. and after that restoration work was carried out several times, the last in 1905.
The exposed position of the church is immediately striking. It stands on the summit of the Graça hill and is visible from afar. The church forecourt is one of the city's loveliest vantage points. The Baroque façade, with the detached bell tower, gives a really dilapidated impression.
The one-aisled interior covers an area of 60 by 30m/197 by 98ft and appears dark, despite the white and pink marble used and the stucco ceiling painted in the same colours. The walls are interrupted by four solid and powerful-looking side chapels which greatly contribute to the overall impression of the interior. Noteworthy is the violet-clad figure of the "Senhor dos Passos" – reached via a flight of steps in the right transept – which is carried in a procession every year on the second Sunday in Lent. This has taken place in Graça since 1587.

Ermida da Nossa Senhora do Monte

Location
Largo do Monte

On a neighbouring hill to the north of the monastery complex of Graça stands the little chapel of Nossa Senhora do Monte. It was built in 1243 on the site where the first bishop of Lisbon, São Gens, was martyred in the 4th c. Many local people took part in the rebuilding of the chapel after the earthquake.
The interior of the small church is relatively bright and noticeably simply fitted out. Unfortunately the main altar was decorated somewhat more lavishly. A crib constructed by Machado de Castro is in a window on the left-hand wall. He also created the cribs in the Basilica da Estrela, the Museu de Arte Antiga and in the Sé Patriarchal (see entries).

Vantage point

In front of the chapel lies a very lovely, tree-lined vantage point from which, when looking to the south-west, a marvellous view of the whole of Lisbon's inner city as far as the Tagus can be enjoyed and which affords perhaps the best view of the Castelo de São Jorge (see entry).

*Igreja do Carmo · Museu Arqueológico — H 3

Location
Largo do Carmo

Trams
24

Lift
Elevador do Carmo

Open
Mon.–Sat.
10am–1pm,
2–5pm
(June–Sept. until 6pm)

The Igreja do Carmo was destroyed by the earthquake and now houses the Archaeological Museum. It is one of Lisbon's most unusual memorials. The ruins are immediately obvious from the Rossio (see entry) and from the bridge leading from the Elevador do Carmo (see entry) but appear less noticeable from the Largo do Carmo. One reason for this is the location of the church. It was built on a slope to the west of the Baixa (see entry) so that, with the western main façade incorporating the entrance portal kept relatively low, the eastern part with the chancel had to be built even lower and is thus more striking.
The construction of the church and the now closed former Carmelite monastery dates back to a vow taken by the Portuguese national hero, Nuno Álvares Pereira, before his troops could secure Portugal's independence against Castille in the battle of Aljubarrota in 1835 and thus the power of the first Avis king, João I. Nuno Alvares himself lived later as a member of the Order in the Carmelite monastery and died there in 1431.
The ruins are the remains of Lisbon's only church built in the almost pure Gothic style. Together with the Sé Patriarchal (see entry), it is one of the few relics of mediaeval building remaining in the Portuguese capital.
The former church is entered through a lovely portal. The style of construction of the three-aisled building is still apparent, the view of the high Gothic arches which now tower up uselessly, being particularly impressive. Only the chancel in the eastern section is still roofed and it is here in particular that the proportions of the former church are apparent. A Manueline window opposite the entrance dates originally from the Mosteiro dos Jerónimos (see entry) in Belém.

The Carmo Church

After the earthquake it was actually planned to rebuild the monastery church but this never happened. The ruins were temporarily completely overrun by ivy. The interior was temporarily used for different purposes and finally turned into an archaeological museum in the middle of the 19th c. In addition, summer concerts often take place in the church ruins.

Museu Arqueológico

The exhibits of the archaeological museum are somewhat indiscriminate, but very effective in their suitable setting, both in the roofless part of the ruins and in the well-maintained eastern chancel. Archaeological finds from Portugal, England, Switzerland and from Middle and South America have been assembled here. The founder of the monastery is called to mind by his original sword and by the wooden copy of a stone sculpture which was destroyed in the earthquake. A 4th c. Roman sarcophagus portraying the Muses as well as the tombs of Fernando I (14th c.) and of Maria of Austria (18th c.) with sculptures by Machado de Castro can be seen. Part of a marble pillar dating from the time of the West Goths has also been retained. It was found during excavations in the Baixa.

Chafariz do Carmo

A lavishly-decorated, lovely fountain stands under trees right in the middle of the Largo do Carmo in front of the church ruins. The Chafariz do Carmo was built here in 1796 on the site of an earlier fountain. The area surrounding the fountain consists of a block decorated with four dolphins and is covered by a cupola borne on four pillars.

GNR Headquarters

The headquarters of the GNR (Guarda Nacional Republicana), a type of riot police, are now accommodated in the former Carmelite monastery next to the church. On the day of the revolution of April 25th 1974, the former dictator and successor of Salazar, Marcelo Caetano, and some other politicians from his regime sought protection from the revolutionary troops in the building. When the GNR headquarters were violently threatened, the politicians gave themselves up: Caetano was taken to the airport and left

In the ruins of the Carmo Church

The Carmo Fountain

the country. A tightly-packed crowd followed the events on the otherwise very quiet Largo do Carmo.

Igreja da Conceição Velha (Church) J 2

Location
Rua da Alfándega

Trams
3, 16, 24

Buses
13A

The Manueline portal of the Igreja da Concão Velha stands out noticeably from the rather inconspicuous, self-contained row of houses on the Rua da Alfándega. The portal comes from the former, important Igreja da Nossa Senhora da Misericórdia which was built here at the beginning of the 16th c., but was almost completely destroyed by the 1755 earthquake. This predecessor of the present church was built on the site of a synagogue on the request of the sister of Manuel I, Leonor von Bragança, who also initiated the Convento da Madre de Deus (see entry).

The form of the Manueline portal is attributed to João de Castilho, who is considered one of the finest architects of this age. Most typically recognisable embellishments are the Knight's Cross of Christ, the armillary sphere (a globe of metal rings representing the equator, tropics, etc.) on the right and the left and the Portuguese coat of arms. The group of people above the portal include Leonor, her brother Manuel and Pope Leo X, above whom Nossa Senhora de Misericórdia spreads her protective coat. The present entrance was the southern side door of the transept in the earlier, considerably larger church. The arrangement of the ground plan has therefore become completely different. Both of the two remaining, preserved windows on the southern façade and the altar chapel in the interior have been included within the new church.

Inside the one-aisled building the painted stucco ceiling, the "M" of Manuel I and a crown make reference to the original church. The chancel is vaulted by a faceted barrel ceiling. All in all, the interior appears isolated from the older entrance portal. While in the early 16th c. Manueline decoration was now and then added to the structure of older buildings already in existence, here the exact opposite was unavoidable. In both cases, however, the impression is easily formed that the different elements of style are isolated and disorganised when placed next to one another.

Igreja da Graça

See Graça

Igreja do Menino de Deus (Church) J 3

Location
Largo do Menino de Deus

Trams
28, 28B

Buses
37

A church well worth visiting, and one which evokes Italian associations, can be found on the eastern edge of the Castelo de São Jorge (see entry) outside the castle walls. The Igreja do Menino de Deus on the square of the same name was commissioned by João V. It is one of the few churches which survived the earthquake relatively undamaged. Construction began in 1711 but even today it has not been completely finished. This is why there are no towers and no sculptures in the niches made for them in the exterior above the main entrance and the side entrance.

The proportions of the interior, built on an octagonal ground plan, and the choice of warm colours radiate harmony and peace. The interior appears light and barely over-ornate. Through its simplicity, the effect of the unusual ground plan comes to the fore. Geometrically stylised flower decorations made from different coloured marbles convey a friendly ease, almost elegance. The wall paintings in the eight discreet side chapels are the work of the Portuguese artists Jerónimo da Silva and Vieira Lusitano. A small three-storey cloister with lovely blue and white tiling on the walls is linked to the church building.

The church is closed apart from when Mass is celebrated, but requests to view can be made at the side entrance on the left.

Caso do Menino de Deus

A small, ochre-coloured building in the same square (no. 4, with an extended bayed entrance), the Casa do Menino de Deus, dates from the 16th c.

*Igreja de Santa Engrácia · Panteão Nacional K 3

Location
Campo de Santa Clara

Trams
3, 16, 24

Buses
9, 12, 13A, 17, 25, 25A, 28, 35 39, 46, 59, 81 82, 90

Open
Tues.–Sun.
10am–5pm

Only since the middle of the 1960s has the dome of the Igreja de Santa Engrácia formed part of Lisbon's typical skyline. The church, one of the most striking in the city and visible from afar, has a long and complicated history. An earlier church on this site dating from the 16th c. and bearing the same name had to be torn down, as it was considered desecrated after a robbery in 1630. The deed was blamed on a Jew, who was executed, although it was later proved that he had nothing to do with the incident and that the only reason he had not spoken out about it was so that his love affair with a nun in the neighbouring Santa Clara convent was not discovered. The convicted man is supposed to have phrophesied that the building of a new church would never be finished as the blame for the theft had been laid on an innocent man.

In fact it took about 300 years to complete the church (in Portugal any work whose completion takes a relatively long time is known as an "Obras de Santa Engrácia"; a Santa Engrácia work). The first new building collapsed in 1681 – probably because of a storm's effect on a construction error. In 1682 work on the present church was begun following plans designed by the architect João Antunes. The lower floors were built, but it obviously appeared too risky to span them with the planned dome, so that for decades the church remained in ruins and was sometimes used temporally

Igreja da Conceição Velha: Doorway

Igreja de Santa Engrácia

and contrary to its proper intention as a store for war materials. In 1916 a further attempt was begun to complete the building. A law decreed that the church should be used as a national pantheon. Only in the Estado Novo under Salazar was the interior construction undertaken, including the risk of spanning the interior with a concrete dome. The building complex was finally completed in 1966 as a temple to honour national heroes.

Exterior

Despite the long time taken in its construction, the national pantheon appears as a really unified building. The Baroque elements date from the first stage of building, but clear, classical lines can be seen when viewing the exterior. All in all the pantheon appears rationally structured with very harmonious proportions. The two-storey façade is divided symmetrically by pillars and simple windows. The dome gives the impression of being massive through the pilasters which have been elongated into little towers with the lantern set on top.

Interior

White, yellow, pink, grey and black marble dominates in the interior and exudes elegance. The emptiness of the interior, which has no seating and is built on a plan of a Greek cross, appears somewhat oversized. The main cupola is surrounded by four semi-cupolas. In order to do justice to the building's planned function,

six large cenotaphs have been placed in the side apses. Six national heroes are honoured by empty tombs: Vasco da Gama, Henry the Navigator, Luis Vaz de Camões, Afonso de Albuquerque (the first viceroy of India), Pedro Álvares Cabral (the discoverer of Brazil) and Nuno Álvares Pereira (who secured Portugal's independence from Spain). Symbolic gravestones honouring President Teófilo Braga, Sidónio Pais and Oscar Carmona as well as the writers Guerra Junqueiro, João de Deus and Almeida Garrett have been erected in two side rooms.
It is possible to walk around the inside of the dome and thus gain a fine view down into the interior, from the exterior of the dome a marvellous view can be enjoyed across Alfama and on to the Tagus.

Igreja do Santo António da Sé

See Sé Patriarchal

*Igreja de São Roque (Church) G/H 3

Location
Largo Trindade Coelho

Buses
15

Lift
Elevador da Glória

Open
Daily 8.30am–5pm (June–Sept. until 6pm; holidays 8.30am–1pm)

This church, which contains Lisbon's most valuable church interior decoration, is located quite inconspicuously in the Largo Trindade Coelho on the corner of the traffic-heavy Rua de São Pedro.
The Igreja de São Roque was built in the second half of the 16th c. on the site of a Manueline Rochus chapel, which João III had granted to the Jesuits. It was erected according to the plans of the Italian architect Filippo Terzi, who also later designed the Igreja de São Vicente de Fora (see entry). The original façade was destroyed by the earthquake and had to be newly rebuilt after 1755. Rythmically articulated by two rows of pilasters, it appears rather cool and unadorned. The one-aisled interior of the church has remained for the most part spared from the effects of the earthquake. Unfortunately the side chapel dedicated to St Anthony was relatively badly damaged and was not restored until the 19th c.
The Manueline style in which the interior is constructed corresponded with the ideas of the Jesuits and embodies, as it were, a religious programme: the restrained interior construction should help worshippers to concentrate fully on the church service. In keeping with the times is the conscious observance of acoustic aspects through the abandonment of side aisles and the inclusion of apertures for natural light. Beams necessary for the flat, extraordinarily wide roof of the nave were unavailable in this size on the Iberian peninsula and thus had to be brought from Germany. The ceiling is decorated with architectural paintings in perspective, which imitate a cupola vault.

Side chapels

The effect of the really sober and clearly calculated internal architecture is almost drowned by the decorations and the large side chapels. The eight side chapels were furnished in the 16th c. and the 17th c. and decorated in parts up until the 19th c.

Capela de São João Baptista

Especially worth seeing is the chapel of São João Baptista, the last chapel added, and dedicated to John the Baptist. The history of the development of this work of art designed in the Italian Baroque style is extraordinary: João V, wasteful and pious, ordered it from Rome in 1740. From 1742 it was constructed by the architects Luigi Vanvitelli and Nicola Salvi and finally blessed by the pope. In 1747 it was taken to pieces and transported by ship to Lisbon, where it was carefully reconstructed. A further two years passed before its completion and installation. As at this time Portugal had the goldmines of Brazil at its disposal, the king thought that he would not have to restrict himself financially; on the other hand he financed the necessary construction of the Aqueduto das Águas Livres (see entry) through taxes. The king only had the most valuable materials imported: agate, alabaster,

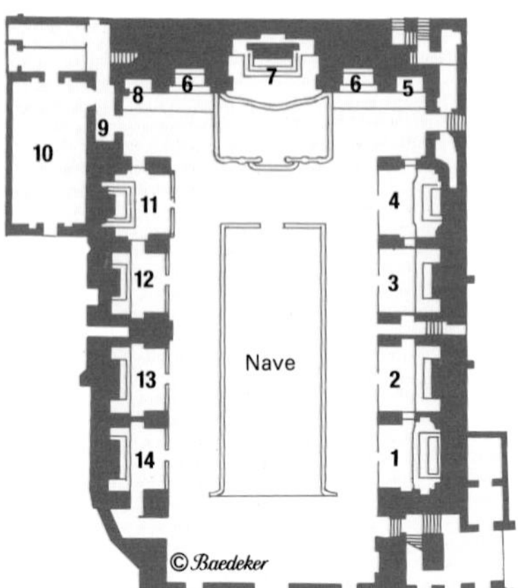

Igreja de São Roque

1 Lady Chapel
2 Chapel of Saint Francisco Xavier
3 Chapel of St Roche
4 Sacramental Chapel
5 Chapel of the Annunciation
6 Reliquary Altar
7 High Altar
8 Marble Altar
9 Crib
10 Sacristy
11 Chapel of John the Baptist
12 Chapel of Our Lady of Piousness
13 Chapel of St Anthony
14 Chapel of the Holy Family

ivory, gold, silver and jewels. The pillars are made of lapis lazuli, the angels of Carrara marble, the altar front of amethyst, for the woodwork precious woods were used exclusively, for the most part from Brazil. The pictures ("Christ's Baptism", "Easter" and "Proclamation") as well as the floor are created from mosaic stones.

Capela de São Roque

The oldest of the side chapels is dedicated to St Roches. It dates from the second half of the 16th c.; in 1584 Franciscode Matos created the tiles

Capela de São João Baptista in the Igreja de São Roque

depicting St Roches. The side picture "The Angel appears to St Roches" is considered to be one of the most important works of Gaspar Dias.

Museu de Arte Sacra

Immediately next to the church, the Museu de Arte Sacra (Museum of Sacred Art) is housed in the former Misericórdia old people's home and orphanage. Included among the exhibits is wonderful Italian gold work, some 17th c. paintings as well as fine priests' vestments.

*Igreja de São Vicente de Fora (Church) K 3

Location
Largo de São Vicente

Trams
28, 28B

Open
Daily: 9am–1pm
3–6pm

The Igreja de São Vicente de Fora, together with the adjoining former Augustinian monastery (now closed), stands on a hill to the east of Alfama and is visible from afar. The Largo das Potas de Sol, on the edge of Alfama and where a memorial to St Vincent was erected in 1970, offers a fine view of the church in the distance. From here the additional name *de Fora* (outside), referring to its position, can be appreciated; at the time of its construction, the church stood outside of the city walls.
Several partly contradictory legends have grown up about the life of St Vincent to whom the church is dedicated. Both Portugal and Spain lay claim to the saint. Confusion reigns mostly about his burial site; one claim holds it to be in Avila in Spain in a church named after him, another points to St Vincent's mother of pearl encrusted reliquary in Lisbon's Sé Patriarchal (see entry), which used to be kept in a former church on the site of São Vicente de Fora. He is commonly considered to be a Spanish saint, but is also held to be a Portuguese one. In Portugal he is the patron saint of sea voyages and of viniculture, and the people of Lisbon have recorded his life in the coat of arms of their city. According to Portuguese tradition, during the 4th c. the body of St Vincent was washed ashore at Sagres in the Algarve in one of two ships accompanied by ravens (Cabo de São Vicente is

Igreja de São Vicente de Fora

thus the name of the most south-westerly rocky plateau near to Sagres). In the 12th c. Afonso Henriques had his remains transported to one of the churches commissioned by him on the site of the present São Vicente de Fora.

The building of the Igreja de São Vicente de Fora was ordered by the Spanish king Philipp II in 1590. Philipp II had the previous 12th c. church on this site torn down and asked the Italian architect Filippo Terzi to design a new church. In his plans Terzi focused on the Il Gesù in Rome. The building style evident in the São Vicente de Fora belongs to the end of the Renaissance. Although the church continued to be built up until the beginning of the 18th c. (the main work being completed by 1629, however), as a whole it appears extraordinarily uniform.

The strongly symmetrical façade is flanked by two towers. Above three great portals can be seen three niches with portrayals of St Sebastian, St Augustine and St Vincent and above them are three windows with triangular and segment pediments.

Interior

The interior is decorated with white marble and also appears very unified. The 74m/243ft long one-aisled construction is vaulted by a coffered ceiling with bright pink and bright yellow fields of marble. The crossing spans a cupola, whose proportions do not appear completely coherent. A larger and more lavish cupola collapsed during the earthquake – its former size can still be imagined from the lower edge of the cupola. Pillars support the careful construction of the present cupola. The enormous Baroque canopy which roofs over the Vincent altar was created by Machado de Castro. It is supposed to emphasise the "Most Holy One", but it almost overpowers the peaceful unity of the rest of the architecture. Of the six side chapels, one completely decorated with Talha woodwork is particularly striking.

Augustinian Monastery

The former Augustinian monastery is reached via the nave. The entrance hall (portaria) and two small cloisters are covered with 18th c. tiles. Those in the hall depict scenes of the conquest of Lisbon and Santarém as well as the construction of São Vicente de Fora. Many of them show typical 18th c. painted tile scenes, although there are some anachronisms: views of the city, fashions and daily life are thoughtlessly mixed. The most original is a

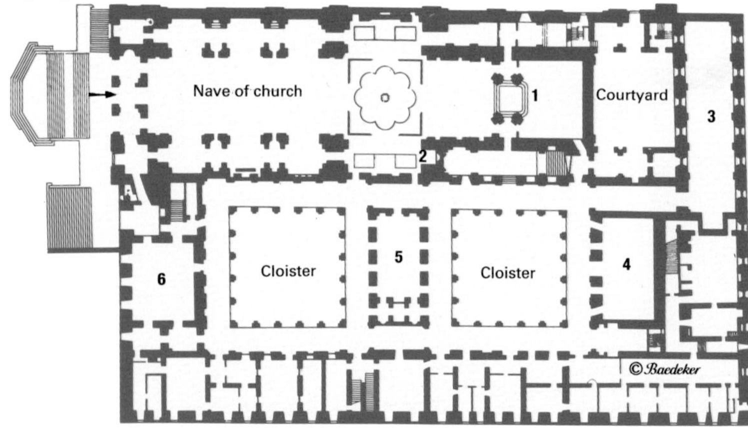

1 Altar of St Vincent
2 St Anthony's Chapel
3 Pantheon of the Braganza Dynasty
4 Pantheon of the Patriarchs
5 Sacristy
6 Convent Entrance Hall

depiction of the capture of Lisbon in 1147 with the Sé Patriarchal (see entry) in the background – the cathedral is shown with two Baroque towers which it did not acquire until the 18th c. The depiction of the construction of São Vicente de Fora shows the present late Renaissance church and not the intended Roman predecessor. Even the conquerors' ships are too Baroque for 1147.
In the cloisters (inside, leading to the transverse courtyard) 38 tiles depicting the fables of La Fontaine can be seen, some of which have been restored very poorly and now and then oddly. The sacristy lies between the cloisters. The walls are completely covered with pink, black and white marble, the wooden ceiling is decorated with 17th c. paintings by André Gonçalves.

Panteão da Familia Real

In 1855 the former refectory was turned into a pantheon for the royal family. Here can be found the graves of almost all of the members of the Bragança dynasty from João IV (died 1656) to Amélia (died 1951); only Maria I and Pedro IV are not buried here. A stone figure in front of the graves of Carlos I and his son Luis Filipe catches the eye. The king and his successor were murdered on February 1st 1908 on the Praça do Comércio (see entry). The stone sarcophagi were ordered by Salazar. Previously the members of the royal family rested in wooden coffins with glass lids.
Also buried here is King Charles of Rumania, who was related to the Portuguese royal family and who died in exile in Portugal in 1953.

Jardim Botânico (Botanical Garden) G 4

Location
Rua da Escola Politécnica

Trams
10, 20, 24, 29, 30

Buses
15, 39, 58

Open
Mon.–Fri.,
9am–7pm
Sat., Sun.,
Holidays
10am–6pm

Lisbon's botanical garden is considered to be one of Europe's finest. It covers an area of 34,000sq.m/365,976sq.ft extending uphill from the Rua da Escola Politécnica to the Avenida da Liberdade.
Inspired by two professors from the adjoining Science Faculty (which had to be evacuated from the rooms of the Escola Politécnica in 1978 owing to a fire) it was set out here in 1873, thus before the construction of the Avenida de Liberdade.

Pleasant walks can be enjoyed here among all manner of species of plants from all over the world, little streams and some modern statues.

A meterological observatory, opened in 1863, and an astronomical institute and observatory have been built on a higher terrace. A department of the Science Museum located in this upper part of the garden can be visited by an appointment.

Museu Nacional de História Naturel

Further premises of the Science Museum are housed in the Escola Politécnica (founded in 1837) at the entrance to the botanical garden. The museum is composed of several smaller museums, some of which are in the process of being built. The Museu de Barbosa du Bocage and the Museu da Ciéncia only open for temporary exhibitions. A permanent exhibition of mineralogical finds can be seen in the Museu e Laboratório Mineralógico e Geológico.

Jardim da Estrela (Estrela Garden) E/F 4

Location
Praça da Estrela

Trams
25, 26, 28, 29, 30

Buses
9, 20, 22, 27, 38

Certainly Lisbon's best-loved garden is the Jardim da Estrela located opposite the Basilica da Estrela (see entry), which was laid out to a variety of designs between 1842 and 1852. Among old trees, lush bushes and herbaceous borders there are ponds with different varieties of water birds, little fountains and an artificial grotto. Especially lovely is a large music pavilion which was built in 1884. It first stood on the Passeio Público, the forerunner of the Avenida da Liberdade (see entry). When the Avenida da Liberdade was constructed it had to move and acquired an excellent site here.

English Cemetery

The entrance to the old English cemetery is situated opposite the north side of the Jardim da Estrela. The author Henry Fielding, whose novels are considered to be "master works of English humour", is buried here. He died on October 8th 1754 during a holiday in Lisbon.

Jardim Zoológico (Zoological Garden) E 8/9

Location
Estrada das Laranjeiras/ Estrada de Benfica

Metro
Sete Rios

Lisbon Zoo was first founded in 1884 but had to change its location twice before it opened its gates here in 1905. The site has some very fine old animal houses, cages and aviaries; animals from all over the world are kept and cared for here. A dogs' cemetery at the north end of the zoo is a very strange feature.

By following a trail of brown arrows through the zoo grounds the most important animal enclosures and further attractions are reached. The zoo can also be toured in a small train. The zoo is open daily from 9am to 6pm, in the summer to 8pm.

Jardim Zoológico
Zoological Garden

1 Children's Zoo
2 Flamingos
3 Administration
4, 5, 6 Restaurants or snackbars
7 Rose Garden
8 Greenhouses
9 Antelopes, Buffaloes, etc,
10 Gorillas
11 Hippopotami
12 Poultry
13 Apes
14 Peacocks
15 Llamas
16 Cranes
17 Tapirs
18 Reindeer, Deer
19 Antilopes
20 Herons
21 Mufflons
22 Camels, Dromedaries
23 Chimpanzees
24 Reptiles
25 Zebras
26 Ostriches
27 Giraffes
28 Bears
29 Elephants
30 Lions
31 Greenhouse
32 Rhinoceros
33 Dogs
34 Beasts of prey
35 Tigers
36 Apes' School
37 Deer
38 Bears
39 Dogs' Cemetery

Lapa (Quarter) D/E 2/3

The little quarter of Lapa, which arose in the middle of the 18th c., is considered to be one of Lisbon's best residential areas. Large old villas and much greenery characterise this peaceful quarter where many embassies and consolates are situated.

Among the small palaces some are striking on account of their unusual architecture, such as the Casa Visconde de Sacavérn in the Rua do Sacramento á Lapa (no. 24), which was built shortly before the turn of the century.

Location
Between Estrela and the Tagus

Trams
25, 26, 29, 30

Buses
13, 27

Mãe d'Água das Amoreiras (Castle surrounded by water) F 5

The large Mãe d'Água das Amoreiras, a castle surrounded by water, at the Jardim das Amoreiras served as a reservoir for the water conveyed across the Aqueduto das Águas Livres (see entry). The architect Carlos Mardel, who later played a large part in the reconstruction of the Baixa (see entry), drew up the plans for the castle in 1752, but it was not finally completed until 1834. From outside the functional-looking building with 5m/16½ft thick walls appears very severe and plain. It occupies 5500 cubic m/21,582 cubic ft. A bust honouring Manuel da Maia, the architect of the aqueduct, stands in front of the entrance.

The interior of the castle is very impressive. The wall leading to the aqueduct has been turned into a grotto, above which the water runs down to the large basin. The foundations of strong pillars, which support the roof of the hall, are buried in the basin. This room, with its unusual atmosphere, is mainly used for art exhibitions – a very successful setting for such a purpose. A flight of steps leads to a roof terrace from which there is a

Location
Praça das Amoreiras 18

Trams
10, 24, 25, 26
29, 30

Open
Times vary (dependent on individual exhibitions)

Arco das Amoreiras

Ermida da N. S. de Monserrate

panoramic view of the city. From the steps it is also possible to look into the interior of the aqueduct.

Arco das Amoreiras

The last part of the aqueduct follows the Rua das Amoreiras. The arch of the Aqueduto das Águas Livres, which spans the road and which was also designed by Carlos Mardel, looks very spectacular. It was constructed in 1748 in the shape of a Roman triumphal arch. At this point the water pipeline turns off at a right angle to the Mãe d'Agua.

Ermida da N. S. de Monserrate

The small Ermida da Nossa Senhora de Monserrate was built in 1763 in one of the arches of the aqueduct (between the Arco das Amoreiras and Mãe d'Agua).

Mafra (Excursion)

Location
50km/31 miles north-west

Buses
Buses of the "Rodoviária Nacional" from Praça Marquês de Pombal; "Mafrense" from Rua Fernandes de Fonseca

The town of Mafra, with its population of about 7000, lies approximately 50km/31 miles north-west of Lisbon and is widely known because of its enormous former royal monastery-palace, the most extensive complex of its type on the Iberian peninsula.
During the reign of José I, the Italian master sculptor Alexandre Giusti founded the "Mafra school" here. This was an important school of sculpture at which such famous artists as José Almeida and Joaquim Machado de Castro studied.
Mafra is an unassuming, small town, its centre dominated by the enormous monastery-palace which is visible from afar. It is also worth visiting the carefully restored 13th/14th c. Gothic church of Santo André, containing the tombs of Dom Diogo de Sousa and his wife.
From Mafra it is easy to visit the resort of Ericeira (see Costa do Sol), about 10km/6 miles to the west.

**Palácio Nacional de Mafra

Open
Wed.–Mon.
10am–1pm,
2–5pm

The Palácio Nacional de Mafra was founded in 1717 by João V and his queen, Maria Anna of Austria, in fulfilment of a vow made in 1711 and in thanksgiving for the birth of an heir (later José I). The Italian-trained German architect Johann Friedrich Ludwig (known as Frederico Ludovice in Portugal) and his son Johan Peter Ludwig were in charge of the construction work. More than 45,000 workmen were used in the building, some of whom had been forced to take part and who were guarded by soldiers (this ambitious project was described by the famous Portuguese poet José Saramago in his novel "The Memorial"). After only thirteen years of work, the monastery was consecrated in 1730, although the complex underwent further extensions up until 1750.
The monastery was originally occupied by Franciscans and later for a time by Augustinians. When it was closed following the dissolution of all religious orders in 1834 parts of it were allocated to the army.
The former royal apartments were hardly ever occupied. King João V and Maria Anna of Austria only spent a few days here. The palace enjoyed its brief heyday at the beginning of the 19th c. when João VI resided in Mafra from 1806 to 1807. With the approach of French troops the royal family made a hurried departure from the palace, en route for Lisbon and subsequently to Brazil, taking most of the valuable furnishings and works of art with them. Later Portuguese rulers did not spend much time in Mafra, usually only stopping here in order to hunt nearby.

Layout

The huge building consists of the monastery church, the monastery accommodation containing the cells and the communal rooms used by the monks, and a further section to serve the royal family as their accommodation.

Palácio Nacional de Mafra

Monastic Palace of Mafra

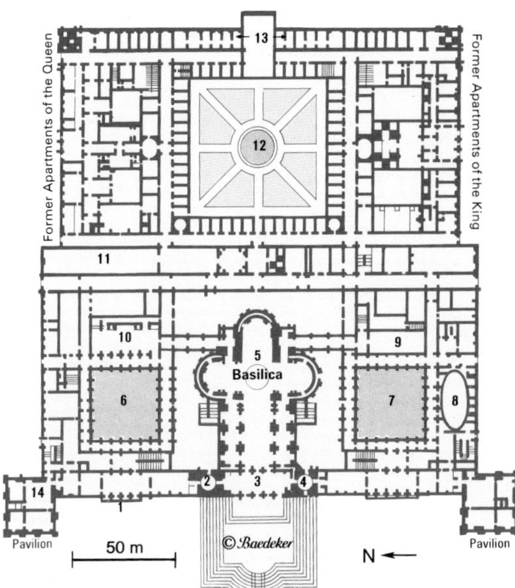

1 Entrance
2 Tower
3 Vestibule (statues of saints)
4 Tower
5 Dome
6 Cloister
7 Cloister
8 Chapterhouse
9 Sacristy
10 Campo-Santo Chapel
11 Refectory
12 Convent garth (gardens)
13 Library (upper floor)
14 Museum of Sculpture (Museu de Escultura Comparada)

The building is often compared to the Escorial in Madrid, but was intended by its founder to surpass even this in size and splendour. Its dimensions alone allow the complex to be described in superlatives: the building as a whole measures 251m/825ft long by 221m/725ft wide and is constructed on an almost square plan and designed with the strictest regard for symmetry. It covers a total area of 40,000sq.m/48,000sq.yds and has 900 rooms, 2500 windows and 5200 doors. The suite of rooms on the first floor of the west side extends unbroken for more than 250m/820ft; 300 monks and 150 nuns lived in the monastery accommodation.

Like no other building in Portugal, the palace at Mafra displays cool Baroque magnificence, lavish extravagance and absolute royal power. The possession of goldmines in conquered Brazil provided the financial means for it.

The church is open to the public, as are parts of the former royal apartments and the monastery accommodation (guided tours). A large part of the palace is now used as barracks.

Basilica

The basilica occupies the central part of the main front, which is precisely articulated and almost without decoration – it later served as a model for the building of the Basilica da Estrela (see entry). Its main façade is flanked by two 68m/223ft high bell towers, which are integrated almost without a transition into the front of the palace. The carillon of 114 bells was made by an Antwerp bell-founder named Lavache.

The single-aisled limestone basilica is reached through the vestibule of the church, with its fourteen large Carrara marble statues of saints by the Italian sculptor Alessandro Giusti. The ground plan of the church is based on a Latin cross. The total length is 58.5m/192ft, and at its widest point in the crossing measures 43m/141ft. The construction of the crossing cupola with a height of 65m/213ft and a diameter of 13m/42½ft and of the 2m/6½ft wide lantern took two years. The interior has a coffered barrel-vaulted

The Monastic Palace of Mafra, an example of absolutist power

ceiling and appears clearly structured by the 62 fluted pillars. Different types of marble in pink, white, black, grey, blue and yellow have been combined into a geometric pattern. German Baroque and Italian Classical influences are apparent: Johann Friedrich Ludwig is supposed to have received inspiration from St Peter's basilica in the Vatican and from the Church of Jesus in Rome.

Striking are the six organs, commissioned by João V between 1792 and 1807 and constructed to the plans of the organ builders Joachim António Peres Fontanes and António Xavier Machado.

The basilica contains eleven chapels. Until the 18th c. works by Portuguese and Italian artists hung here. Extensive dampness damaged the paintings, however, and they had to be replaced by the current flat reliefs made of Carrara marble. These reliefs are the work of artists at the school of sculpting. The altar paintings in the large chapels of the crossing are the combined works of Alexandre Giusti and his famous pupil Machado de Castro.

The marble statues in the side chapels portray various saints. They were made in Italy and transported to Mafra. Together with the statues on the outer façade and in the vestibule they form the most important collection of Italian sculpture in Portugal.

Monastery buildings, Royal apartments

During a guided tour it is possible to view some parts of the monastery buildings and the royal apartments. The juxtaposition of spartan monks' cells and the lavishly-furnished royal apartments is striking.

Within the monastery the old pharmacy, the kitchen and the infirmary, with its cells for the sick monks, can be seen. The wooden couches have gaps in the centre, which served to relieve strain on the patients' spines.

The furnishings and works of art in the former royal apartments date from the 18th and the 19th centuries. Several bedrooms, the throne room, the Hall of Discoveries, the music room as well as a comically-furnished hunting room follow on from one another. One room contains various lutes, some of which were made for different purposes. In the games room there are two old billiard tables and forerunners of present-day gambling machines. A bust in the vestibule is of the founder of the palace, João V, wearing a laurel wreath on his head.

Sculpture Museum

In one of the rooms used to accommodate the Sculpture Museum casts of famous works by Portuguese, Italian and French sculptors of the 12th c. to 16th c. can be seen.

Library

In the eastern wing of the palace is located the 88m/290ft long and, in the middle, 20m/65ft wide royal-monastery library. It contains 40,000 volumes, including valuable incunabula and manuscripts, first editions of Camões' "Lusiads" and the plays of Gil Vicenteas as well as a trilingual Bible of 1514 and the earliest edition of Homer in Greek.

Tapada de Mafra

To the rear of the palace extends the Tapada de Mafra, the royal deer-park enclosed by a wall 20km/12½ miles long, in which the royal family still hunted at the beginning of the 20th c.

Monumento Cristo Rei (Statue of Christ the King)

Location
South bank of the Tagus, by the Ponte 25 de Abril

Buses
From Cacilhas

Open
Daily 9am–7pm (July/Aug. until 7.30; in winter until 6pm)

The Monumento Cristo Rei stands on top of a hill about 110m/361ft high on the south bank of the Tagus and can be seen from afar immediately above the exit of the Ponte 25 de Abril (see entry). Any resemblances to the Statue of Christ at Rio de Janeiro are not incidental: the Cardinal-Patriarch of Lisbon saw it in 1934 on a visit to Brazil and thereafter entertained the idea of having a similar monument erected in Portugal. At an assembly held in 1940 in Fátima the bishops of Portugal took a vow to commission the construction of a statue of Christ, if Portugal were not drawn into the Second World War. The architect António Lino, the engineer Francisco de Mello e Castro and the sculptor Francisco Franco worked on the project. The laying of the foundation stone took place in 1949, and in 1959 the monument was officially opened. The statue of Fátima with miraculous skills was also transported here for the opening celebrations, while Pope John XXIII sent a radio address.
The four arches in the 82m/269ft high concrete base are supposed to represent the four directions and thus the universitality of the Kingdom of Christ. A small chapel is located in the foot of the base. The figure of Christ itself is 28m/92ft tall, while the representation of the heart measures 1.89m/6ft.
A lift takes visitors up to a platform below the Christ figure from where a unique view of Lisbon and its surroundings can be enjoyed.

**Mosteiro dos Jerónimos (Hieronymite Convent)

Location
Belém, Praça do Império

Trams
15, 16, 17

Buses
27, 28, 43, 49, 51

Train
From Estação Cais do Sodré, Station Belém

Open
Tues.–Sun. 10am–6.30pm (Oct.–May until 5pm)

In the suburb of Belém, parallel to the bank of the Tagus and measuring almost 300m/985ft, stands one of Portugal's most famous buildings, the former Hieronymite Convent (Mosteiro dos Jerónimos). The convent complex originally stood on the water's edge. However, a gradual and natural shift of the river combined with the building of the harbour basin have meant that its once important proximity to the Tagus can now only be imagined. The Praça do Império (see Belém), laid out as a park, the wide Avenida da India, the suburban railway to Cascais as well as some harbour basins and the Padrão dos Descobrimentos (see entry) now lie between the convent and the Tagus.

The choice of site dates back to a hospice which was affiliated to the small chapel of Nossa Senhora de Restelo. This was built here by Henry the Navigator at the time of the first great voyages of discovery in the first half of the 15th c. The Knights of Christ began their journeys from the nearby port of Restelo, the hospice served as their home, the chapel as a place to

Mosteiro dos Jerónimos de Belém

Hieronymite Monastery of Belém

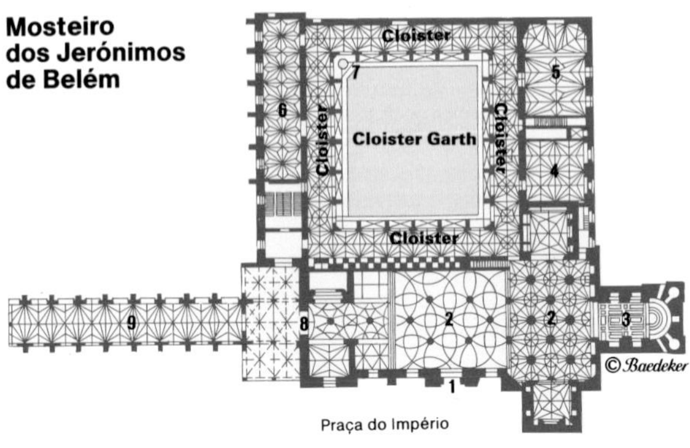

1 South door
2 Church of Santa Maria de Belém
3 Choir
4 Sacristy
5 Chapterhouse
6 Refectory
7 Lion Fountain
8 West Door
9 National Museum of Archaeology in former dormitory

pray before beginning their voyages into the unknown. Even Vasco da Gama is supposed to have prayed here in the summer of 1497 before his first voyage to India. After the successful return from the expedition, Manuel I commissioned the building of a convent on the site of the chapel. The location of the Mosteiro dos Jerónimos has thus been a focal point for Portugal's most important events. The construction of the Manueline building was begun around 1502 following the plans of Diogo de Boytaca (see Famous People), between 1517 and 1522 the detailed work was carried out under the direction of João de Castilho and the high choir was only completed in 1571 thus belonging to the Renaissance. The more than 182m/597ft long western part of the convent complex, in which the maritime museum and the archaeological museum are housed, was rebuilt and partly restored at the end of the 19th c. in the neo-Manueline style.
After part of the roof above the Chapterhouse collapsed in the winter of 1989/90 there followed a frank discussion about the sorry state of many Portuguese monuments. It was felt necessary to place the Mosteiro dos Jerónimos under the special protection of UNESCO as an endangered world monument. Reasons given for the roof collapse were the generally bad state of repair of the convent complex as well as possibly the building work undertaken for Belém's new cultural centre next to the convent forecourt.

Igreja de Santa Maria

The south side of the Igreja de Santa Maria (facing the Tagus, in the eastern part of the complex) is characterised by the richly-decorated Manueline south portal. Both the portal and the filigree-style balustrade, which forms the upper border, lessen the strong impression of the actually very compact façade. The octagonal cupola tower above the west portal also appears rather light due to the embellishments and the continuation of the eight corner pillars into little pointed towers. The cupola dates from the 19th c., before this the tower had a somewhat lower helm roof. The Manueline window decorations appear clear and less eroded. Considerably less decorative, however, is the external wall of the main chancel at the eastern end, which was only added in the second half of the 16th c.
The south portal is the work of the architect João de Castilho, who also created the portal of the Igreja de Conceição Velha (see entry), which escaped the earthquake undamaged. Above the edge of the roof two projecting buttresses flank the portal. The central axis is interrupted by a window above both entrances. Two lions are depicted between the doors – they act as reminders of the heraldic animal of St Jeronimus. Above them Henry the Navigator can be seen portrayed as a stylised figure. In front of the window, at the true end of the archway, stands a figure of Mary, at the top beneath the main baldachin with the Cross of the Knights of Christ an

South doorway of the church . . .

. . . and the west range

angel holds the royal coat of arms. The reliefs above the two doors portray scenes from the life of St Jeronimus. A total of 25 figures have been erected between piers and pillars and below decorated baldachin, including the twelve apostles, kings and queens and bishops.
The less impressive west portal is the work of the Frenchman Nicolas Chanterène. Depicted to the left next to the door are the founder of the convent complex, Manuel I, on his knees, and his patron saint, St Jeronimus. Opposite on the right is Maria of Castille, Manuel's second wife, and her patron saint, John the Baptist. Scenes from Bethlehem (Belém) can be seen in the tympanum: the birth of Christ – including two angels carrying the Portuguese coat of arms – and the adoration of the shepherds.
The conscious synthesis of worldly rule and representation of Godly power stands out in the decoration of the south and west portals.

Church Interior

The three-aisled interior of the hall church, chiefly the work of João de Castilho, conveys an extraordinary effect. From the west portal to the east choir measures 92m/302ft, the width 22m/72ft. The nave and the side aisles have a uniform height of 25m/82ft. The Gothic fan vault spans six slender-looking pillars in the nave and two somewhat stronger crossing pillars. The dainty effect of the octagonal pillars is strengthened more by the fine embellishments which decorate them. The transepts, measuring 49m/161ft across, support the overall impression of spaciousness.
The main choir, not added until 1571 and whose style assigns it to the late Renaissance, is most impressive. Corinthian and Ionian pillars as well as the clear, geometric arrangement of the paintings have nothing more in common with the opposing, almost playful effect of the decoration of the rest of the building. The Monstranz of Belém, a work by the goldsmith and playwright Gil Vicente, used to stand here – it can now be seen in the Museu Nacional de Arte Antiga (see entry).
The west gallery (reached via the cloister) offers a marvellous view of the interior. The organs on both sides date from the 18th c.

Cloister of the Hieronymite convent

Monuments to various famous people from Portuguese history are located inside the church. On the right next to the western entrance is the sarcophagus of the poet Luis Vaz de Camões (see Famous People), who glorified the voyages of discovery of Vasco da Gama in his "Lusiadas". The sarcophagus on the right honours Vasco da Gama. Both monuments were erected during the course of the recollection of the "Golden Age". All the important symbols of that epoch – the Portuguese coat of arms, the Cross of the Knights of Christ, armillary sphere and a caravel – have been integrated in a Manueline style.

In the transept can be seen the sarcophagi of various members of the royal family, including in the southern section the empty grave of the apparently lost, but still "longed for" King Sebastião (see Famous People). On the left of the high choir the memorials to Manuel I and his wife Maria are borne by elephants, on the right rest João III, under whom the construction of the convent continued after the death of Manuel, and his wife Catarina.

Cloister

Passing the west portal of the convent church we reach the famous cloister (Claustro), called by art historians the "most impressive cloister in the world". Its importance lies without doubt in the pure Manueline decoration, which is only equalled in Portugal in the cloisters of Batalha and Tomar.

The square garth – once laid out as a pond, now as a small garden – is surrounded by two-storey arcades, each of which measures 55m/180½ft long. The lower storey is the work of Diogo de Boytaca, the upper of João de Castiho. Extensive Manueline decoration has been incorporated into the moderate Renaissance site. On closer inspection armillary spheres, crosses of the Knights of Christ, the royal coat of arms and stylised plants can also be found here. In the north-west corner is the Lion Fountain – the heraldic animal of St Jeronimus – which once stood in a basin in the middle of the cloister. A monument to the poet Fernando Pessoa (see Famous People) was erected in 1985 in the middle of the northern arcade. The transfer of his grave from Prazeres cemetery to Belém represented an acknowledgement of the most important 20th c. Portuguese writer, whose work only became famous after his death.

Chapterhouse

The graves of further famous people can be found in the former Chapterhouse in the north-east corner of the cloister. The poet and historian Alexandre Herculano (1810–77) and the writer and politician Almeida Garrett (1799–1854) are buried here, as well as the writer and first president of the republic Teófilo Braga (1843–1924) and the long-serving president, Oscar Carmona (1869–1951), who performed his duty from 1928 until 1951 alongside Prime Minister Oliveira Salazar with little influence.

Refectory

The large refectory, the former dining hall, is situated on the north-west side and is particularly striking on account of its 17th c. wall tiles and fan-vaulted ceiling.

Museu Nacional de Arqueologia e Etnologia

Open
Tues.–Sun.
10am–12pm
2–5pm

Admission free on Wednesday

The dormitory was originally housed in part of the unfinished 182m/597ft long wing of the convent, which adjoins the Igreja de Santa Maria. In 1834, after the dissolution of the convent, the Casa Pia, an orphanage for about 800 children, was set up here. Restoration and partial renewal of this part was completed at the end of the 19th c. and today the National Museum of Archaeology and Ethnology (founded in 1893), which was reopened in 1990 after several years of extensive reorganisation, is located here.
The museum contains a collection of archaeological finds. Neolithic, Bronze Age, Iron Age and Roman tools are displayed and explained (in Portuguese) and arranged according to their epoch. A film introduces Portuguese sites where finds have been made. The museum also contains a separate exhibition of jewellery dating from 20–150 A.D., which has been found in Portugal.

Museu da Marinha

Open
Tues.–Sun.
10am–5pm

The Maritime Museum (Museu da Marinha) is housed in the western part of the former convent wing as well as in the modern extension opposite.
Luis I had the museum built in 1863 and it moved into its current accommodation in 1962. As the collection was started quite late most of the exhibits here are model ships and not originals. Portugal's military and colonial history until the 20th c. is documented by means of historical paintings, original nautical charts, navigational aids, weapons, portraits and busts of famous people. In addition are exhibited replicas of so-called padrões, round stone pillars with the Cross of the Knights of Christ or an armillary sphere, which the Portuguese placed everywhere they landed on their voyages of discovery mainly along the African coast. Of interest are some model ships from river voyages and fishing as well as authentic rooms from the royal yacht "Améllia".
Original 18th c. and 19th c. galleys can be seen in the new part of the museum, including those commissioned by João V, Miguel I and Maria I. Also exhibited here is the seaplane "Santa Clara", painted with crosses of the Knights of Christ, which crossed the Atlantic from Lisbon to Rio de Janeiro in 1922.

Planetário Calouste Gulbenkian

Presentations
Tues. 3pm, 4.15pm;
Sat. 4pm, 5pm;
Sun. 11am, 4pm, 5pm

Between the west wing of the convent and the modern extension of the Maritime Museum stands the Calouste Gulbenkian Planetarium. It was built in 1964 according to the plans of the architect Frederico George, who was also responsible two years before for the extension of the

Maritime Museum (the presentations given at 5pm are also in English and French).

Mouraria (Quarter) J 3

Location
Between Castelo de São Jorge, Graça and Largo Martim Moniz

Trams
3, 12, 17, 19, 20, 25, 26, 28

Buses
7, 8, 40

Mouraria is one of Lisbon's oldest districts. It contains a tangled street layout just as in Alfama (see entry), which has remained since the times of the Moors. The Arabs withdrew into this quarter after Lisbon was conquered by the Portuguese – a ghetto for people of different faiths arose which at that time was located outside of the city gates. In the 19th c. prostitution and fado, which at this time was considered to be indecent, brought the quarter a bad name. Now Mouraria is an extremely neglected, poor part of the city. Renovation of houses, which are threatened with falling into ruins, and an improvement in the living standards of the inhabitants of Mouraria has only begun recently. In contrast very grandiose buildings are being constructed on the edge of the quarter: this difference is felt most acutely when leaving the modern shopping centre at the Largo Martim Moniz and turning into the immediately neighbouring little alleyways of Mouraria.

The quarter is still today quickly associated with fado, which has been heard in the streets here throughout the last century. The Casa de Severa in the Rua do Capelão 36 – hopefully being turned into a fado museum – was the home of the legendary fadista Maris Severa Onofriando, who died aged 26 on November 30th 1846. A stylised fado guitar can be seen on the newly-surfaced road. The memory of the singer is also kept alive in house no. 32: there is a pub here called "Os Amigos da Severa" (the Friends of Severa). Another great fado interpreter, Fernando Mauricio, was born in house no. 23.

Museu d'Água Manuel da Maia (Water Museum) L 3

Location
Rua do Alviela 12

Trams
3, 16, 24

Buses
13A

Open
Tues.–Sat.
10am–12.30pm
2–4pm

The history of Lisbon's water supply is documented in a very clear and imaginative way in the city waterworks museum EPAL (Empresa Pública das Águas Livres). Opened in October 1987, the museum – named after the architect of the Aqueduto das Águas Livres – has been assembled in a former pumping station. Four enormous steam engines dating from 1880, which were used for pumping, are kept in a machine room: one of them has been reconditioned and can be seen working in demonstrations.

In the rest of the museum the first water system from Roman times is explained; model figures of water-carriers, pictures of old wells, plans of the aqueduct and of the castle surrounded by water, and a water meter dating from 1856 are some of the exhibits. At the end of the exhibition, water quality control, chlorination of Lisbon's water and so on is explained. Its exemplary arrangement earned the Museu d'Água Manuel da Maia the 1990 first prize from the European Museums Council.

Museu Arqueológico

See Igreja do Carmo

Museu de Arte Decorativo (Museum of Decorative Art) J 2

The 17th c. former city palace of the Count of Azurara stands on the Largo das Portas do Sol and currently houses the Museum of Decorative Art. The banker Ricardo do Espirito Santo Silva, whose family was one of the richest in Portugal, acquired the palace in 1947 and donated his collection to be the museum.
Portugal's most important furniture collection can be viewed here during a guided tour. Valuable wooden Portuguese, French and English furniture dating from the 16th to the 19th c. are presented in suitable surroundings. Bedrooms, dining rooms, function rooms, music rooms and dressing rooms from different eras have been reconstructed in their original forms here. The furniture is completed by wall hangings, silver work, porcelain, ceramics, collections of old books as well as some original tiling and ceiling paintings.
Part of the collection includes furnishings belonging to José I and his wife Maria: a bedroom and a children's room, both retained in the Manueline style. One of José I's coaches stands in the entrance hall.
The museum contains a training workshop for craft workers, which is likewise affiliated to the foundation. Bookbinders, gilders and cabinet-makers are trained here in traditional techniques.

Location
Largo das Portas do Sol

Trams
28, 28B

Buses
37

Open
Tues.–Sat.
10am–1pm,
2.30–5pm

Museu Calouste Gulbenkian

See Fundação Calouste Gulbenkian

Museu da Cidade (City museum) G 11

In 1739 João V had the Palácio Piomenta on the northern end of the Campo Grande (see entry) built for his mistress, the nun Madre Paula from the Odivelas convent. In 1962 the city of Lisbon set up in this palace a museum in which the history of the development of the city is extensively documented.
On view are Roman excavation finds, historical paintings of the conquest of the Castelo de São Jorge (see entry) by the Portuguese, old navigation charts, documents from the "Golden Age", architectural models and pieces saved from buildings after the earthquake (such as the "diamond stones" from the Casa dos Bicos (see entry). Panoramic views of the city before the earthquake occupy a wide room, together with pictures of the earthquake itself and a collection of foreign reactions to the catastrophe. A large 1959 model of the city and its surroundings before 1755 is very interesting. Various plans for the reconstruction of the Baixa (see entry), drawings of old wells and of the Aqueduto das Águas Livres complete the exhibits.
It is also worth seeing the fully equipped kitchen of the old palace, some living rooms and lovely azulejo wall pictures.

Location
Campo Grande 245

Buses
1, 7, 17B, 33, 36
36A, 46A, 47, 50

Open
Tues.–Sun.
10am–1pm
2–6pm

Museu Etnográfico (Museum of Ethnography) H 3

The Museum of Ethnography is attached to the Geographical Society (Sociedade de Geografia). This was founded in 1875 and moved into its present accommodation in 1907. The building in the Rua das Portas de Santo Antão contains conference rooms, several fine old halls and a specialist library. Statues of the most important people in Portuguese history stand in the spacious entrance hall.
The somewhat antiquated Museu Etnográfico on one of the upper floors was founded in 1892. A guided tour includes the opportunity to look at

Location
Rua das Portas de Santo Antão 100

Metro
Restauradores

Sala de Portugal in the Geographical Society Building

Tours
Mon., Wed., Fri., 11am, 3pm

exhibits from overseas which document Portugal's era of colonialism. Tools, weapons, textiles, masks, wooden carvings, old toys and ceramics can be seen in show cases arranged according to their country of origin. Of interest is a wooden statue of Anthony, who was held in Angola to have magic powers, in direct contrast to the importance which St Anthony has for Lisbon (see Sé Patriarchal, Igreja do Santo António da Sé). Also included among the exhibition pieces is a chair belonging to Pedro V (1855–91), king of the Congo.
The old rooms in which the collection is housed are also very impressive: the large hall (Sala de Portugal) with its beautiful gallery, which is also used for conferences and concerts, and several smaller halls (Sala Algarve, Sala Padrões, Sala da India), which have recently been partly renovated.

Coliseu dos Recreios

Adjoining the building housing the Sociedade de Geografia stands the Coliseu dos Recreios (see Rua das Portas de Santo Antão).

Museu de Etnologia (Museum of Ethnology)

Location
Avenida Ilha da Madeira

Buses
28, 32, 49, 51

Open
Tues.–Sun.
10am–12.30pm, 2–5pm

The Museum of Ethnology on the northern edge of the Lisbon suburb of Belém (see entry) contains an extensive collection of materials and information from the former Portuguese colonies in South America, Africa and India.
The modern building on the Avenida Ilha da Madeira was not officially opened until 1985; however, there is only sufficient space to show the most important exhibits on a permanent basis. The museum's collection is therefore shown as a rotating series of very interesting, technically-excellent exhibitions, each based around a different theme and well worth visiting.

Museu da Marinha

See Mosteiro dos Jerónimos

Museu da Marionета (Marionette Museum) J 3

The small Marionette Museum, located close to the east side of the Castelo de São Jorge (see entry), was founded by puppeteers with a view to reviving the spirit and characteristics of the Opera Buffa and to adapting/rearranging new theatrical and musical concepts. Puppet theatre has a long tradition in Portugal. It reached its cultural zenith in the 18th c. with a marionette opera written especially for this form of theatre. The originality of the opera has led it to be described as unique in the history of the theatre. The members of the internationally-famous Marionetas de S. Lourenço theatre also present archaic, medieval and Baroque theatre and undertake theatre tours through Portugal.
The collection, which is supported by the Gulbenkian Foundation, includes almost everything that should be in a marionette museum: puppets, props, sets, old illustated broadsheets, posters and some oriental puppets. The exhibition rooms are named after famous Portuguese puppeteers or authors.

Location
Largo Rodrigues de Freitas 19 A, First Floor

Trams
12, 28, 28B

Open
Tues.–Fri. 10am–1pm, 3–6pm (Closed during performances without notice)

Museu Militar (Military Museum) K 2

The 18th c. classical building on the Largo dos Camnihos de Ferro houses the Museu Militar (Military Museum; entrance on the west side). In 1851 General José Baptista da Silva founded the Artillery Museum here and since 1926 it has been known as the Military Museum. A site was chosen with a relevant past history. Since the beginning of the 1th c. guns had been manufactured in an earlier building which burnt down in 1726. Weapons were produced in the present building up until the 20th c. For a long time the building served as the "Royal Arsenal". The main portal was built in the 18th c. by the French architect Maurice de Larre, the portal on the west side was completed by the Portuguese sculptor Teixeira Lopes at the beginning of the 20th c. On display are a variety of historical war documents, rows of weapons from different eras: cannons of all sizes, rifles, clubs, crossbows and a sword belonging to Vasco da Gama. Two rooms are devoted to the origins and development of Portuguese weapons. The museum's collection also includes reports from the Colonial Wars between 1961 and 1974. Parts of the ceilings and walls are extensively painted with glorified battle scenes.

Location
Largo dos Caminhos de Ferro

Trams
3, 16, 24

Buses
9, 12, 13A, 17, 25, 25A, 28, 35 39, 46, 59, 81, 82, 90

Open
Tues.–Sat. 10am–4pm; Sun. 11am–5pm

Museu Nacional de Arquelogia e Etnologia

See Mosteiro dos Jerónimos

**Museu Nacional de Arte Antiga (Museum of Ancient Art) D/E 2

The Museum of Ancient Art has been housed since 1884 in a palace built by Count Alvor in 1690 in which the Pombal family later lived for some time. Both the name of the street and the common nickname for the museum, "Casa das Janelas Verdes" – house of green windows – originate from the building's shutters which were formerly painted green. The original palace was renovated several times and finally enlarged with a modern extension.

Location
Rua das Janelas Verdes 95

Trams
15, 16, 17, 18, 19

The Military Museum (see page 117)

Buses
14, 27, 28, 32, 40, 43, 49

Open
Tues.–Sun. 10am–5pm

A small chapel which belonged to the St Albert Carmelite monastery, founded in 1584, stood in the path of the planned extension and was integrated into the new building.

As well as an extensive art gallery the museum houses a collection of Egyptian, Greek and Roman sculptures, ceramic and porcelain, and excellent silver and gold work. Vestments, Portuguese furniture, carpets, Gobelin tapestries, Indo-Portuguese handiwork and Namban works of art also form part of the collection.

The main entrance lies on the narrow west side of the building on the Jardim 9 de Abril. From this small park a marvellous view across the Alcântara harbour area to the Tagus and the Ponte 25 de Abril (see entry) can be enjoyed.

Ground Floor (Extension)

The tour of the museum begins on the ground floor of the new extension. On view are pieces of Portuguese furniture and interior furnishings dating from the 15th c. to the 17th c. as well as tapestries and vestments.

St Albert Monastery chapel

A few steps lead to the St Albert monastery chapel. Blue and white azulejo scenes and Talha Dourada cover the walls right up to the ceiling. Two tall side chapels are completely decorated with azulejos. One of Machado de Castro's Christmas cribs, dating from the beginning of the 19th c., is in the anteroom. This artist's works also include the cribs in the Basilica da Estrela (see entry), the Sé Patriarchal (see entry) and in the Ermida Nossa Senhora do Monte (see Graça), as well as the bronze statue of José I on the Praça do Comércio (see entry). Machado de Castro has located the crib scene in a typically Portuguese landscape.

First Floor

The tour next proceeds to the first floor of the extension. Exhibits include Indo-Portuguese handiwork, 18th c. Chinese and Japanese faience, Portuguese glassware and 16th–19th c. Portuguese and Chinese ceramics.

The collection of so-called Namban art is of historico-cultural interest. It refers to handiwork produced as a result of the contact between Portugal

Museu Nacional de Arte Antiga

Casa das Janelas Verdes

National Museum of Ancient Art

SECOND FLOOR

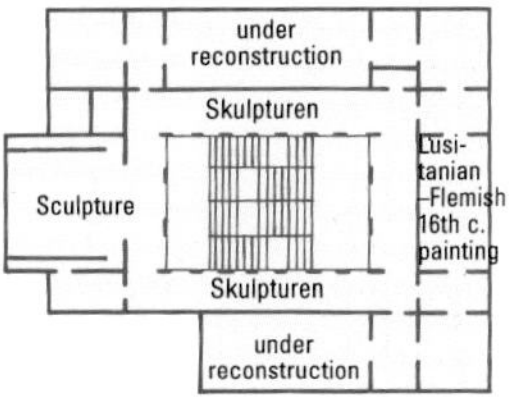

under reconstruction
Skulpturen
Sculpture
Lusitanian-Flemish 16th c. painting
Skulpturen
under reconstruction

FIRST FLOOR

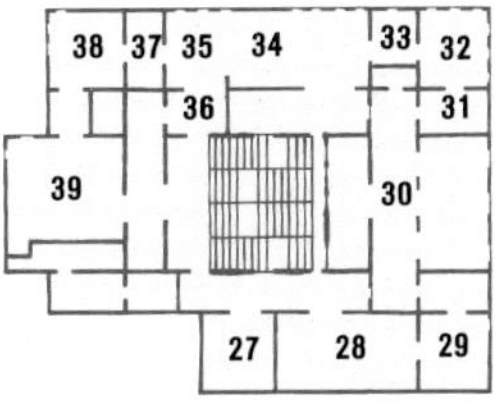

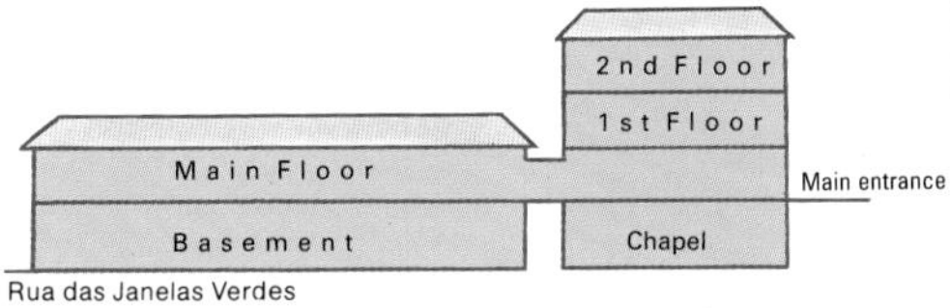

2nd Floor
1st Floor
Main Floor
Basement
Chapel
Main entrance
Rua das Janelas Verdes

© Baedeker

Portuguese Furniture and Applied Art

MAIN FLOOR

Foreign Art
WC
Sales
Vestibule
Convent Chapel

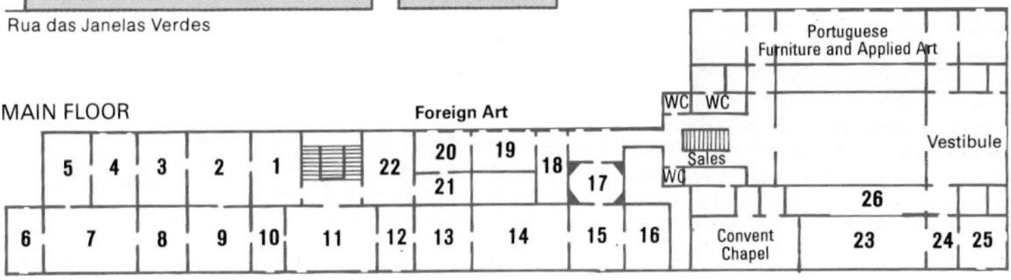

1 Sala Calouste Gulbenkian (sculpture)
2 14th/15th c. painting
3 15th/16th c. Flemish and Spanish painting
4 15th/16th c. painting (including a Bosch altar and Cranach)
5 15th/16th c. painting (including Dürer and Holbein the Elder)
6 Italian faience (16th c.)
7 16th c. painting
8 17th c. painting
9 15th–18th c. portrait painting
10–12 Applied Art (16th–18th c.)
13–17 Temporary exhibitions
18 18th c. portrait painting
19–22 18th c. applied art
23 Nativity crib
24–26 Ecclesiastical robes and tapestries
27 Namban art
28/29 Indo-Portuguese handicraft (17th/18th c.)
30 Chinese and Japanese faience (18th c.)
31, 32 Oriental porcelain (16th–19th c.)
33 Portuguese porcelain
34 Portuguese ceramics (16th–19th c.)
35, 36 16th–19th c. glass
37/38 Gold and silversmiths' work (17th–19th c.)
39 Gold and silversmiths' work (14th–16th c.)

BASEMENT

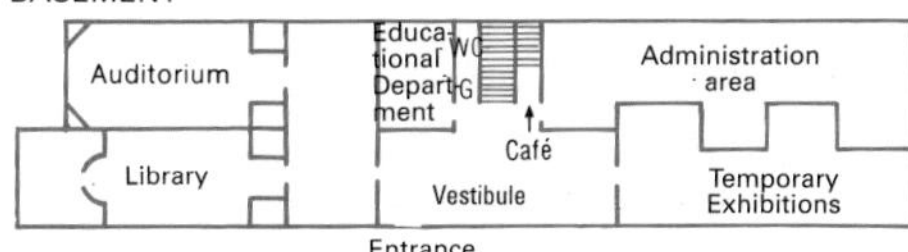

© Baedeker

and Japan between 1543 and 1639. Portuguese immigrants to Japan were called "Nanban-jin". Japanese artists portrayed the arrival of their conquerors from their point of view on large-size screens and some pieces of lacquer work. The collection of Indo-Portuguese and Afro-Portuguese furniture resulted from the influence of reciprocal relations.
Among the silver and gold work of the 12th–19th c. some pieces are particularly outstanding: a cross commissioned by Sancho I in 1214, a

Manueline gold monstrance dating from 1506 from the Mosteiro dos Jerónimos (see entry), attributed to the famous goldsmith and playwright Gil Vicente, and a processional cross from Alcobaça from the 14/15th c.

Second Floor

Many of the rooms on the second floor are at present closed for a comprehensive re-organisation.

Main Floor

The ground floor of the extension leads into the main floor of the original palace. Mainly European art from the 14th–19th c. is exhibited in this part of the museum.

The most important of the Portuguese paintings is, without doubt, the polyptych from St Vincent's altar, which was found in the São Vicente de Fora monastery and restored in 1910. Uncertainty has surrounded the origins of the "Adoration of St Vincent" ("Veneração a São Vicente"). Both the exact date of the work and the artist have not been clearly identified until now. It is generally accepted that Nuno Gonçalves, who was Afonso V's court artist from 1450 to 1467, painted this six-part altarpiece. The work is held to be an important historico-cultural document, as some prominent personalities from 15th c. Portuguese society are depicted on it. However, art historians are not always agreed on the identity of the people portrayed. A total of 60 people can be seen, including the most important from the age of Portugal's voyages of discovery. Men and women from the royal house of Avis, the most important sailors from this era, priests, knights, fishermen, navigators and beggars can be recognised in the picture.

Whoever the artist may ultimately prove to be, it is thought that he studied in Flanders. Although the stylistic originality of the work stands out it cannot actually be attributed to a particular European school. In contrast with the general custom of that time, the people have not been positioned in front of a background of countryside or architecture but stand alone. In this way concentration is completely directed on the serious faces and individual expressions of those portrayed.

Of the six large panels the two middle ones stand out. While all the people are only portrayed once, St Vincent appears on both the middle screens. His central position on these main screens underlines the importance the artist placed on Portugal's patron saint. As the two depictions of St Vincent are turned towards the centre it is thought that there was eventually meant to be a seventh screen. This is allegedly contradicted by the lines of the

Polyptychon "Veneração a São Vicente"
Painted by Nuno Gonçalves c 1460–70

Museu Nacional de Arte Antiga

ground which provide the only spatial clue; apart from that it is not known with certainty how the panels were hung, one above another, one below another on one next to another.
Particularly important people can be recognised in the left-hand panel. Members of the family of King Afonso V surround St Vincent. Below on the right kneels Afonso V himself, behind him on the edge of the picture stands his son João, the later João II. Without doubt the most well-known is the portrayal of Henry the Navigator (see Famous People), who was an uncle of Afonso V. On the left next to St Vincent kneels the wife of Afonso V, Queen Isabel, behind her stands Isabel of Aragón, a sister of Henry the Navigator and thus the king's aunt. In the background real people are also portrayed, although controversy reigns over their actual identities. Both the person on the very left and in the second panel on the left are thought to be self portraits of the altarpiece's supposed creator. Others maintain that Nuno Gonçalves immortalised himself on the right of the middle panels as the second person on the right in the row in the background.
On this second main panel priests and knights are gathered around St Vincent. Below on the left is Prince Fernão, Afonso V's brother and father of Manuel I. Archbishop Jaime of Lisbon can be recognised by his mitre. Clearly identifiable is the historian Gomes Eanes de Azurara on the top right, who dedicated himself in a chronicle to Henry the Navigator.
The smaller outer panel on the right shows the second duke of Bragança, Fernão, and a Moorish knight. On the three remaining smaller side panels Cistercian monks from the Alcobaça monastery, fishermen and navigators can be seen. On the panel on the extreme right a beggar, a Jewish scholar with the Torah and a priest with the remains of St Vincent are depicted (chronological authenticity was apparently not adhered to).

European Art

Much Portuguese art from this time comes from schools of painting. Paintings signed with "estilo Gonçalves", "estilo Gregório Lopes" or "escola portuguesa" point to this. The museum owns 16th c. works by Vasco Fernandes, Cristovão de Morães, Cristovão de Figueredo, Frei Carlos and Francisco Henriques. A painting dating from the 16th c. shows the arrival of the relics of Santa Auta in Lisbon, which had been acquired in Cologne; this picture served after the earthquake as a model for the restoration of the Manueline entrance portal of the Convento de Madre de Deus (see entry). Exhibits include 17th c. paintings by Josefa de Obidos, Francisco Vieira Portuense and Filipo Lobo, in the 18th c. the respected portrait artist Domingos António de Sequeira was particularly outstanding. As well as works by the Portuguese artists, paintings by French Italian, Flemish, Spanish, German, English and Dutch can be seen, including Hans Memling ("Virgin and Child"), Piero della Francesca ("St Augustine"), Dürer ("St Jeronimos"), Cranach ("St Catherine", "Salome"), Holbein the Elder ("Virgin and Child with Saints"), Bassano ("Virgin and Child"), Pieter Brueghel the Younger ("The Boy"), Velázquez, van Dyck, Reynolds, Hoppner and Romney.
The triptych "Temptation of St Anthony" by Hieronymus Bosch is one of the museum's most important works. Thanks to thoughtful arrangement the black-white Golgatha scenes on the rear can be seen.
A smaller section includes a collection of European art of the 16th–18th c. with tapestry, faience, furniture, silver and porcelain.

Sala Calouste Gulbenkian

In the Sala Calouste Gulbenkian are exhibited works which Gulbenkian (see Famous People) endowed to the museum in the 1950s, including a Greek torso of Apollo (450–400 B.C.) and the "Danaide" by Rodin.

Museu de Arte Contemporânea (Museum of Contemporary Art) H 2

Location
Rua Serpa Pinto
Chiado 6

The Museu Nacional de Arte Contemporânea has evolved from a former state-owned art museum, which was divided in 1911 into the Museum of (then) Contemporary Art and the Museu Nacional de Arte Antiga (see

Trams
28, 28B

Open
Tues.–Sun.
10am–12–30pm,
2–5pm

entry). At the time of this division all Portuguese works of art created after 1850 were moved from the museum in the Rua das Janelas Verdes into the rooms of a former monastery, where the Biblioteca Nacional (see Cidade) was then and the art college (Academia das Belas Artes) is now accommodated. Works by Portuguese artists on view date up to about the turn of the century. Modern paintings are exhibited by the Centro de Arte Moderna in the Fundação Calouste Gulbenkian (see entry).

Columbano Bordalo Pinheiro, the brother of the well-known caricaturist and potter (see Museu Rafael Bordalo Pinheiro) was the first director of the museum. He also belonged to the "Grupo do Leão" (Group of Lions), which consisted of the most important artists of that time. The works of many artists belonging to this circle are on view in the museum.

Museu Nacional do Azulejo

See Convento da Madre de Deus

*Museu Nacional dos Coches (National Coach Museum)

Location
Praça Afonso de Albuquerque, Belém

Trams
15, 16, 17

Buses
14, 27, 28, 29, 43, 49, 51

In 1726 João V had a riding school built on the east side of the Palácio de Belém (see Belém) within which the Museu Nacional dos Coches (National Coach Museum) was set up in 1902. Initiated by Queen Amélia and Colonel Alfredo d'Albuquerque a collection of former royal coaches and ceremonial carriages was assembled. These coaches dating from the 16th–19th c. certainly form the most extensive and valuable collection of its type and is well worth seeing.

Included among the exhibits are various presents from popes and foreign princes as well as a wedding present from Ludwig XIV; some of the

Philip II's carriage: a simple exterior and a grandiose interior

coaches were even driven from Rome or Austria to Lisbon. The oldest exhibit is a 16th c. Spanish coach, in which Philipp II entered Lisbon at the time of the Spanish domination of Portugal. Simply decorated externally, the interior is richly embellished. Pompous baroque coaches, which demonstrate different principles of construction, form the largest part of the collection – clear evidence of the increasingly abundant great love of splendour among the nobility. They include some coaches built in the early 18th c. which are without doubt the most valuable, for example a carriage commissioned by João V for a Portuguese ambassador on the occasion of a papal visit. Also on show are two 18th c. processional coaches and several sedan-chairs, which had to be carried by men or by mules.
On view in the second room is a forerunner of the first Lisboan taxi-cab, a small coach coloured green and black just like the current taxis – although in reverse order. In the entrance hall stands the coach in which Elizabeth II enjoyed a tour of Lisbon when she first came to Portugal in 1957.
For those interested in the appearances of members of the Portuguese royal family there are about 20 portraits of the members of the Bragança family on show upstairs in the gallery.
In contrast to the splendour of the coach museum there is a collection of model cars upstairs at the exit, the gift in 1986 of José Pinheiro da Costa.

Trains
From Estação Cais do Sodré, Station Belém

Open
Tues.–Sun. 10am–1pm, 2.30–5.30pm (June–Sept. until 6.30pm)

Museu Nacional do Teatro

See Parque do Monteiro-Mor

Museu Nacional do Traje

See Parque do Monteiro-Mor

Museu Rafael Bordalo Pinheiro H 11

At the northern end of the Campo Grande (see entry) two interesting museums stand opposite each other: the Museu da Cidade (see entry) and the museum dedicated to the artist Rafael Bordalo Pinheiro (1846–1905). Rafael Bordalo Pinheiro came from an artistic family; his younger brother Columbano Bordalo Pinheiro, who for a time led the group of artists "O Grupo do Leão", which was famous in Portugal, also became well-known. At first Rafael Bordalo Pinheiro mainly drew caricatures. He lived and worked for some time in Brazil. After his return to Portugal he began to work with ceramics in his mid-thirties.
The museum is located in a lovely old villa dating from 1912. It contains predominantly ceramics, which clearly demonstrate the caricatural bent of the artist. Figures or faces are portrayed in the form of vases, cups or teapots, with the nose or a cigar serving as a spout, etc. The rest of his everyday pottery, plates, bowls, terrines, is remarkable for its unusual ideas. One service is painted with the motif of the Torre de Belém (see entry). Much of the work alludes to Portugal's history, the differing art styles of the country are, in part, mixed indiscriminately. Pinheiro's Art Nouveau bowls and tiles, decorated with the reliefs of plants and animals, are very lovely. Some pieces of faience, more than 2m/6½ft tall, were produced in his factory in Caldas da Rainha north of Lisbon. His figure of "Zé Povinho", a caricature of the typically small Portuguese man, has gained great popularity. Various models of the "Zé Povinho" can also be seen in the museum. A portrait painted by his brother shows Rafael Bordalo Pinheiro at the age of 45.

Location
C. Grande 382

Buses
1, 7, 36, 46A, 47

Open
Tues.–Sun. 10am–1pm, 2–6pm

Paço Real

See Sintra

Paços do Conselho (City Hall) H 2

Location
Praça do Municipio

Trams
15, 16, 17, 18, 19, 25, 26

Buses
1, 2, 7, 13, 13A, 14, 17, 40, 43, 44, 45, 83

Lisbon's city hall, called the Paços do Conselho (or Câmara Municipal), stands on the east side of the Praça do Municipio. A building, whose east wing accommodated the city council, was built on this site in 1774 but was completely burnt down in 1863. In 1875 the current building was completed.

The neo-Classical façade appears very plain in contrast to the interior. Allegorical figures in the tympanum represent freedom, the arts, the sciences, trade, etc. The interior of the city hall has been lavishly and prestigiously arranged in an eclectic stringing together of the most varied styles. Enormous wooden doors lead off from the stair well, which is covered by a cupola roof, into the individual rooms. The walls are wood panelled and covered in part with lavish wood carving. Vivid wall decorations and painting made to look like carving have been closely juxtaposed just like neo-Baroque and neo-Classical creations of form. The ceiling decoration in the rooms is by famous Lisbon artists such as José Malhoa and Columbano Bordalo Pinheiro; various busts are the work of the sculptor Teixeira Lopes.

Pelourinho

A so-called pelourinho, an 18th c. pillory, stands on the rather unspectacular square in front of the city hall. From the 12th until the 18th c. pelourinhos were erected in many towns in Portugal; they served less to punish convicts but were far more a symbol of the town's jurisdiction. The rather fragile-looking pillory in front of the Lisbon city hall evokes Manueline associations: it consists of three stone bands which in turn have been wound into a spiral. The pillars are crowned by a bronze armillary sphere.

*Padrão dos Descobrimentos (Monument to the Discoveries)

Location
Avenida de Brasilia, Belém

Trams
15, 16, 17

Buses
27, 28, 29, 43, 49, 51

The Padrão dos Descobrimentos (Monument to the Discoveries) was completed as a model for the Portuguese world exhibition (see Belém) and erected on the bank of the Tagus in its current form in 1960. The official reason for the opening of the monument was the celebration of the 500th anniversary of the death of Henry the Navigator (see Famous People), who gained great honour in the "Estavo Novo". The monument clearly shows above all else the artificial revival of the most important epoch of Portugal's national history under the Salazar dictatorship.

Cottinelli Telmo, the architect who was responsible for creating the whole area of the world exhibition, built the 54m/177ft high Monument to the Discoveries, the figures on the two external sides are the work of the sculptor Leopoldo Almeida.

Viewed from the side, the symbolic meaning of the monument becomes clear: it is shaped like a ship's bow and projects out above the water across the Tagus. Henry the Navigator himself stands right at the top of the prow, behind him are a row of over-sized figures, each from a different profession, yet each of which took part in some way in the voyages of discovery and conquest. Immediately behind Henry the Navigator are Manuel I (see Famous People) and the poet Luis de Camões (see Famous People). Stylised armillary spheres on both sides of the construction stand as symbols of the Portuguese sea voyages of that time. The front entrance is shaped like a huge sword.

In 1985 several rooms in the monument were furnished and these are now used for small temporary exhibitions or conference rooms. Concepts from

The Discovery Monument in Belém ▶

the "Golden Age" gave the rooms their names. The vantage point on the seventh floor offers a marvellous view of the Tagus as far as the Atlantic, of the Praça do Império with the Mosteiro dos Jerónimos (see entry) and of a compass measuring 50m/164ft in diameter let into the ground in the square in front of the monument, a present from the Republic of South Africa. The Portuguese routes of discovery and of conquest have been portrayed in the centre with exact dates.

Espelho de Água

A restaurant called "Espelho de Água" (Water Mirror) is at present housed in the building surrounded by water to the west of the monument. The building was constructed as part of the world exhibition and is the work of the architects Cottinelli Telmo and António Lino.

Palácio da Assembleia Nacional

See Palácio de São Bento

Palácio da Independência (Independence Palace) H 3

Location
Largo de São Domingos

Metro
Rossio

Buses
1, 2, 9, 11, 21, 31, 32, 36, 39, 41, 44, 45, 46, 80, 83, 90

The Palácio da Independência is located close to the Rossio (see entry) on the north side of the Largo de São Domingos and is known by two names. It was given its original name of Palácio de Almada in honour of its former owner, the Count of Almada. The building's foundation stone was laid in 1509 and some Manueline details from this time can still be detected in the inner courtyard, for example the door decorations. Two conical kitchen chimneys are reminiscent of the royal palace at Sintra (see entry).

The name Palácio da Independência (Independence Palace) recalls a curious event that occurred in 1640. Philipp II of Spain had occupied Portugal in 1580, a year later he was recognised as King of Portugal. The loss of some colonies and the intense pressure of taxes levied to finance the Spanish wars led about 80 years later to a conspiracy among several of the Portuguese nobility. On December 1st 1640 there ensued a successful rebellion, followed by the restoration of Portugal's independence. About 40 conspirators prepared for the action under the leadership of the Duke of Bragança in the grounds of this palace. The Duke, from whose grandmother the royal family descended, was crowned João IV, King of Portugal. From a neighbouring monastery the nobles reached the palace garden from across part of the old 14th c. city wall and gathered there in a small, isolated pavilion. It has even been suggested that there was an underground path linking the garden with the Baixa along which people could pass unseen.

The Sociedade Histórica da Independência de Portugal has its seat in some of the rooms of the Palácio da Independência. This society has awarded itself the task of keeping alive the memory of the happenings of December 1st 1640 and the general consciousness of Portugal's national history.

A museum is planned for the palace, which is to be equipped with the most modern technical equipment. The completely neglected garden, to which part of the old city wall still belongs today, is to be newly laid out, old tiles restored, the pavilion renovated and called the Sala dos Conjuradores (Room of the Conspirators). Apart from this, it is planned to open a specialist library and a restaurant offereing typical national dishes.

Every year on December 1st official memorial events take place both in the Palácio da Independência and at the Praça dos Restauradores.

*Palácio dos Marqueses de Fronteira C/D 8

Location
Largo de São Domingos de Benfica

It is certainly worth visiting the somewhat remote private palace and attractive garden of the Mascarenha family on the northern edge of the Parque Florestal de Monsanto (see entry).

João Mascarenha had the house built in the Italian Renaissance style in

1670. At that time his family lived in Lisbon and only moved here in 1755, after their city residence had been destroyed by the earthquake; members of the family still live on the estate today. In 1989 a foundation was set up to deal with the maintenance of the palace and the garden and the staging of cultural events. The family bears the title of the Count of Mascarenha following an honour bestowed on a Mascarenha during the wars of restoration.

Buses
16, 41, 46, 54, 58

Trains
From Estação Rossio, Station Cruz da Pedra

In the course of a guided tour an interesting view can be had of some of the rooms. The Sala das Batalhas (Hall of Battles) is decorated with tiles depicting scenes of different encounters, which helped restore to Portugal independence from Spain in 1640. Concerts are sometimes staged in this room, its good acoustics have led to it being used as a recording studio. A private library with 17th c. works has been installed in the formerly open veranda. From here there is a fine view of the well laid out garden. In another room tiles can be seen which are some of the first imported into Portugal from Delft in the 17th c. The pictures show pastoral scenes and hunting scenes as well as musical instruments, from which it can be deduced that a music room was once located here. The Juno room, whose ceiling is painted with a picture of the goddess Juno, is used today as a reception room.
In some of the living rooms and also in the dining room there are striking examples of valuable tiled panels as well as furniture and porcelain from Portugal, France, China and India dating from the 17th c. and the 18th c. and family portraits from the early 19th c.

Chapel

By following a long terrace, decorated with mythological figures and 17th c. tiles portraying the arts, a small chapel is reached. It was built in 1584, before the palace was built on the later landholding.

Venus Garden

From here the part of the park known as the Venus Garden, enclosed by the palace and the mountains, is reached. It owes its name to the Venus

Fronteira Palace: the King's Gallery

Grotto in the Venus Garden

A fountain in the Italian Garden

fountain in the centre: three dolphins carry a shell from which the goddess is climbing.

In one corner of the estate is a former pool with many gargoyles, behind this an artificial grotto, whose walls incorporate pieces of broken pottery. It is thought that a royal feast took place at the official opening of the palace; to ensure that the crockery was only used once for this purpose it was broken at the end of the meal and the pieces set into the wall of the grotto. The so-called Italian Garden is particularly worth visiting. This approximately 4000sq.m/43,056sq.ft garden area was laid out in the Italian style in the 17th c. At that time some natural springs were used in the construction of several fountains and a particularly fine large pond. This pond is flanked by two wide flights of steps giving access to a gallery extending the whole length of the pond. Especially impressive is the blue of the 17th c. tiles: they were used to keep away insects and, according to a local explanation, angry ghosts. The tiles with the semi-three-dimensional pattern of fir cones are of Spanish origin. Busts of former Portuguese kings stand in small niches, hence the name "Kings' Gallery". Blue-white tiles on the pool itself depict different knights. a fountain in the middle of the garden bears an armillary sphere as a symbol of Portugal's "Golden Age" and the coat of arms of the Mascarenha family.

On the façade of the palace facing the garden there are a variety of tiled pictures depicting hunting and expedition scenes, allegories of ancient gods and seasons as well as depictions of everyday life. The poet Luis de Camões (see Famous People) can be recognised in one picture.

Palácio Nacional da Ajuda

Location
Calçada da Ajuda

The Palácio Nacional da Ajuda was built as a replacement for the royal castle at Terreiro do Paço (see entry), which was destroyed in the 1755 earthquake. A first, provisional, wooden building at Ajuda burnt down in 1794; in 1802 construction of the large-scale project designed by the Italian architect Fabri was begun – it has remained incomplete until today. The royal family's flight to Brazil in 1807 and the Miguelist wars of 1832–34 contributed to the building work stopping temporarily. The original plans were altered several times, first by Manuel Caetano de Sousa, then by J. Costa e Silva and later by Francisco Rosa. It was not until the end of the 19th c. that the building was in any way almost finished.

Buses
40, 42

Open
Mon., Tues., Thur.–Sun.
10am–5pm

The plans for the castle complex envisaged a construction of more than twice the size of the current building. Looking into the inner courtyard the unfinished state of the building becomes clear: instead of the planned windows, merely useless openings in the wall are to be seen on the west side of the courtyard. On the south wall also, which was really intended to be the main façade, there are quite a few signs of the unfinished nature of the building. The announcement of an architectural competition has now begun a new attempt finally to complete the construction of the former royal palace.

Located on an exposed site above the river Tagus, the Palácio da Ajuda is visible from afar. The enormous complex appears compact and strong. The large-scale front façade, with three large central windows above three entrance portals lined by Doric pillars, at first hides the fact that the building is incomplete. More than 20 allegorical marble statues stand in arrow niches in the hall; they were made in the 19th c., some of them being the work of the famous sculptor from the Mafra school, Machado de Castro.

Only Luis I used the palace as a proper residence from 1861 to 1889; Maria Pia von Savoyen, his wife, lived here until she left Portugal in 1910. The royal family's living rooms can be viewed today; valuable tapestries and furniture as well as portraits of members of the royal family can be seen. The rooms are sometimes used for state receptions or for extensive temporary exhibitions (then from time to time not all of the royal living rooms are open to the public). Part of the palace is used as an administrative wing, in addition a library with an adjoining archive is located here.

Jardim Botânico da Ajuda

The Ajuda Botanical Garden, which was commissioned by Pombal in 1768 and was laid out in the Italian style, lies somewhat to the south-west of and below the palace grounds, with its entrance on the Calçada da Ajuda. A collection of rare plants, including an approximately 400-year-old dragon tree, can be seen here. A view of the Tagus and of the Ponte 25 de Abril (see entry) can be enjoyed from a higher terrace.

Open
Daily 10am–6pm

Palácio Real das Necessidades — D 3

The Palácio Real das Necessidades today accommodates the foreign ministry and is therefore not open to the public. The building was constructed between 1745 and 1750 on the order of João V, who had taken a vow after a serious illness to have a royal palace built after his recovery. The building suffered little damage during the 1755 earthquake.

Location
Largo das Necessidades

Trams
19

Buses
13, 27, 40, 49

Maria II and her husband, Ferdinand of Saxe-Coburg-Gotha, who had the Pena Palace in Sintra (see entry) built, lived in the palace. Three of their sons died of a fever epidemic here. Manuel II resided in the building before he fled to Brazil in October 1910 after the revolution.

The palace was built in a style typical of the reign of João V with Baroque and Classical elements. The two-storey main building which stands on the Largo das Necessidades forms only a small part of the entire complex. A portal with an arcaded porch stands out strikingly from the uniform main façade. The tower of a castle chapel projects above the north side of the building.

Palácio Real das Necessidades: seat of the Foreign Minister

Largo das Necessidades

An impressively lavish fountain with fantastic figures and an 18th c. obelisk stands on the Largo das Necessidades.

Tapada das Necessidades

An extensive area of parkland extends behind the palace. The Tapada das Necessidades, earlier used for hunting, can be visited on weekdays.

Palácio de São Bento F 3

Location
Largo de São Bento

Trams
28, 28B

Buses
6, 13, 39, 49

The Palácio de São Bento, a sweeping white building complex above the Largo de São Bento, is the seat of the Portuguese parliament; the alternative names for the palace, Palácio da Assembleia Nacional or Palácio da República, reflect this function. The official residence of the prime minister is also located in the complex.

The position of the parliament buildings is curious: the forecourt, the somewhat lower lying Largo de São Bento, is, in contrast to the palace itself, hardly prestigious. The elevated position of the spacious building and the almost over-sized flight of steps linking it to the small square below make it appear over-imposing and almost isolated. The houses in the nearest residential area seem minute by comparison.

The Palácio de São Bento originated in a former Benedictine monastery, which was built in 1598 under the direction of the architect Balthasar Alvares. In 1834, after the Benedictine order had been dissolved, the São Bento monastery was converted into parliament buildings. The present neo-Classical appearance arose after a fire in 1895. The building continued to be reconstructed to the plans of the architect Ventura Terra until the 1940s; little remains of the former monastery.

The interior is prestigious with a white and pink coloured marble floor and similarly coloured marble pillars. Statues and wall paintings serve as decorative details. It is worth viewing one of the semi-circular senate rooms with

Palácio de São Bento: Assembly room of the Portuguese Parliament

its Corinthian pillars. Both here and in the chamber there are areas set aside for the public. The seven pillars in the chamber, symbolising justice, eloquence, law, etc., are impressive. Paintings by Columbano Bordalo Pinheiro hang in the elegant hall in front of the chamber which is called "Passos Perdidos" (Lost Steps). Wall-paintings by Domingos Rebelo, which date from 1944, depict scenes from the age of discovery and conquest and can be seen in the Salão Nobre. On the ground floor two bells from the earlier monastery recall the origins of the building.
Until recently the Torre do Tombo national archive was located in parts of the east wing, but is now housed in a new building next to the old university (see Cidade Universitária).

Panteão Nacional

See Igreja de Santa Engrácia

Parque Eduardo VII

F/G 5/6

The severe and cool Parque Eduardo VII, which actually forms a continuation of the Avenida da Liberdade, does not really appear "Portuguese". It was developed in the first decade of the 20th c., considerably later than the boulevard, and was named after the English king, who paid a visit to Lisbon in 1903. Prior to that the fallow area at the top end of the Avenida was called the Parque da Liberdade.

Location
North of the Avenida da Liberdade

Buses
1, 2, 11, 12, 18, 20, 21, 22, 23, 27, 31, 32, 36, 38, 41, 42, 44, 45, 46, 48, 49, 51, 53, 83, 90

With an area of about 25ha/62 acres it is by far the largest park within the inner city. The middle section consists of two parallel wide paths, joined by a dull and monotonous strip of grass lined by symmetrical hedgerows. The

The "cold greenhouses" in the Parque Eduardo VII

Metro
Rotunda, Parque

Trams 24, 27

park ends at the top with a 450m/1404ft long and 55m/181ft wide viewing terrace, whose pillars and lanterns date from the 1940s and can be seen from a distance. In good conditions it is possible to see as far as the Serra da Arrábida (see Costa de Lisboa). The two less artificial outer areas are more attractive than the centre.

Estufa Fria

The complex known as "Estufa Fria" (open daily 9am–4.30pm) is located in the north-west corner of the park and is worth visiting. Within this "cold greenhouse", developed in 1929, there is a garden with native and tropical plants, which grow among ponds, bridges and aviaries to form a pleasant setting. The complex is protected by a large roof made of wooden bars.

Pavilhão Carlos Lopes

Opposite, on the east side, stands the Pavilhão Carlos Lopes (named after a marathon runner and Olympic winner), also known as the Pavilhão dos Desportos. It was built in 1932 as a copy of a past building style and accommodates an old sports hall. Nowadays far more concerts and meetings, etc. take place here than sports events. The azulejo pictures on the outside walls and in the entrance hall are noteworthy.

Parque Florestal de Monsanto — A–D 5–9

Location
West of the city

Buses
11, 23, 24, 29, 48

The wooded Parque Florestal de Monsanto extends across hilly land to the west of Lisbon. With the exception of some well-used traffic routes, the area is very quiet and not to be recommended for long walks. The possibility of creating a popular leisure area here, close to the city, has been completely ignored up until now. However, efforts are at present being made to increase the general leisure value of Monsanto Park and to create a recreation area near to Lisbon with proper barbecue areas and pathways. With several viewpoints and well-sited restaurants, a good basis is already available for new development.

Parque do Monteiro-Mor G 14

Although threatened by the surrounding and ever-encroaching satellite quarters, the Monteiro-Mor Park lies in such a pleasantly idyllic location on the northern edge of Lisbon that it proves possible to go for a "country" walk there, without feeling spoilt by the proximity of the city. The park belongs to an 18th c. palace complex (Palácio do Monteiro-Mor), within which two interesting museums are currently accommodated.
An extensive plant collection, interspersed with pools and ponds, has been laid out in the front part of the park. The mixture of formal and wild nature, fountains and weathered stone statues creates a unique and peaceful charm. The furthermost part of the park appears more rambling and lighter and is more in tune with the neighbouring pastureland.
An exclusive restaurant, which is always busy, is pleasantly situated on a terrace.

Location
Lumiar

Buses
3, 4, 7, 7A, 36

Open
Daily 10am–5pm (May–Oct. until 7pm)

Museu Nacional do Traje

In 1977 the National Costume Museum was set up in one of the palace buildings, which were built in the 18th c. and have been owned by various families. Not only national costumes are on view in the museum; the collection includes a wide variety of clothing of all types. The museum owns more than 20,000 exhibits from different centuries and from all parts of the country, most of which have been donated by private individuals and other Portuguese museums. In interesting temporary exhibitions marginal or overlapping themes are covered, e.g. the survey of a particular era by means of clothes and fashions.

Open
Tues.–Sun. 10am–1pm, 2.30–5pm

Museu Nacional do Teatro

The National Theatre Museum was set up in 1985 in a previously burnt-out building, which has been rebuilt to incorporate the most modern museum techniques. The museum's collection includes costumes, designs, stage props, tickets, posters, programmes, records, etc. and documents in a series of temporary exhibitions the lives of stage stars and landmarks of the Portuguese theatre.

Open
Times vary (often closed for long periods for the preparation of exhibitions)

*Ponte 25 de Abril (April 25th bridge) B 1/2

After the Tagus has expanded into the 13km/8 mile wide lake-like "Mar da Palha" (Straw Sea) about 30km/18½ miles from its estuary into the Atlantic, it flows once again just before its mouth through a river basin only about 2km/1¼ miles wide, which immediately afterwards opens out funnel-like into the Atlantic. This natural condition made it possible to build a bridge at the narrowest point, shortly before the Tagus enters the Atlantic and thus to provide a traffic link for the south of Portugal to the capital city. Until 1966 the Tagus could only be crossed 30km/18½ miles north of Lisbon via a bridge at Vila Franca de Xira or by ferry. The building of the bridge also made a direct link between the capital and the river bank lying opposite it – once the bridge was opened the number of inhabitants living on this side of the river rose dramatically.
The construction of the steel and concrete bridge was based on the plans of an American firm. Its total length measures almost 2.3km/1½ miles, the height of the carriageway about 70m/230ft, the foundations 82m/269ft below water-level. The two pylons each measure 190m/623½ft tall, the distance between the pillars a good 1000m/3282ft. The bridge was officially opened on August 6th 1966 with the name Ponte de Salazar; after the end of the dictatorship it was renamed Ponte 25 de Abril in memory of the

Location
Between Alcântara and the Statue of Christ

Buses
52, 53 (from Praça de Espanha; cross the bridge)
14, 27, 28, 32, 43, 49, 51, 56 (to the bank of the Tagus, as high as the bridge)

Trams
15, 16, 17

Toll

revolution. The bridge offers a very impressive view of the whole of Lisbon and across to the west over Belém to the Atlantic.
Since its opening the ever-increasing amount of traffic using the bridge has long exhausted its capacity. In particular, on summer Sundays and after bank holidays kilometre-long queues build up on both sides of the bridge and even daily commuter traffic overloads it. For years discussions have been held to try to solve the traffic problem. Suggestions include the construction of a second bridge, a tunnel or a second carriageway below the existing one. (The last idea has been under consideration for some time for rail traffic; however, a train link with south Portugal has not yet been created.) For the moment the construction of a fifth lane, which can be opened either in a north–south or a south–north direction according to need, has been of help.

*Praça do Comércio H2

Location
South of the city-centre on the river bank

Trams
15, 16, 17, 18, 19, 25, 26

Buses
1, 2, 7, 9, 11, 13, 13A, 14, 17, 25, 25A, 28, 32, 35, 39, 40, 43, 44, 45 46, 59, 80, 81, 82, 83, 90

From the time before the earthquake until the present day, the name Terreiro do Paço (Palace Square), has been customarily used by the people of Lisbon to mean the Praça do Comércio (Trade Square). The royal palace Paço da Ribeira, into which Manuel I moved in the 16th c., stood on this site on the river bank until 1755. The Terreiro do Paço was consequently used as a place to receive kings and guests, who arrived by ship – although it was also used as a setting for burning heretics and for bullfights.
After the Terreiro do Praça was completely destroyed by the earthquake and had been flooded, the present Praça do Comércio was built in conjunction with the rebuilding of the Baixa (see entry) by the architect Santos Carvalho. Uniform arcaded façades line three sides of the square, approximately 180m/591ft by 190m/624ft. It enjoys an unrestricted view of the Tagus and has been called "Lisbon's reception room". A further tribute – "one of the loveliest squares in Europe" – was presumably made at a time before the spacious inner area was used as a car-park. The architectural balance of the buildings is hardly set off by the parked cars or the heavy traffic, which surges around the square. The buildings are mainly occupied by public authorities or ministries. A large post office is located in the north-west corner of the square, while the complex on the east side accommodates the stock exchange.

Arco Triunfal

The uniform north front is interrupted in the middle by the Rua Augusta, forming a direct link to the Rossio (see entry). The opening is spanned by a lavish triumphal arch, which was not completed until 1873. The marble statues, which flank the royal coat of arms, portray (from left to right) Viriatus, the legendary leader of the Lusitanians in the battle against the Romans, the mariner Vasco da Gama (see Famous People) and Nuno Álvares Pereira, who defended Portugal's independence against the Spanish. The figures on the sides are allegories of the Tagus (left) and the Douro (right). On top of the arch stands a group of allegorical figures, in the middle of which Glory crowns Genius and Courage. The triumphal arch is expected to be made accessible to the public in future so that it becomes a fine viewing platform for the Baixa.

José I Memorial

The equestrian statue of José I, the work of Machado de Castro, the famous sculptor from the Mafra school, was erected in the centre of the Praça do Comércio in 1755. It is dedicated to the king, under whom Minister Pombal had a completely free hand in the rebuilding of the city after the earthquake. Pombal himself is immortalised in a bronze medallion on the pedestal of the statue. The medallion was removed on the orders of Maria I, who extensively undid Portugal's reforms, but was returned in 1833.
The whole statue measures 14m/46ft tall, the equestrian statue alone is a good 7m/23ft and weighs about 30 tonnes. It was the first bronze memorial

◀ *The April 25th Bridge*

Triumphal Arch and Monument to José I on the Praça do Comércio

to be cast in Portugal, in the military arsenal at the foot of Alfama, in which the Museu Militar (see entry) is now housed. It was brought to the Praça do Comércio in a specially prepared vehicle accompanied by a carnival procession of more than 1000 citizens. Models of the memorial and the vehicle are on view in the Museu Militar. The English name for the square, Black Horse Square, is derived from the original dark bronze of the equestrian statue.

Café Martinho da Arcada

The Café Martinho da Arcada, located somewhat inconspicuously in the north-east corner of the square under the arcades, has a long history. It was founded in 1782, but did not get its name until later from the owner Martinho. A regular of the café was Portugal's most famous 20th c. poet, Fernando Pessoa (see Famous People). Pessoa worked and lived for a long time in the Baixa and is said to have written pieces of his work in the Martinho da Arcada after closing time. Until the autumn of 1989 the café was retained in the style in which Pessoa enjoyed it. Following suggestions made by a Pessoa society, which calls itself the Friends of the Martinho da Arcada, the café has been restored and renovated and was reopened early in 1990 as a quality restaurant and esplanade café. Now it is chiefly the employees of the surrounding ministries who meet here for lunch.

Cais das Colunas

The south side of the Praça do Comércio, which opens onto the waterfront, ends in the Cais das Colunas (Quay of Pillars); a small flight of steps leads gently into the water, with their end marked by two pillars. From here the view below the Ponte 25 de Abril extends to the Atlantic. To the north the whole square is visible in front of the backdrop of the Castelo de São Jorge (see entry).

Estação Sul e Sueste

The "river-railway" Sul e Sueste, constructed in 1931 by the architect Cottinelli Telmo (see Practical Information, Stations), is located on the south-east edge of the square.

The Cais da Alfândega is located immediately next to the Estação Sul e Sueste, the mooring place for passenger ferries sailing to and from Cacilhas, Seixal, Barreiro and Montijo.

Praça de Dom Pedro IV

See Rossio

Praça da Figueira

H 3

The Praça da Figueira (Fig Tree Square), located immediately next to the Rossio, is part of the urban development concept of Pombal's lower city (see Baixa). It is directly linked to the Praça do Comércio (see entry) by the lively Rua da Prata. Although the square has many shops, in comparison to the neighbouring Rossio, it appears considerably quieter, a result essentially of the fewer cars using it. This may also be one of the reasons why the typical uniformity of building in the Baixa is more noticeable here than in the Rossio.

Location
East of Rossio

Metro
Rossio

Trams
3, 17, 19, 25, 26

Buses
7, 14, 37, 40, 43, 59 (and all lines to neighbouring Rossio)

Before the earthquake a large hospital, the Todos-os-Santos Hospital, stood on this site. It is easily recognisable in old views of the city. In 1755 the hospital was housed in the 16th c. former Jesuit monastery of Santo Antão-o-Novo, where it still exists today as the Hospital de S. José. In the same year a large market was set up here and in 1885 covered markets were built which gave the square a completely different character. Lively business was the order of the day here, especially in the mornings, and the square with the all-day market became a popular tourist attraction. In the middle of the 20th c. the covered markets were pulled down.

In their place, in the middle of the Praça da Figueira, there now stands a

Praça da Figueiral Monument to Joãs I

Pombal Memorial in the same square

bronze statue which commemorates the first king of the House of Avis, João I, depicted astride a horse. The statue is the work of the sculptor Leopoldo de Almeida.

Praça Marquês de Pombal G 5

Location
Northern end of the Avenida da Liberdade

Metro
Rotunda

Buses
1, 2, 11, 12, 20, 21, 22, 23, 27, 31, 32, 36, 41, 44, 45, 46, 48, 49, 53, 83, 90

At its northern end the Avenida da Liberdade (see entry) opens onto one of Lisbon's busiest squares, the Praça Marquês de Pombal, usually known for short as the Rotunda. The only interchange station in Lisbon's metro system below the traffic junction bears the same name. The square can be crossed by pedestrians by means of an underpass and in this way the Parque Eduardo VII (see entry), which borders the square to the north, and the monument in the centre of the roundabout can be relatvely easily reached.

Lisbon's coat of arms has been carefully depicted as a mosaic picture in the cobbled square in front of the colonaded statue. Shortly after the construction of the Avenida da Liberdade the present position had been determined for the erection of a memorial to the Marquês de Pombal (see Famous People), José I's minister, who was chiefly responsible for the reconstruction of the city which had been destroyed by the earthquake – at least about 100 years after the Avenida da Liberdade was created. In 1913 an open competition to build the memorial was finally announced, the first stone was laid four years later and the second in 1926. A further eight years passed before the statue was finally officially opened in 1934.

The 9m/30ft tall statue of the Marquês de Pombal, accompanied by a lion, stands on a 36m/118ft high pillar. The gaze of the ambitious and controversial politician is directed on to the lower city (Baixa) created by him. Depicted on the pedestal are agricultural and educational scenes – areas where the minister carried out extensive reforms. Below the pedestal an allegory of the earthquake with shattered stone cubes and overflowing waves from the Tagus can be seen. The people sitting at the back of the statue embody the reformed Coimbra University.

Praça dos Restauradores H 3

Location
Southern end of the Avenida da Liberdade

Metro
Restauradores

Buses
1. 2. 9, 11, 21, 31, 32, 36, 39, 41, 44, 45, 46, 83, 90 (and all lines to Rossio)

The southern end of the Avenida da Liberdade (see entry) is formed by the Praça dos Restauradores. The square's name refers to the time of the restoration, the re-establishment of Portuguese independence after 60 years of Spanish rule. On December 1st 1640 a successful revolt against Spain occurred, for which a large group of Portuguese noblemen had secretly prepared nearby in the Palácio da Independéncia (see entry). Today December 1st is celebrated as one of Portugal's national holidays, with a commemoration taking place every year on the Praça dos Restauradores.

A 30m/99ft tall obelisk stands in the centre of the busy square. The Monumento dos Restauradores de Portugal was unveiled in 1886. The bronze figure on the pedestal represents Victory (holding a palm leaf and a crown) and the spirit of independence. Place names and the dates of the battles of restoration are inscribed on the sides.

Hotel Avenida Palace

The old-established Hotel Avenida Palace on the corner of the Largo de Dom João da Câmara was designed – like the neighbouring neo-Manueline Estação Rossio – by the architect J. Luis Monteiro. The luxurious hotel was built in 1892, five years after the station. The building evokes a cosmopolitan and liberal impression, reminiscent of the first years of the Avenida da Liberdade.

On the corner opposite to the hotel stands a kiosk which was built in the Art Nouveau style shortly before the turn of the century. Tickets can be bought here in advance for all types of events.

Obelisk on the Praça dos Restauradores

Bullring

Eden-Teatro

Built in the 1930s by Cassiano Brànco, the Eden-Teatro on the west side of the square was for a long time one of Lisbon's leading cinemas. Today it is closed; it is being discussed whether a hotel should be built in its place, retaining the original façade.

Palácio Foz

Shortly after the earthquake, in 1755, the Marquês de Castelo Melhor had this palace built by the Italian architect Fabri. It owes its present name to the Marqués da Foz, who inherited the palace in 1869. At the beginning of the 20th c. some of the rooms were used for theatre, cinema, *revista*, variety and dance presentations. Today the palace houses the main tourist information office, a small gallery and a media and press department.

Elevador da Glória

A funicular railway, the Elevador da Glória, adjoins the Palácio Foz. It carries passengers up westwards to Bairro Alto. The railway's upper exit is located next to the lovely viewpoint of São Pedro de Alcântara. The Elevador da Glória was opened in 1885.

Praça de Touros (Bullring) — H 8

Location
Campo Pequeno

Metro
Campo Pequeno

Buses
1, 17B, 21, 27, 32, 36, 38, 44, 45, 46A, 47, 49, 54, 56, 83, 90

The bullring, built in the neo-Manueline style in 1892 to the plans of the architect António José Dias, stands on the Campo Pequeno, next to the busy Avenida da República. Bullfights were already being held on this spot in the 18th c. The building appears very colourful on account of its red brick, which is rare for Lisbon. Arabic associations are evoked in particular by the twin windows and the four tower-like porches, which bear the Moorish-inspired double dome. Crescent moons decorate the points of the domes. The main entrance is flanked by two additional domed towers linked by a stepped gable. The diameter of the arena measures 80m/263ft.
Bullfights usually take place here once a week during the summer season (see Practical Information, Bullfights); the arena can seat more than 8000

spectators. Recently the Praça de Touros has also been used frequently for concerts.

Queluz (Excursion)

Location
About 15km/9 miles north-west of Lisbon

Trains
From Estação Rossio, Station Queluz-Belas; from there about 1km/½ mile through the town in a south-easterly direction

Queluz, which lies about 15km/9 miles north-west of Lisbon, owes its importance to the attractive Palácio Nacional de Queluz ("What Light!"), a rococo-style summer residence of the royal house of Bragança. Today the palace is used for state receptions and state visits.

Queluz, like neighbouring Amadora and Brandoa, has almost joined up with the Portuguese capital. This former country area has developed during the course of the 20th c. into one of Lisbon's largest satellite suburbs. More than 200,000 people live here in concrete blocks; the area is one of the city's focal points of social problems. Within this setting the relaxed idyll of the Queluz summer palace today appears somewhat too carefree.

**Palácio Nacional de Queluz

Opening hours

With the exception of holidays, the palace and gardens are open Mon., and Wed.–Sun. 10am–1pm and 2–5pm. However, as the complex is used for official receptions it is always worth inquiring at the Tourist Information office in Lisbon to see if the palace and grounds are open to the public.

History

Queluz palace was built as a summer residence on the order of Pedro III. and his wife, the former Queen Maria I. The Portuguese architect Mateus Vicente de Oliveira was first commissioned with the renovation of an old

The Palace of Queluz

country house into a palace in 1747. Mateus Vicente was a pupil of the architect Ludovice, who designed the enormous monastery-palace at Mafra (see entry), later he drew up the plans for the Basilica da Estrela (see entry), The mid section of the palace, which overlooks the gardens, was designed by Mateus Vicente. After the earthquake, when the Portuguese architect was heavily involved in the rebuilding of the destroyed city, the Frenchman Jean Baptiste Robillon took over the work. During this period the west wing of the palace was completed, many of the rooms were decorated and the surrounding garden area with the Lions' Staircase was laid out. Building work was completed in 1794.

Palace rooms

The three-winged palace radiates a light and friendly atmosphere. It has often been compared to Sanssouci Castle in Potsdam and occasionally also with Versailles. When inside, the many large windows constantly draw the eye out to the palace gardens.

The interiors of the rooms and the furniture demonstrate a French influence. Gold-painted ornamentation in rocaille or garland designs, wall tiling and ceiling paintings are to be found everywhere and illustrate the original function of the individual rooms and halls.

The throne room, which is often used for state receptions and balls, was decorated with Rococo wood carving by Faria Lobo. The allegorical ceiling paintings and heavy chandeliers appear overpowering in the otherwise empty hall. Between 1749 and 1768 work was carried out on the music room. Today some smaller chamber concerts still take place here in worthy surroundings.

The Corredor das Mangas (Corridor of Shirtsleeves), which was used as the anteroom to the Hall of the Ambassadors, forms the link between the two wings of the building. It bears its second name of Azulejo Corridor on account of the tiles depicting the seasons, the continents and hunting scenes which were put up in 1784 in place of the paintings which originally hung here. A coach, in which Maria I went for drives, stands in this connecting hall.

Before entering the Hall of the Ambassadors, visitors pass through the Sala da Tocha (Torch Room), the Sala dos Archeiros (Archers' Room) and the Sala dos Particulares (Private Room), all of which contain 18th c. Portuguese furniture.

The Hall of the Ambassadors has a baldachin ceiling and two thrones, with two chairs for visitors standing opposite. The royal family is depicted in the ceiling paintings, together with musical scenes, reflective of the time when Pedro III used to hold concerts in this room.

The walls of the Sala do Despacho (Excursion Room) are painted with old-fashioned country scenes, featuring drives taken by the family; during the reign of João VI, the room was used for ministerial meetings. The Sala do Toucador, the queen's former dressing room, is lined with gold-embellished mirrors. The ceiling is decorated with flowers, as well as pictures showing children dressing in state robes. The furnishings in the bedroom belonged to Carlota Joaquina and date from the early 19th c. A room with a small altar was used as a prayer room. The round room adjoining this was one of the king's rooms and is painted with scenes from the life of Don Quixote as well as musical scenes. Porcelain and silver, once belonging to the royal family, is displayed in the dining room, most of it is Chinese.

Today the former palace kitchen accommodates the high-class restaurant Cozinha Velha (entrance on the palace forecourt).

Palace gardens

The palace gardens were laid out by Jean Baptiste Robillon in the Rococo style, based on the designs of the French landscape gardener Le Nôtre, and are well worth visiting. Allegorical figures, vases and azulejos are integrated with box hedges, geometric beds and flower borders. Some lead sculptures were cast in England. Interspersed with the plants are fountains and streams, the mirror-effect on the calm waters was consciously included at that time as an element of form. In the lower part of the garden the Jamor-Baches watercourse was dammed into a 115m/377ft long "river" decorated with azulejos. Members of the royal family would come to this part of the garden to fish, to sail, to play or to have their meals in a former summer house at the water's edge. The palace, which stands considerably higher than the gardens, is reached via the wide Lions' Staircase, named after the lions which flank it.

Palace square

The Largo do Palácio, a wide square in front of the palace, features a statue of Maria I. The royal barracks and the Palace Chapel, in the purest Rococo style and containing the military music school, is separated from the rest of the palace buildings by a wide road.

*Rossio · Praça de Dom Pedro IV — H 3

Location
City centre

Metro
Rossio

Buses
1, 2, 9, 11, 21, 31, 32, 36, 39, 41, 44, 45, 46, 80, 83, 90

Like many of Lisbon's squares, Rossio also has an official and an unofficial name. Its official name, Praça de Dom Pedro IV, commemorates Portugal's first liberal king; however, the square is usually simply referred to as Rossio, the Portuguese name for any large square. This says a great deal about the character and importance of Rossio for the Portuguese capital. Other names, such as the "heart" of Lisbon, emphasise that this is the pulsating centre of the city. Today Rossio is not only a meeting place for both citizens and tourists but also the workplace of countless newspaper vendors, shoe-shine boys, street traders and lottery ticket sellers. Many buses also stop in the square; the main taxi rank is located here, as is the most southerly Metro station and a railway station serving many suburbs; it is the most congested area for traffic in the city centre. Amid all this pandemonium Rossio's cafés are popular for sitting and watching the world go by. At lunchtime and after work many shop and bank workers from the Baixa come here.

During the Middle Ages Rossio had already become a central stage for the life of the city. Until the end of the 18th c. the burning of heretics, carried out as part of the Inquisition, took place here and bullfights were still being

staged here up until the last century. The square was used for major events of all types – from carnival balls to mass rallies.
In its present form it arose as part of the newly-rebuilt post-earthquake Baixa (see entry). Rossio, the Praça da Figueira (see entry) and the Praça do Comerçio (see entry), together with the grid-like arrangement of connecting streets, form a united area of urban development. Its architectural design originates from plans drawn up by the Hungarian Carlos Mardel.
The Classical Teatro Nacional Donna Maria II (see entry) stands on the northern side. Three of the Baixa's eight straight streets join the square on the opposite side; the entrance to the Rua dos Sapateiros is spanned by the decorative Arco do Bandeiro. This bears the name of the wealthy sponsor Pires Bandeiro who commissioned it at the end of the 18th c.
In the mid 19th c. the whole inner area of the square was cobbled with a lovely wave-like mosaic pattern; today only a small, central part of this remains. There are two impressive fountains and a statue of Pedro IV here.

Pedro IV Statue

In 1870 the 23m/75ft tall marble pillar topped with a bronze statue of Pedro IV was set up in the middle of this extensive square. After 1807, when the royal family fled from Napoleonic troops, the son of King João VI stayed in Brazil. He remained there after his father returned to Lisbon and became in 1822 Pedro I, emperor of Brazil, which was henceforth an independent country.
An international competition, in which 87 artists took part, was held to undertake the statue. The work was finally awarded to a sculptor and an architect from France. The four figures on the plinth symbolise Justice, Wisdom, Courage and Restraint – attributes ascribed to Pedro IV.

Café Nicola

Of the numerous cafés and restaurants bordering the square special mention must be made of the Café Nicola (Nos 24/25). This establishment, which dates from 1929, is known particularly for its association with the poet Manuel Maria Bocage (1765–1805). He was a regular customer of the

View of the Rossio

old Café Nicola which stood here at the end of the 18th c. and which was a meeting place for artists who were active in both the literary and political fields. In the Café Nicola, Bocage improvised sonnets and satirical poems. In 1797 he was arrested, as his bohemian way of life and his emotional poetry were not to the liking of the state authorities. In the new Nicola a statue, a wall-painting and printed sugar packets commemorate the celebrated customer.

Tabacaria Mónaco

The narrow Tabacaria Mónaco (no. 21) dates from 1894. The beautiful tiles next to the entrance are the work of the well-known artist Rafael Bordalo Pinheiro, whose ceramic work can be seen in the museum named after him on the Campo Grande. It is worth taking a look inside: the paintings by António Ramalho and the wood fittings by Frederico Augusto Ribeiro were part of the original furnishings. At the beginning of the 20th c. the Tabacaria Mónaco was a popular meeting place where Lisbon's latest news was exchanged.

São Domingos

The small Largo de São Domingos, on which a church of the same name stands, lies at the north-east corner of the Rossio. In the 13th c. a Dominican monastery was founded on this site but was completely destroyed by the 1755 earthquake. The portal of the original chapel was incorporated into the reconstruction of the Dominican church, built to plans by the architect Carlos Mardel. The façade and the chancel are the work of Ludovice, the architect of the monastery-palace at Mafra (see entry). In 1959 the interior was almost completely destroyed by fire, the damage can still be clearly seen today. The single-aisled bare church interior, which was originally richly decorated with talha, now appears almost bizarre. The eight side chapels have been temporarily furnished with statues of saints. Despite its somewhat morbid appearance the church is popular with the people of Lisbon.
The Palácio da Independéncia (see entry) stands on the north side of the square.

Rua das Portas de Santo Antão — H 3/4

Location
Centre

Metro
Restauradores

The lively Rua das Portas de Santo Antão is one of the parallel streets lying to the east of the Avenida da Liberdade (see entry). The street name dates from the 15th c. when a gate in the former town wall stood here. The street is mainly well-known for its many restaurants offering a wide selection of seafood. There are also some interesting buildings to be seen here.

Casa do Alentejo

The Casa do Alentejo, a meeting place for the people from the historic province of Alentejo (além Tejo = beyond the Tagus) who live in Lisbon, is hidden behind a rather unprepossessing exterior (no. 58). The main function of the Casa do Alentejo is to introduce the country region to the capital and to cultivate its unique culture. The people from Alentejo moved into the Palácio Alverda in 1932. The building is notable on account of its unusual interior. The palace dates from the last quarter of the 17th c., but its current appearance is a result of considerable alterations carried out in 1918. The Moorish-looking covered inner courtyard with a small fountain in the centre is impressive. Copies of the original architectural features give some impression of the Arab-influenced Mudejar style which is to be found particularly in Spain, but also in southern Alentejo.

Coliseu dos Recreios

The Coliseu dos Recreios (nos. 92–104) was built in 1888 to the design of the architect Goulard. The façade was designed by the Italian César Janz, the large glass dome was constructed in Berlin. The architect Cassiano Branco carried out larger renovations in 1929. With room for more than 7000 visitors, the Coliseu was for a long time the city's largest location for events. Circus and variety performances used to take place in the octagonal hall, nowadays not only classical concerts given by large orchestras but

Church of São Domingos

Courtyard in the Casa do Alentejo

also a variety of stars from the field of light music can be heard in the Coliseu.

The Sociedade de Geografia is based in building no. 100. The Museu Etnográfico (see entry) is affiliated to it.

Museu Etnográfico

*Sé Patriarchal (Cathedral) J 2

Location
Largo da Sé

Trams
28, 28B

Buses
37

Lisbon's cathedral, called the Sé Patriarchal, is the city's oldest church and is one of the largest constructions of Romanesque origin in Portugal. The Portuguese word *Sé*, meaning cathedral, comes from the word *sede* meaning bishop's seat. The building stands within the old, densely-built quarter on the southern hillside – there is insufficient room available here for the spacious square which would allow the church to appear more striking.
The origins of the church date back to the 12th century. After the conquest of the city by the first king of Portugal, Afonso Henriques, the construction of a church was quickly begun on a site on which a mosque had stood until then. This was meant to demonstrate who held power in Lisbon from then on. It is thought that old building materials dating in part from the time before the Moors, were incorporated. Apparently after the conquest of the city the Arabs converted a church, which had existed since the early 4th c., and used it as a mosque. Materials dating from pre-Arabic times were found, including a West-Gothic frieze, which was damaged by the gases emitted by the destruction. It has been restored and can be seen in the cloister.
During the centuries the church has been destroyed several times by earthquakes, the first time in 1344. Rebuilding of the cathedral has resulted in a continual change of appearance. At the beginning of the 14th c. Afonso IV had the church enlarged. In 1380, after a powerful earthquake, the

Sé Patriarcal

Cathedral

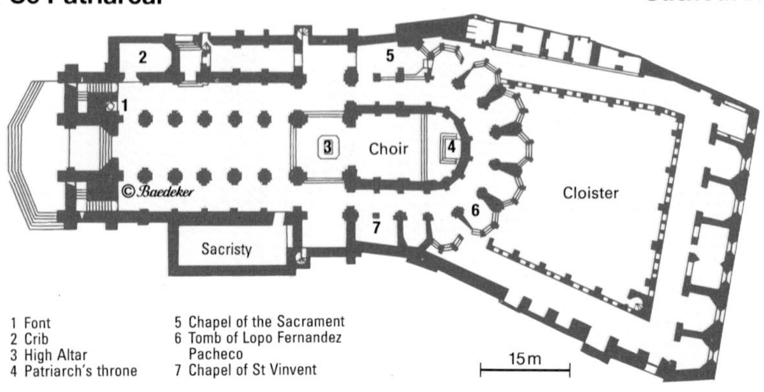

present façade, with its merlon-crowned, fortress-like towers, was erected. In the 18th c. two Baroque spires were added of which the northern tower was for a long time decorated with an octagonal, helm-like top. It was removed in order to emphasise the Romanesque overall impression and with that the solid character of a fortress. For that reason the merlons were added. The pair of Romanesque-style windows replaced two former rectangular ones. In place of the rosette, a window in the form of a second portal was included above the main entrance. A considerable amount of these changes took place during the government of Salazar.

Interior

After some restoration work the interior of the cathedral appears very uniform. It consists of two low side aisles and a higher nave, with a barrel-vaulted and cross-vaulted ceiling. The appearance of the front of the interior is predominantly Romanesque. The chancel and ambulatory are, by contrast, Gothic. In the crossing remains of Romanesque arches can be seen alongside Gothic ones. The eastern limit of the first small church can be recognised by the stone floor in the right ambulatory. The ceiling paintings and the decoration of the chancel as well as one of the two organs are Baroque.

In the Franciscan chapel, on the left next to the entrance, a tiled picture can be seen which shows the saint preaching to the fishes. Also in the chapel is a font, in which St Anthony (to whom the Igreja de Santo António da Sé is dedicated) is supposed to have been baptised in 1195.

One of the Baroque nativity scenes created by the well-known Machado de Castro, whose works also include the statue of José I on the Praça do Comércio (see entry), can be found in the first small chapel on the left. The original event has been moved into the Portugal of the 18th c. with the nativity crib framed by depictions of everyday Portuguese life. In accordance with taste of that time the figures in the background have been foreshortened in order to intensify the impression of depth. The scene was made from terracotta and painted.

The tombs of King Afonso IV and his wife Beatrix have been placed at the sides of the santuary, with the main altar in the centre and the patriarch's throne visible in the background.

Nine chapels have been incorporated into the ambulatory which was built later. St Vincent's Chapel used to contain the reliquary of St Vincent. Also in the ambulatory are the 14th c. sarcophagi of Lopo Fernandes Pacheco and his wife Maria Vilalobos. Pacheco became a follower of King Afonso IV after successfully supporting him in the last battle fought against the Arabs as part of the Reconquista. A further sarcophagus with similar features

appears to be the work of the same sculptor; the person depicted has, however, never been identified.
The sacristy includes the silver, mother of pearl-inlaid reliquary of St Vincent positioned on a marble altar. A statue of the saint holding a caravel and a quill stands behind it.

Cloister

The Gothic cloister, lined by several chapels, is reached via the ambulatory. Particularly impressive is a wrought-iron Romanesque screen, typical of religious art of that time on the Iberian peninsula. the West-Gothic frieze can be seen in the first chapel on the left. Excavations are to be carried out in the cloister garth as it is thought that an underground tunnel still exists leading from the Castelo de São Jorge (see entry) to the cathedral.

Igreja de Santo António da Sé

To the west of and below the cathedral stands a lovely Baroque church dedicated to St Anthony. An earlier 16th c. church was destroyed by the earthquake. Mateus Vicente de Oliveira, who also built the Basilica da Estrela (see entry) and Queluz palace (see entry), completely rebuilt the Igreja de Santo António da Sé.
St Anthony, who gave the church its name, has become known as Anthony of Padua. His real name was Fernando Martins de Bulhões. He was born at the end of the 12th c. in Lisbon and apparently lived for some time in a Franciscan monastery at Santo António dos Olivais near Coimbra. He spent part of his life in Italy, dying in 1231 in Padua. Tradition has ascribed several miracles to him: fish are said to have listened to his words, he is supposed to have cured the ill and brought the dead back to life. On the other hand he is also said to have been one of the leaders in the extermination of the Albigeois who were being persecuted in the south of France. He is generally portrayed as a saint with a popular touch, a helper of the forgotten and

Igreja de Santo António da Sé

a protector of lovers and children. Many illustrations above front doors show him in the dress of a Franciscan carrying the Christ child in his arms. Lisbon has chosen St Anthony as its saint, and Alfama is considered to be "his" quarter. The traditional St Anthony's festival is celebrated there every year on June 13th.

The Igreja de Santo António da Sé is situated on the site of the house where the saint is supposed to have been born. It is said that the crypt, which remains from the original church, was built exactly where the room of his birth was located.

From 1910 to 1926 the church was used by the city for storage and for a time the idea was mooted of accommodating the Museu de Cidade (see entry) here. In honour of the Franciscan jubilee the council relinquished its control of the church. The proportions of the single-aisled interior make it appear very harmonious. A pleasant lighting effect results from the fanlights in the small cupola. The statue of St Anthony, which is carried every year in the procession on June 13th, stands on the high altar. The newer sacristy is decorated with flower-patterned tiles. Pope John Paul's visit on the occasion of the 750th anniversary of St Anthony's death is recorded for posterity on a tiled picture in the crypt.

Museu Antoniano

A small museum has been set up next to the church in memory of the saint (see Practical Information, Museums).

Sintra (Excursion)

Location
About 30km/18 miles north-west of Lisbon

Trains
From Estação Rossio, terminus Sintra

The little town of Sintra lies at a height of about 300m/656ft between Lisbon and the Atlantic at the northern feet of the extensively wooded Serra de Sintra, on one of two mountain ledges bordered by ravines. The Sintra mountains reach a maximum height of 540m/1772ft at the Cruz Alta peak. Sintra enjoys an extremely mild and pleasant micro-climate, which, despite its southern warmth, has sufficient humidity to ensure lush vegetation. It has long been a favourite destination for outings and a popular resort. Lord Byron, who stayed in Portugal at the beginning of the 19th c. and who could find nothing positive about the city of Lisbon, praised Sintra in contrast as a "glorious Eden". The Englishman's praise of the "magical garden of Eden" attracted not only his compatriots, but foreigners from every country imaginable, who settled in Sintra and built mansions and palaces, some of which were rather curious-looking. Many important artists have been inspired by the romantic mountainous scenery here. The opening of the railway between Lisbon and Sintra in 1887 led an increasing number of citizens of Lisbon to escape here from the hot capital in the summer.

The Sintra region was settled very early, traces have been found from prehistoric and early times. The lovely scenery and marvellous climate tempted Moorish leaders to settle here. In 1147 Afonso Henriques vanquished the Arabs, and about 1400 the royal family chose Sintra as the seat of their summer residence. A number of buildings, some very attractive, dating from a variety of different eras still exist in and around Sintra.

Town

The town is centred on the Largo Rainha D. Amélia with the magnificent Palácio Nacional de Sintra on its north side. In front of the Palácio stands a Late Gothic pelourinho (pillory) which has been made into a fountain.

The largo Rainha D. Amélia leads on its south-western side into the Praça da República. This is bordered by the Igreja de São Martinho, originally a 12th c. church and subsequently much altered, and the Museu Municipal (municipal museum; open: Tues.–Sat. 9.30am–noon and 2–6pm), which also accommodates the tourist office. Some few hundred metres to the west is a toy museum (Museu do Brinquedo; open: Tues.–Sun. 10am–12.30pm and 2–6pm).

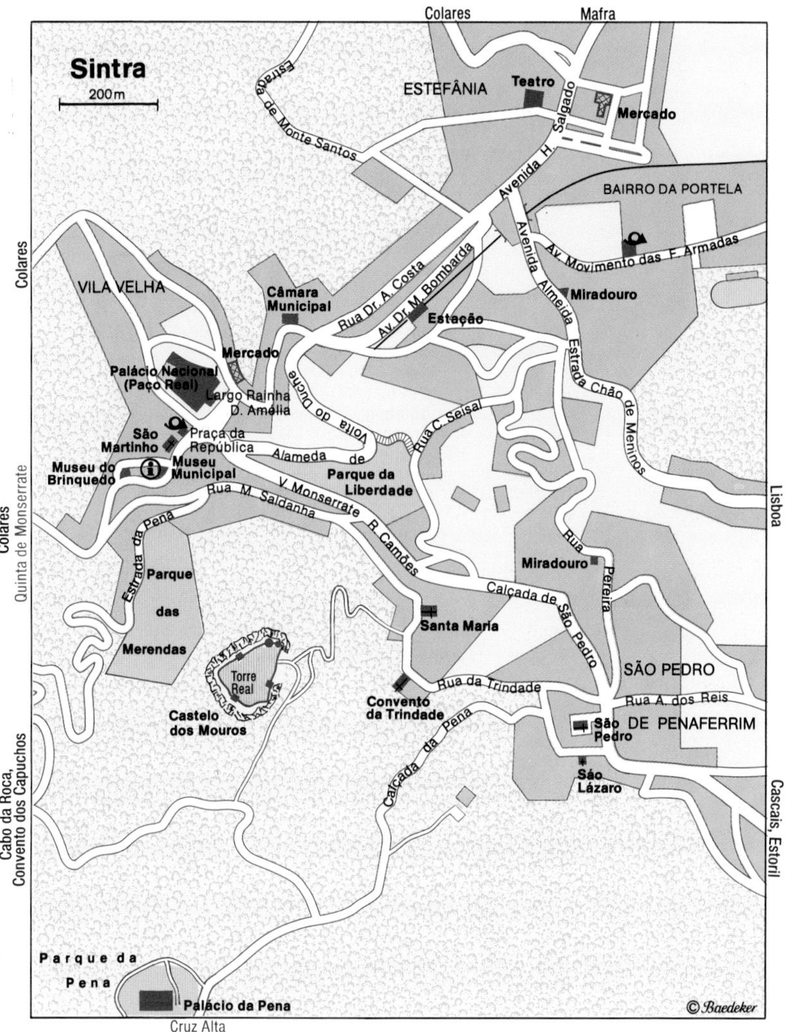

Past Parque Liberdade (Liberty Park), the Igreja de Santa Maria, another much-altered 12th c. church, and the Convento da Trindade, lies the São Pedro part of town with a single-aisled parish church. A large popular market takes place here every second and fourth Sunday in the month.
Immediately above Sintra, on its steep rocky perch, stands the Moorish castle which Afonso Henriques captured in 1147, and then, higher up, the Pena topped by its palace.
Visitors to Sintra should not just visit the places of interest, but allow a little time to go for a stroll through this lovely town.

Festivals

From June to September some first-class concerts and the famous festivals of works by the Romantic composers are staged in and around Sintra (tickets can be bought in advance from the tourist office in Sintra and at Valentim de Carvalho in the Amoreiras Shopping Center – loja 2109).

**Palácio Nacional de Sintra (Paço Real)

Location
Largo Rainha D. Amélia

Open
Thur.–Tues. 10am–1pm, 2–5pm

At the beginning of the 15th c. João I, the founder of the Avis dynasty, had a royal palace built as a summer residence on the 10th c. foundations of a Moorish palace. Later Manuel I extended the east wing. During the reign of Maria II in the 19th c. the castle was completely restored and the rooms partly refurnished. It became the favourite residence of Luis I and his widow, Maria Pia, who lived here after his death.

The palace is not a single, uniform building, but consists of various linked individual units. Its gradual extension and the ensuing variety of styles afford the whole complex a unique charm. Through its history it has brought together Moorish, Gothic and Manueline architectural elements, together with Renaissance features.

The palace frontage on the Largo Rainha D. Amélia, with its gently sloped flight of steps and the five so-called Joanine twin windows, remain from the first phase of the building. These windows were carried off by the Portuguese in the conquest of Ceuta in 1415. João I had them incorporated into the palace walls. It is thought, however, that they are not of North African but of Italian origin as Arabic princes had a preference at that time for embellishing their palaces with Venetian window arches.

The six typically Manueline windows on the right on the east wing are impressive. The two conical towers, easily visible from a distance, are kitchen chimneys, they were only added in the 18th c.

It is well worth visiting the palace interior but this is only possible as part of a guided tour. Particularly impressive is the gorgeous azulejo wall decoration in almost all of the rooms. Some of the tiles date from the 16th c. and show many typical, common patterns and designs of that time. The tour of the palace usually begins in the Guardroom.

Kitchen

The size of the white-grey tiled kitchen is particularly impressive. Visitors stand immediately beneath the two conical chimneys which are believed to be built in a Moorish style. Similar, though smaller, chimneys are often found in Portugal.

Hall of Arabs

A small 15th c. fountain located in the centre of the Hall of Arabs is of note. The lovely tile decoration on the walls achieves its effect through its play

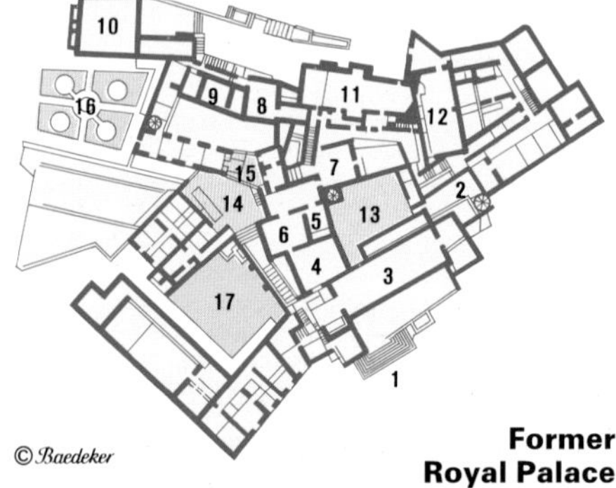

Palácio Nacional de Sintra

with the perspective. The azulejos are some of the oldest in the palace, they were manufactured in Seville in the 16th c. The tile frieze was made in Portugal. The room has the atmosphere of an old Moorish palace.

Chapel

The chapel dates back to the time of João I, his coat of arms can be seen on the ceiling above the high altar. The chapel is apparently located on the site where the Moors built a mosque inside the palace. The beautifully tiled floor is from the early 16th c.

Afonso VI Room

Afonso VI was imprisoned in this room. A family intrigue resulted in him being declared mentally deficient and dethroned. His wife, Maria Franziska Isabella, married Afonso's brother Pedro, who first acted as regent and then had himself crowned Pedro II. Pedro kept his brother captive here for the last eight years of his life until he died in 1683.

Armorial Hall (Hall of Stags)

The hall has an octagonal, wooden cupola, which was painted with stags – featured on the coat of arms of 72 noble familes – on the orders of Manuel I between 1515 and 1518. Manuel I's coat of arms is depicted in the centre of the cupola, surrounded by those of his eight children. The walls of the hall are clad with 17th c. tiles portraying hunting scenes. The tiles were manufactured at the Fábrica do Rato in Lisbon.
A marvellous view can be enjoyed from seven windows, of which two are Late Gothic double windows featuring the characteristically narrow central pillars.

Hall of Magpies

The Hall of Magpies owes its name to the 136 magpies painted on the ceiling, each one holding in its beak the motto of King João I, "por bem", i.e. for the best. The story goes – it has not been historically authenticated – that João's wife caught him kissing a lady-in-waiting. The King's cool response was "foi por bem" ("I did it for the best"). Since the ladies-in-waiting delighted in repeating this ever-afterwards on every possible occasion, their chatter goaded João into commissioning the ceiling. The roses are the symbol of the House of Lancaster, from which his wife, Phillipa, was descended.

Hall of Swans

This room is the largest in the palace and also owes its name to its painted wooden ceiling, which depicts 27 white swans, each in a different position. Each swan wears a crown around its neck. The hall's windows and doors were embellished in the 16th c. in a sumptuous Moorish-Manueline style. The former banqueting hall is still used today on festive occasions.

**Palácio Nacional da Pena

Location
Parque da Pena

Open
Tues.–Sun.
10am–1pm,
2–5pm

The relatively long distance between the centre of Sintra and the Palácio da Pena can be covered either by a long walk, by car or taxi. Horse-drawn carriages can also hired from in front of the Palácio Nacional de Sintra for the journey. The visit to the castle is coupled with one to the Castelo dos Mouros (see below), located half-way along the route.
Visible from afar and easily recognisable by its unique silhouette, the Palácio da Pena stands at a height of more than 500m/1641ft, surrounded by the Parque de Pena, in the middle of the Sintra mountains. Often called the "Portuguese Neuschwanstein", the castle was once used as a summer residence. The royal family fled here on October 4th 1910 when the revolution in Lisbon led to calls for a republic. Manuel II and his wife began their flight to Great Britain from here. The Palácio da Pena is now owned by the state.
In 1511 Manuel I had a small mountain monastery built on the same site for the monks of the Hieronymite order. A 14th c. chapel had stood here previously. The monastery was badly destroyed by the earthquake of 1755 and the ruins inherited by the husband of Maria II, Ferdinand of Saxe-Coburg-Gotha (Ferdinand II) in 1838 after the dissolution of the order.
Wilhelm von Eschwege – baron, engineer, geologist and colonel – was commissioned to build a romantic palace incorporating all the building styles which had hitherto appeared in Portugal and Germany. In addition the remains of the Moorish monastery were to be integrated into it. Eschwege clearly applied himself to this task: Gothic, Manueline, Renaissance and Rococo elements can be seen as well as Moorish and Far Eastern ones. The German architect sought inspiration on journeys to North Africa and southern Spain and from castles in Bavaria and on the Rhine. The copy of a Portuguese landmark is clearly evident: the palace's principal tower is an imitation of the Manueline Torré de Belém (see entry). Features of two Renaissance palaces in Lisbon have also been included: the "diamond facets" of the Casa dos Bicos (see entry) and the hemispheres of the building on the corner of the Rua da Rosa and the Cunhal das Bolas (see Bairro Alto) have been incorporated next to the first entrance gate in the wall.
The mixture of styles continues to be criticised by art specialists. However, a visit to this unusual building is always worthwhile – not least for the extensive view it offers: to the west along the Atlantic coast and to the east as far as the edge of the city of Lisbon. On clear days even the Caparica coast (see Costa de Lisboa) can be seen.

Interior

Even in the furnishing of the royal apartments no stylistic uniformity has been followed appropriate to the idea of the whole complex. Most of the rooms contain an interesting but curious collection of furnishings and everyday objects of all types. Much value was placed on the presentation of details such as Malutensilien or bathroom furnishings. An extensive and valuable collection of porcelain is of interest.
Also noteworthy is the integrated part of the original 16th c. monastery, of which the two-storey Manueline cloister and the monastery chapel of

Palácio Nacional de Pena ▶

Nossa Senhora da Pena have been retained. In the small cloister the fan vault and the azulejo wall tiling in particular are striking. Equally lovely old tile decorations dating from 1619 can be admired in the chapel. The upper part of the altar, dating from 1619, is of particular art-historical interest. It is supposed to be the work of Nicolas Chanterène, who also created the west portal of the monastery-church Mosteiro dos Jerónimos (see entry). The marble and alabaster Renaissance altar was commissioned in 1532 by João III as a thank-offering for the birth of a son. Almost architecturally designed, with pillars and columns, the altar together with the ornamental decoration and the figurative representations create a balanced unity.

*Parque da Pena

Ferdinand of Saxe-Coburg-Gotha was also responsible for the laying out of the Parque da Pena (the park is closed at night; cars are admitted for a fee, but there is no admission to the castle car park). The estate, which covers about 200ha/494 acres, contains over 400 species of trees and shrubs, including tree ferns; it is particularly beautiful in the spring-time when the camellias, rhododendrons and azaleas are in bloom. That sub-tropical plants now grow on this terrain, where originally species of oak predominated, is made possible by the location of the mountains, the volcanic earth, the proximity of the Atlantic, the mild micro-climate and the abundance of water. Groups of trees arranged to give a great variety of contrast, strips of forest with well laid-out paths and little gardens with ponds demonstrate clearly the romantic ideas, which lie behind the realisation of this park.
Cars can be driven up to the Cruz Alta (540m/1771ft), a stone cross (1522) on the highest point in the Serra de Sintra, from where the best view of the Palácio da Pena can be enjoyed.

Castelo dos Mouros

Open
Daily 10am–5pm

High above Sintra, 429m/1408ft above sea level, stands the Castelo dos Mouros. From the south side of the town a road forks right and snakes uphill, with many hairpin bends, first through fine old gardens and then park-like woodland. After about 3km/2 miles a side-road branches off to the left to the Moorish castle, which is about a ten-minute walk from the car park.
Ramparts and towers still standing are of the castle, which was originally built in the 8th or 9th c., captured from the Moors in 1147 by Afonso Henriques and subsequently much altered. In the mid-19th c. Ferdinand of Saxe-Coburg-Gotha had trees planted in the inner courtyard. There is a marvellous view from up here of the town lying far below.

Palácio de Seteais

The Palácio de Seteais occupies an exposed position on the N375 as it leaves Lisbon in the direction of Colares, a town famous for its wines where many citizens of Lisbon have their holiday homes. The name "Palace of the Seven Sighs" is supposed to get its name from the fact that the Treaty of Sintra – the surrender declaration of the French forces – was signed here in 1808. Another version has it that if the sound *ai* is called from the palace forecourt, its echo will return seven times.
The palace was built in the last quarter of the 18th c. by Gildemeester, a Dutch trader and consul, and was extended early in the 19th c. It was a meeting place for the Portuguese nobility and the venue for lively parties. The triumphal arch, which links the two wings of the palace, commemorates a visit by Maria I and her son João VI. The medallion high up in the arch portrays João and his wife Carlota Joaquina.
In 1954 a luxury hotel with a gourmet restaurant was opened in the palace.

*Quinta de Monserrate

Open
Daily
10am–5pm

A few kilometres past the Palácio de Seteais, on the road to Colares, is the entrance to the Quinta de Monserrate, a Moorish-looking villa built in the second half of the 19th c. and set in a lovely park. It was built for one of the wealthiest men in Europe, the Englishman Francis Cook, whom one of the Bragança kings had created Earl of Monserrate. The estate has since been auctioned and is now owned by the state. As a result, the world's largest travel library has been broken up and sent to all four corners of the earth. A rich Englishman had already owned a house on this site in 1790, in which the English author William Beckford lived for a time.

It is worth strolling round the unusually lovely, hilly park, where there is an abundance of tall tree ferns along with many other species of sub-tropical plants.

*Convento dos Capuchos

The Convento dos Capuchos, a former Capuchin monastery, lies 10km/6 miles along the road to the Palácio da Pena south-west of Sintra. The monastery, in its woodland setting, was founded in 1560 by Alvares de Castro. A visit to this very remote monastery is very impressive and gives the visitor the feeling of being transported into a different world. The monks' small cells have been partly hewn out of the rock of a northern slope and insulated against damp and cold with cork. The cells are tiny, the doors very low – it seems impossible that anyone could enter a cell upright or sleep stretched full out. The Capuchin order first developed in Portugal around 1500. The monks led an extremely spartan life in poverty, simplicity and at one with nature. A sick room, a kitchen, a dining room with a simple stone tablet as a table, and a simple little chapel can be seen.

The Spanish king Philipp II, who ruled Portugal from 1580 to 1598, is supposed to have said after visiting the monastery: "In my kingdom I own the richest and the poorest monastery on the earth – the Escorial and the Convento dos Capuchos".

Monte Peninha

A little road goes from the Convento dos Capuchos to Monte Peninha (489m/1604ft), with good views over the Serra de Sintra and the sea. The small Capela da Peninha (open: Wed.–Mon. 9am–5pm) was built in 1711. It is decorated with lovely blue and white tiles and mosaics in the Florentine style.

Teatro Nacional Dona Maria II H 3

Location
Praça D. Pedro IV (Rossio)

Metro
Rossio

Buses
1, 2, 9, 11, 21, 31, 32, 36, 39, 41, 44, 45, 46, 80, 83, 90

The Dona Maria National Theatre (or Teatro Nacional de Almeida Garrett) on the north side of the Rossio (see entry) was built by the Italian Fortunato Lodi on the initiative of the author and temporary liberal politician Almeida Garrett, and is named after Queen Maria II, daughter of Pedro IV.

The Palácio dos Estaus, a palace used by the Inquisitors to carry out their work, originally stood on this site. The foundation stone of the present Classical building was laid in 1842 and it was officially opened four years later. The interior was destroyed by fire in 1964 and not reopened until 1978, as this was seen as an opportunity to renovate completely the theatre and equip it with modern technology.

The Classical façade dominates the north front of the Rossio. Two rows of windows are interspersed with Ionian pillars and surmounted with a row of semi-circular windows. The busts of famous Portuguese poets have been incorporated above the 17 windows of the middle floor. Apollo and seven muses are depicted in the triangular tympanum above the six pillared

Teatro Nacional de Dona Maria II

portico. The original designs for it were by the Portuguese António Manuel da Fonseca, with the Italian Cesarino completing the work. Thalia and Melpomene, figures symbolising Comedy and Tragedy, stand to the right and the left of the gable. Rising above all of this is Assis Rodrigues' statue of Gil Vicente, the forefather of Portuguese theatre in the 16th c.

Teatro Nacional de São Carlos (Opera) H 2

Location
Largo de São Carlos

Trams
10, 20, 24, 28, 28B, 29, 30

Buses
15

The Lisbon opera house is situated on the south side of the inconspicuous Largo de São Carlos in Chiado (see entry). It was built in 1792 to the plans of José da Costa e Silva to replace an earlier opera house which had been completely destroyed by the earthquake. In contrast to the first opera house the new one was not purely the domain of the royal family but became at that time increasingly more popular with the rising bourgeoisie. It was, in fact, some wealthy citizens who commissioned and paid for the new building. Performances of predominantly Italian operas – with mainly Italian casts – gave the Lisbon opera a good name for some time in the 19th c. Musical guests to the Lisbon opera included Toscanini, Saint-Saëns, Liszt, Richard Strauss, Paganini, Rubinstein and Padarewsky.

The Teatro Nacional de São Carlos is regarded as one of Portugal's earliest Classical buildings. The architect based his designs on the Milanese Scala and the Naples opera. The outer façade is simply and harmoniously proportioned. The entrance is covered by a three-arched arcaded balcony surmounted by a veranda. The internal decoration is moderate and elegant. The ceiling painting in the entrance hall is the work of Volkmar Machado. The large concert hall has an elliptical ground plan, above which are five circles one above the other. Smaller-scale chamber concerts take place in the Salão Nobre.

Teatro Nacional de São Carlos

Opposite the opera house, also in the Largo de São Carlos, stands the house where the famous author Fernando Pessoa (see Famous People and Chiado) was born.

Birthplace of Fernando Pessoa

**Torre de Belém (Belém Tower)

The Torré de Belém (Belém Tower) is certainly Lisbon's most famous construction and at the same time most well-known symbol. It stands surrounded by lawns on the bank of the Tagus to the west of the Hieronymite monastery (see Mosteiro dos Jerónimos). At this point the Tagus widens into a large bay.

Location
Avenida da India, Belém

Trams
15, 17

Buses
29, 43

Trains
From Estação Cais do Sodré, Station Pedrouços

Open
Tues.–Sun. 10am–5pm (June to Sept. until 6.30pm)

Originally conceived as a lighthouse and simultaneously a defensive fortress for the port of Restelo, Manuel I had the tower built in 1515 on a small island off the river bank. Many old views of the city show the Torré de Belém at a distance from the mainland surrounded by the waters of the Tagus. A former, older tower on the opposite bank and Belém's fortress tower were supposed to afford maximum protection for the harbour. A general shift in the location of the river bank has resulted in the tower now standing on the mainland right on the water's edge: a footbridge leads across an artificial basin to the entrance to the tower.

Francisco de Arruda began the construction in 1515. De Arruda came from Alentejo and was one of the most famous architects to use the Manueline style. He had studied with his older brother Diogo de Arruda, had then worked for some time in north Africa and was thus acquainted with the elements of the Arabic style – one of the reasons for the obvious Moorish influences in his work.

The Torré de Belém has been the setting for many historical events. These included the onset of Spain's 60-year rule of Portugal after the conquest of the tower in 1580. After Lisbon was taken by Napoleonic troops in 1807 the two upper storeys of the tower were destroyed and wooden houses built in their place. In 1845 Minister Terceira had the tower restored to its original state.

Exterior

The whole complex comprises a four-storey tower, easily visible from a distance, and ramparts which face the river and are built on a hexagonal ground plan. This was consciously created in the shape of a snub ship's bow jutting into the water. The main façade of the fortress is turned towards the sea and gives a completely different impression of the Torré de Belém than from the river bank side. The character of a fortress is expressed particularly in the offshore, lower bastion. Embrasures have been incorporated into the walls, battlements, formed by the juxtaposition of coats of arms, surround the top of the bastion. Small Arabic-influenced, domed watch-towers accentuate the corners. The same elements of form can be observed on the external walls of the square tower: the small domed towers crown the four corners, two lower oriel towers have been fashioned in the same way. A platform at the top of the tower is lined by small battlements with pyramid-shaped helm roofs. The three sides of the tower visible from the river bank incorporate twin windows and dainty, roofed balconies. The double arched windows, the small exits and a seven-arched loggia on the side facing the river evoke Venetian associations.

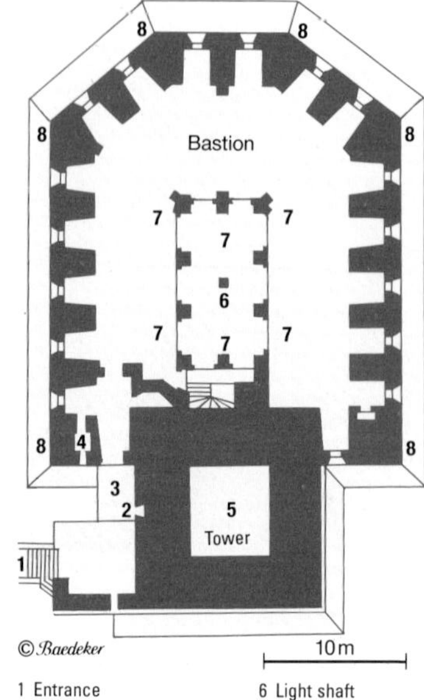

Below the protective, richly-decorated baldachin of the bastion stands a Gothic statue of the Virgin Mary: Nossa Senhora do Bom Sucesso (Our Lady of Good Fortune), the name also borne by the bordering harbour basin. A navigation light was previously installed here.

An interesting story is hidden behind one of the very weathered corbels on the tower. The heads of lions, dolphins and rams can be seen below the bastion's small watch-towers. A rhinoceros' head is visible below the western tower which faces the land. It is supposed to commemorate a rhinoceros that Manuel I received as a present from India – the first rhinoceros in Europe. It was immortalised in a woodcut by Albrecht Dürer, which has since become famous. At that time it was hoped that the rhinoceros would fight an elephant on the Praça do Império to discover which was the strongest creature on earth – but apparently the elephant fled in fear at the sight of his opponent. Manuel wanted to send the rhinoceros by sea to Pope Leo X as a present but the ship was wrecked and sank off the coast of Italy.

Many typical elements of Manueline decoration are clearly recognisable: the coats of arms forming turrets and the railings on the small balconies bear the Cross of the Knights of Christ, while the Portuguese coat of arms

The Tower of Belém, the landmark of Lisbon

with a crown can be seen on the main façade together with armilliary spheres on both sides. A stone rope, which on the side facing the land is entwined into a large knot, encircles the whole tower. Other nautical ropes contribute to the horizontal structuring. The embellishment of the corner towers and, in particular, the baldachin of the figure of the Madonna incorporates pillars, points and stylised organic leaf elements of unmistakably Manueline style.

Interior

The interior of the complex is kept very plain. Store-rooms for weapons and food were set up on the ground floor. The upper storeys housed the Governor's Chamber and, above that, the King's Chamber (no longer furnished) with a small chapel above. The ceiling of the chapel has Gothic supporting beams, the crossing points bear Manueline decoration. The platform on top of the tower affords a fine view of the Tagus, the Atlantic to the west and inland, in good weather conditions, along a valley to the Sintra mountains (see entry) and the Palácio da Pena (see entry). The lower rooms were used for some time as a prison. When the water level was high the prisoners had to stand in water up to their hips.

Practical Information

Accommodation

See Camping, Hotels, Pousadas, Turismo de Habitação, Youth Hostels.

Advance Booking

See Theatres, Concerts.

Airlines

Air Portugal (TAP)
Praça Marquês de Pombal 3–3°; tel. 54 40 80
Airport; tel 8 48 91 81

British Airways
Avenida da Liberdade 36–2°; tel. 3 46 09 31

Air Services

Airport (Aeroporto)

The international airport "Portela de Sacavém" is situated about 13km/8 miles north of Lisbon city centre. For information: tel. 80 45 00.

Connecting bus services

The "Linha Verde" provides a direct connection from the airport to the centre and to Santa Apolónia railway station.
Bus lines 44, 45 and 83 also operate to the town centre. Bus line 8 terminates relatively close to the centre at Largo Martim Moniz, bus line 22 passes the upper end of the Avenida da Liberdade at the Praça Marquês de Pombal.

Flight connections

Air Portugal (TAP) operates several connections each day between Lisbon and Porto, Lisbon and Faro, and Lisbon and Portimão. There are also daily connecting flights to Funchal (Madeira) and Ponta Delgada (São Miguel, Azores).
Fares are reasonably priced. It is recommended to purchase tickets for onward flight connections in Portugal rather than in advance.

Car rental

Car rental company desks are located directly adjacent to the arrivals hall. Cars should be returned outside the airport building near the entrance to the departure hall.

Banks

Opening times

Most banks are open Monday to Friday, from 8am to 3pm, some close for lunch between noon and 1pm. A few banks in the city centre open again from 6–11pm Monday to Saturday.

◀ *High-rise tower block in the Amoreiras Shopping Center*

Exchange machines — There are also some automatic exchange machines in the centre which change various foreign currencies.

Currency — See Currency

Beaches (praia)

Lisbon's beaches are to be found to the north and south of the Tagus estuary in an area referred to as the Costa de Lisboa, comprising the west of Lisbon, the Costa do Estoril and to the south the Costa Azul ("Blue Coast") which includes the wonderful, clean beaches of the Costa de Caprica. A favourite area with the people of Lisbon is the coast further to the south of Setúbal on the Tróia peninsula.

Dangers — Bathing in the Atlantic can be hazardous. On the Costa de Caparica and the beach at Guincho are particularly deceptive whirlpools and currents. Many beaches, especially the more remote, are not supervised even in high season. On attended beaches flags are flown to indicate whether bathing is safe: red flag = no bathing (not even close to the beach); yellow flag = no swimming; green flag = bathing and swimming permitted; blue-white checked flag = beach not always supervised.

Access

Costa de Caparica	Buses from Areeiro, Praça de Espanha, Cacilhas
Sesimbra	Buses from Praça de Espana, Cacilhas
Tróia	Ferry from Setúbal
Estoril	Local train to Cascais
Praia de Guincho	Bus from Cascais
Praia das Maçãs	Bus from Sintra

Boat Services

Boat excursions — Some tour operators organise excursions in small boats along the Tagus (see Excursions). It is possible to travel independently to the opposite bank where there are several places of interest to visit. Most boats are passenger ferries, some take cars.

From the marina at Terreiro do Paço, next to the Praça do Comércio: organised round trips along the Tagus and to Cascais.
From Cais da Alfândega, opposite Estação Sul e Sueste (passenger ferries): Cachilhas (bus service from here to Monumento Cristo Rei and to the Costa Azul); also to Burreiro, Seixal and Montijo.
From Cais do Sodré (car ferry): Cacilhas.
From Estação Fluvial in Belém: Trafaria and Porto Brandão.

Further information is available from the tourist information centres (see Information).

Breakdown Assistance

See Motoring.

Business Hours

See Opening Times.

Bullfighting

Portuguese bullfighting is less brutal than it is in Spain as the bulls leave the arena alive. However, the bull is slaughtered afterwards at the abbatoir.

Portuguese bull fights are governed by complicated rules which are unintelligible to the outsider.
Bull fights take place every Thursday evening and occasional Sundays from April to October at the Lisbon bull ring at Campo Pequeno (see A–Z, Praça de Touros).

Bus Stations

General

Portugal has a close and very well organised network of overland buses, operated by the Rodoviária Nacional (RN). Comfortable express buses are used mostly on longer routes. Tickets for longer journeys can be bought one day in advance.

Bus stations

Av. Casal Ribeiro 18
(express buses, international services, buses to the north and north-east)

Av. 5 de Outubro 75
(only buses to the Algarve and Alentejo)

Camping

Camp sites

Parque de Campismo de Monsanto
Parque Florestal de Monsanto
Tel. 70 44 13/70 83 84
Open: throughout the year
Buses: 14, 43 from Praça da Figueira via Praça do Comércio

Note

Information can be obtained from the AA and major tourist offices.

Cafés

Selection

Café Nicola
Praça D. Pedro IV (Rossio) 24/25
(See A–Z, Rossio)

Café Suissa
Praça D. Pedro IV (Rossio) 99
(See A–Z, Rossio)

Café A Brasileira
Rua Garrett 120 (Largo do Chiado)
(See A–Z, Chiado)

Pastelaria Bénard
Rua Garrett 104–106

Café Martinho da Arcada
Praça do Comércio/Rua da Prata
(See A–Z, Praça do Comércio)

Confeitaria Nacional
Praça da Figueira 18 B/C

Pastelaria Versailles
Av. da República 15 A

Confeitaria dos Pastéis de Belém
Rua de Belém 84/86

The Café Nicola, once the haunt of artists and writers

Cerca Moura
Largo das Portas do Sol 4

Outdoor cafés

Café in the Parque Eduardo VII
between the Pavilhão dos Desportos and Rua Eng. Canto Resende

Café in the Jardim do Campo Grande
north of Av. do Brasil

Car Rental

General

To rent a car in Portugal drivers must be at least 21 years old and have held a full driving licence for one year. Car rental can often be arranged through the operator at the time of booking a package tour.

International car rental companies

Avis
Av. Praia da Vitória 120; tel. 3 56 11 76
Airport; tel. 8 49 48 36

Budget
Av. Fontes Pereira de Melo 6; tel. 53 77 17
Airport; tel. 80 17 85

Europcar
Quinta da Francelha, Lote 7, Prior Velho, 2685 Sacavém; tel. 9 42 40 24
Airport; tel. 80 11 76

Hertz
Av. 5 de Outubro; tel. 57 90 77
Airport; tel. 8 49 27 22, 80 14 96

National car rental companies

Enauto
Rua de Entrecampos 6–1; tel. 7 96 89 08, 7 97 40 81

Turim
Rua D. Estefânia 15 A; tel. 54 41 64

Chemists (farmácias)

Medicines

As well as medicines manufactured in Portugal well known brands from other countries are also obtainable from chemists, often at much lower prices than in the country of origin.

Opening times

Regular opening hours are: Mon.–Fri. 9am–1pm and 3–7pm, Sat. 9am–1pm.

Emergencies

Addresses of chemists on duty at night and on Sundays are posted in every chemists. Information on duty chemists (farmácias de serviçio) can be obtained by dialling 118.

Cinemas

Lisbon has 30 cinemas with over 50 screens. Here, too, most of the large cinemas have been divided into several smaller ones. One of the few remaining old-style cinemas with just one large hall is the "Condes" on Avenida da Liberdade. For the most part American films are shown; all foreign films have the original soundtrack and are sub-titled. The "Cinemateca" (Rua Barata Salgueiro 39) has a more unusual programme, with old Portuguese films being shown; at the cinema in "Forum Picoas" (Av. Fontes Pereira de Melo) the latest Portuguese films can be seen and premières are held. The daily newspaper, Diario de Noticias, carries details of cinemas, films and times. Monday is half price and often sold out in advance so buy your tickets early.

City Sightseeing

Note

Information about up-to-date sightseeing programmes in the city is obtainable from the tourist information offices (see Information).

Bus tours

Various tour operators offer bus tours round Lisbon, mostly of half a day's duration. The tours start fom the Praças Marquês de Pombal at the southern end of Eduardo VII Park. As well as the main sights in the city centre the suburb of Belém is generally included, with a visit to a museum in Belém.

City tours by tram

Since the municipal public transport company, Carris, realised the value of its old, increasingly unprofitable trams as a tourist attraction, it has organised tours of the city by "eléctrico". There are two attractive lines on offer, one runs to Belém from July to mid-Sept., the second round the centre through several quite different quarters of the city (this second tour also takes place after dark) from May to Sept. They depart from Praça do Comércio. Fares are payable on board the tram at the beginning of the tour.

Tours on the River Tagus

The beauty of the view of Lisbon from the river has long been acknowledged. The tours follow the direction of the river estuary and take in the entire panorama of the city, above which many of the sights visibly tower. Tours commence and terminate at the marina at Terreiro do Paço, near the Estação Sul e Sueste at the Praça do Comércio. There are also trips from Lisbon to Cascais and vice versa.

Currency

Unit of currency

The Portuguese unit of currency is the escudo (abbreviated to esc. or $), which is (theoretically) subdivided into 100 centavos. There are bank notes for 500, 1000, 5000 and 10,000 escudos and coins are in denominations of 1, 2½, 5, 10, 20, 50, 100 and 200 escudos, as well as 50 centavos.

Exchange rate

Exchange rates are subject to fluctuation; they can be obtained from banks and tourist offices and are published in the national press.
As is generally the case for countries with weak currencies, it is advisable to change money in the country, rather than beforehand. A commission of between 11 and 30% is levied for buying back Portuguese bank notes.

Import and export of currency

There is no limit on the amount of escudos and foreign currency which can be taken into Portugal. However, visitors entering Portugal must possess at least 10,000 escudos, or the equivalent in foreign currency, plus 2,000 escudos for each day of their stay. It is advisable to declare large quantities in order to avoid problems when leaving.
No more than 100,000 escudos per head in Portuguese currency may be taken out of the country and no more than the equivalent of 500,000 escudos in foreign currency, or the declared amount if higher, may be taken out.

Eurocheques

Eurocheques up to a value of 30,000 escudos can be encashed.
It is advisable to take money in the form of travellers' cheques.

Credit cards

Banks, larger hotels, certain restaurants, car rental firms and some shops accept most international credit cards. Visa and Eurocard are widely recognised, American Express and Diner's Club are not so widespread.

Portuguese currency

Customs Regulations

Entry from EC countries

Visitors from EC countries can import into Portugal certain articles free of duty for their personal use: (for visitors over 15) 1000g coffee or 400g instant coffee and 200g tea or 80g tea extracts, also (for visitors over 17) 1.5 litres of alcohol over 22% or 3 litres of alcohol below 22% or 3 litres of sparkling wine and 5 litres wine as well as 300 cigarettes or 150 cigarillos or 75 cigars or 400g of tobacco and 75g perfume and 0.375 litre of toilet water. Visitors over 15 may also bring in goods and presents to the value of 60,000 escudos.

Entry from non-EC countries

In addition to personal effects visitors over 17 from non-EC countries may import 200 cigarettes or 100 cigarillos or 50 cigars or 250g of tobacco and 1 litre of alcohol over 22% or 2 litres of spirits below 22% and 2 litres of wine as well as 50g perfume and 0.25 litre toilet water. Visitors over 15 may also bring in goods and presents to the value of 7,500 escudos.

Diplomatic Representation

United Kingdom

Embassy/Consulate
Rua São Domingos à Lapa 37
1200 Lisbon; tel. (01) 3 96 11 22

United States of America

Embassy
Avenida Forças Armadas, 1600 Lisbon; tel. (01) 72 66 00

Canada

Embassy
Avenida Liberdade 144–156, 1200 Lisbon; tel. (01) 3 47 48 92

Electricity

The current is supplied at 220 volts AC/DC. In the large hotels standard European two-pin plugs can be used, otherwise an adaptor (for North American visitors, a voltage transformer and an adaptor) is necessary.

Emergencies

Emergency telephone number

For police, fire, medical and rescue services throughout Portugal telephone 115.

Medical assistance

See entry

Events

March

Procissão do Senhor dos Passos da Graças: procession on the second Sunday in Lent.

May

Procissão da N.S. da Saúde: procession on the second Sunday in May.

June

Festivals of the Saints, street festivals with cabaret, music, etc. June 13th of particular importance for Lisbon, "Dia de Santo António", the patron saint of the city; street festivals the night before in many districts, large procession on the Avenida da Liberdade with individual districts competing for first prize. June 23th, "Dia de São Pedro", in São Pedro near Sintra.
Fundaçao Calouste Gulbenkian: contemporary music concerts.

June to September	Various festivals of classical music in Sintra and surroundings and in Queluz castle gardens.
September	Festo do Avante: the festival of the party magazine of the Communist PCP on the second weekend in September has become something of an institution not only for the party faithful. It celebrates the lifting of press censorship in 1974; information about life and culture in the different regions of the country, stalls, music by Portuguese groups. art exhibitions, etc.
October	Days of old music in the Fundaçao Calouste Gulbenkian.
November	Jazz festival in Cascais.

Excursions

Destinations

The following places in the surroundings of Lisbon are described in the A–Z section: Cascais, Monumento Cristo Rei, Costa Azul, Costa do Estoril, Estoril, Mafra, Queluz and Sintra.
Most of these destinations can be reached by public transport.

Organised excursions

In addition several companies organise bus excursions into the surrounding area of Lisbon. There are also trips to destinations further afield, such as Coimbra, Evora, Fatima, Obidos and Tomar or longer excursions of several days' duration to the Alentejo or the Algarve. Entrance fees to palaces, etc. are included in the price.
Information and departure times can be found at the lower end of the Parque Eduardo VII at the Praça Marquês de Pombal.

Boat trips on the Tagus

The company "Transtejo" operates boat trips on the Tagus. Excursions are from April to October and usually last 2 hours. Information and departure times from the Marina at Terreiro do Paço, next to the Praça do Comércio, or tel. 87 50 58.

Fado

Fado live

Hearing fado live can be an experience which conveys much about Portugal and the Portuguese way of life. It can still be heard in its original form in a few bars in the districts of Alfama, Bica or Bairro Alto. There are countless restaurants in the Bairro Alto with singing during or after dinner where with luck an impression of the real fado can be gained

Fado venues

Most restaurants open about 8.30pm with the performances commencing somewhat later. Generally there is no admission charge but the meals and drinks tend to be more expensive, or else a minimum price policy operates. It is advisable to book for many of the fado restaurants listed.

Senhor Vinho
Rua do Meio à Lapa 18
Tel. 67 26 81 (closed on Sundays)

Adega Machado
Rua do Norte 91. Tel. 3 42 87 13, 3 46 00 95

Arcadas do Faia
Rua da Barroca 54/56. Tel. 3 42 19 23

Taverna d'El Rei
Largo Chafariz de Dentro 14/15. Tel. 87 67 54

Live Fado, a speciality of Lisbon

Adega Mesquita
Rua Diário Noticías 107. Tel. 3 46 20 77

Adega do Ribatejo
Jd Regendor 27. Tel. 3 46 09 46

A Severa
Rua das Gáveas 51. Tel. 3 42 83 14

Lisboa à Noite
Rua das Gạveas 69. Tel. 3 46 26 03

Painel do Fado
Rua São Pedro de Alcântara 65–69. Tel. 32 54 71

Fado Menor
Rua das Praçąs 18. Tel. 67 18 56

Santa Cruz
Largo Santa Cruz do Castelo 5. Tel. 86 77 63

Records

See Shopping

Food and drink

General

As is the case in many other Mediteranean countries breakfast is not a very substantial meal. In hotels and pensions, however, coffee, rolls, butter and jam are usually served.
Lunch (almoço) and dinner (jantar) are more important. Many Portuguese eat a cooked meal twice a day, often in restaurants. Going out for a meal is

almost always an occasion to meet friends and acquaintances. Birthdays, at any age, are celebrated in restaurants. The meal consists of three courses. The first course is usually soup, the main course is a choice of meat or fish with potatoes (often chips) or rice, and dessert is fruit or a sweet. A basket containing bread, butter and sometimes cheese or olives is always placed on the table at the beginning of the meal.

Meal times

Lunch is usually taken between 12.30 and 2pm and dinner between 8.30 and 10.30pm.

Cuisine

Portuguese cuisine is typified by simple, palatable and digestible dishes. The best examples of Portuguese cooking are often to be found in unpretentious restaurants. Portugal is known for simple tasty soups which can serve as a first course or as a snack. Portugal is paradise for the lover of fish and shellfish. Otherwise the selection of main courses is rather limited and there is little variety between restaurants. Meat and fish dishes are often served with just a small salad or portion of vegetables and ordering a separate salad is recommended. Fish is frequently served with very fine potatoes, meat with chips or rice. The desserts are delicious, very sweet almost always homemade regional creations, followed by strong black coffee.

Soups (sopas)

Sopa de Legumes	Vegetable soup
Sopa de Feijão	Bean soup
Sopa de Peixe	Fish soup
Creme de Marisco	Shellfish bisque
Caldo Verde	Cabbage and potato soup with small slices of sausage
Canja	Chicken broth
Açorda à Alentejana	Clear bread soup with a poached egg, seasoned with a lot of garlic and coriander, typical dish from the Alentejo
Gaspacho	Spicy cold vegetable soup
Caldeirada	Fish stew
Cozida à portuguesa	Vegetable soup with assorted meats
Feijoada	Bean stew

Fish dishes (peixe)

Bacalhau	Dried cod is one of the national dishes. Each region has its own particular recipe.
Bacalhau cozido	Boiled dried cod
Bacalhau à Bras	Dried cod baked with egg, potatoes and onions
Sardinhas assadas	Grilled sardines
Linguado	Sole
Cherne, Robalo	Perch
Lulas grelhadas	Grilled octopus
Atum	Tuna fish
Enguia	Eel
Peixe espada	Swordfish
Salmão	Salmon
Truta	Trout

Shellfish

Camarão	Prawns
Lagosta	Crayfish
Amêijos	Cockles
Açorda de marisco	Garlic and bread soup with shellfish
Arroz de marisco	Rice with shellfish

Meat dishes

Carne de porco	Pork
Carne de porco à Alentejana	Pork with clams
Carne de vaca	Beef
Espetada de carne	Kebab with various meats

Leitão assado	Roast suckling pig
Lombo de porco	Roast leg of pork
Bife	Steak
Costeleta	Cutlet
Borrego	Lamb
Cabrito assado	Roast kid with potatoes and peppers in a white wine sauce and garlic
Frango assado	Roast chicken
Peru	Turkey

Egg dishes (ovos)

Ovos mexidos	Scrambled eggs
Ovos estrelados	Fried eggs
Omeleta	Omelette

Vegetables (legumes)

Ervilhas	Peas
Cenouras	Carrots
Cogumelos	Mushrooms
Alho francês	Leeks
Pimentos	Peppers
Feijões	Beans
Alface	Lettuce
Salada Mista	Mixed salad

Fruit

Salada de fruta	Fruit salad
Maçã	Apples
Pera	Pears
Morangos	Strawberries
Pêssego	Peach
Melão	Melon
Melancia	Water melon
Laranja	Orange
Uvas	Grapes

Desserts (sobremesa)

Gelado, Sorvete	Ice cream
Arroz doce	Milk pudding
Leite creme	Baked pudding with eggs, milk and sugar
Ovas moles	Sweetened egg yolks with almonds
Pudim flan	Crème caramel
Pudim Molotov	Meringue
Mousse de chocolate	Chocolate mousse
Toucinho do céu	Dessert made from sugar, eggs and ground almonds
Tarte de amêndoa	Shortcrust pastry tart with split almonds
Bolo de chocolate	Chocolate cake

Drinks

Long drinks

Mineral water (*água mineral*) has a long tradition in Portugal, its medicinal properties were recognised by the Romans. It is usually served still (*sem gás*) but can be carbonated (*com gás*).
Good quality fruit juices are found in Portugal together with the internationally known brands of long drinks.

Coffee

Coffee is served with milk in a glass (*galão*) or strong in a small cup (*café* or *bica*).

Beer

Beer (*cerveja*) is very popular in Portugal. The best known brand is "Sagres", brewed in Vialonga near Lisbon, and "Superbock", a light, sweet beer is also widely drunk. A *cerveja* is a bottled beer, an *imperial* a small draught beer, and a *caneca* is a large one.

Spirits

Ginjinha is the best known spirit, a sweet cherry liqueur which is sometimes the only drink available in tiny bars. *Bagaço*, a marc, or an *aguardente velha*, a mature brandy, are popular after a meal. *Medronho* is made from the fruit of the strawberry tree, *cana* is spirit distilled from sugar cane.

Wine

Vinho da casa (house wine) or *vinho de mesa* (table wine) are served with meals. Wine is either *vinho tinto* (red wine) or *vinho branco* (white wine). The best known wines come from the Dão, Douro, Ribatejo regions and from Colares, west of Lisbon. *Vinho verde* is a light, sparkling fresh wine which comes from the region north and east of Oporto and accounts for about 20% of Portuguese wine production. The description "green wine" refers to the production method: the grapes are harvested early and only fermented for a short time.

The most famous Portuguese wine is without doubt port wine, which gets its name from the northern town Oporto. The chief wine growing area on the upper slopes of the Douro is on slate-rich soils which give the wine its individual flavour. A mixture of partly fermented red wine and brandy is stored for years in barrels or, in the case of certain quality ports, in bottles. Dry port wines are popular as an aperitif, whereas the sweet ports are preferred as dessert wines.

Moscatel de Setúbal is a popular dessert wine which is pressed from the Muscatel grapes grown to the south of Lisbon.

Getting to Lisbon

By air

There are direct scheduled services from London and Manchester to Lisbon and direct services from the major cities in the United States and Canada. Seats are often also available on many charter services.

Lisbon airport "Portela de Sacavém" is situated to the north of the city, about 13km/8 miles from the city centre. Several connecting bus services operate to the city centre, including the green-white "Linha Verde" (No. 90), which provides a direct link from the airport via the town centre to the international railway station Santa Apolónia.

By car

There is a wide choice of cross-Channel car ferry services between Britain and France. From the French Channel ports it is approximately 1300 miles/2090km to Lisbon, 1200 miles/1930km to Oporto and 1350 miles/2170km to Faro. The recommended route is Paris–Bordeaux–Hendaye/Irún (French-Spanish border)–Burgos–Salamanca–Vilar Formoso (Spanish-Portuguese border)–Coimbra. An alternative is the car ferry to Spain (Plymouth to Santander) taking 24 hours, then travel onwards by road; information from Brittany Ferries, tel. (0752) 21321. From Santander to Lisbon is approximately 580 miles/934km. It is only worth taking a car to Lisbon to visit places which are not accessible by public transport. Portugal has few stretches of motorway. Driving in Lisbon itself is inadvisable.

By motorail

There is a motorail service from Paris to Lisbon. Passengers travel on the "Sud Express" and cars on a separate train, the car arriving in Lisbon a day later. Information from French Railways, 179 Piccadilly, London W1V 0BA; tel. (071) 409 3518.

By rail

There is daily service – the "Sud Express" – between London (Victoria) and Lisbon via Paris and Irún/Hendaye. This journey from Paris to Lisbon takes 25½ hours. Information from British Rail Travel Centres.

By bus

Eurolines operates a weekly service from London to Lisbon taking just over 18 hours. Tickets are available from any National Express or Eurolines agent. Alternatively, from Paris there is a service to Lisbon everyday except Monday.

Hospitals (hospital)

Central exchange

The central exchange for eight Lisbon hospitals (Hospitais Civis de Lisboa): tel. 87 22 40.

Hospitals

Hospital S. José
Rua José António Serrano. Tel. 8 86 08 48

British Hospital
(English-speaking doctors)
Rua Saraivo de Carvalho 49. Tel. 60 20 20 (day), 60 37 85 (night)

Hospital de Santa Maria
Av. Prof. Egas Moniz. Tel. 7 97 51 71, 7 97 51 91

Red Cross

Emergency service: tel. 3 01 77 77

Hotels (hotel)

Categories

There are five official categories of hotel. The scale ranges from luxury hotel (five stars) to modest hotels (one star).

Pensions

In Lisbon there are many smaller pensions, which are no less comfortable than the lower category hotels and are often cheaper. Pensions are classified into four categories, some are unclassified. A "residencial" is comparable with a pension in terms of comfort and price, an "albergaria" corresponds to a top category pension.

Reservations

There are numerous hotels and favourably-priced pensions in the city centre on both sides of the Rossio and the Avenida da Liberdade. It can be difficult, particularly in the summer months, to find accommodation after 6pm. The mid-range and lower-priced hotels are often fully booked. The tourist information centre in the Palácio Foz (see Information) is often helpful in finding accommodation. It is generally advisable to book in advance.

Tariffs

Room tariffs vary considerably according to the season. In the following table recommended seasonal prices for a double room with bath for one night are given, prices for single rooms are some 30% below those of double rooms. One night for two people in one of the listed pensions costs between 3000 and 10,000 escudos.

Category	Double room
*****	25,000–40,000 esc.
****	12,000–25,000 esc.
***	8000–17,000 esc.
**	5000–10,000 esc.
*	3000– 6000 esc.

Hotels
*****

Alfa Lisboa, Av. Columbano Bordalo Pinheiro; tel. 7 26 21 21, 375 r.
Altis, R. do Castilho 11; tel. 52 24 96, 307 r.
Avenida Palace, R. 1 de Dezembro 123; tel. 3 46 01 51, 92 r.
Lapa, R. Pau da Bandeira 4; tel. 3 95 00 05, 94 r.
Lisboa Sheraton & Towers, R. Latino Coelho 1; tel. 3 56 39 11, 386 r.
Meridien, R. do Castilho 149; tel. 69 04 00, 318 r.
Ritz Inter Continental, R. Rodrigo da Fonseca 88; tel. 69 20 20, 290 r.
Tivoli, Av. da Liberdade 185; tel. 53 01 81, 344 r.

Hotels
****

Continental, R. Laura Alves 9–13; tel. 7 93 66 22, 220 r.
Diplomático, R. do Castilho 74; tel. 3 56 20 41, 90 r.
Dom Manuel I, Av. Duque de Avila 189; tel. 57 61 60, 60 r.
Fénix, Pr. Marquês de Pombal 8; tel. 53 21 21, 114 r.
Flórida, R. Duque de Palmela 32; tel. 57 61 45, 108 r.
Holiday Inn Lisboa, Av. António José de Almeida 28 A; tel. 7 93 50 93, 169 r.
Lisboa, R. Barata Salgueiro 5; tel. 3 55 41 31, 61 r.

The Lisbon Sheraton

Hotel Meridien

Lisboa Penta, Av. dos Combatentes; tel. 7 26 40 54, 588 r.
Lisboa Plaza, Tr. do Salitre 7; tel. 3 46 39 22, 93 r.
Lutécia, Av. Frei Miguel Contreiras 52; tel. 89 70 31, 151 r.
Mundial, R. D. Duarte 4; tel. 86 31 01, 146 r.
Príncipe Real, R. da Alegria 53; tel. 3 46 01 16, 24 r.
Tivoli Jardim, R. Júlio César Machado 7; tel. 53 99 71, 119 r.

Hotels
***

Berna, Av. António Serpa 11–13; tel. 7 93 67 67, 154 r.
Botânico, R. Mãe de Agua 16–20; tel. 3 42 03 92, 30 r.
Dom Carlos, Av. Duque de Loulé 121; tel. 53 90 71, 73 r.
Eduardo VII, Av. Fontes Pereira de Melo 5; tel. 53 01 41, 121 r.
Embaixador, Av. Duque de Loulé 73; tel. 53 01 71, 96 r.
Flamingo, R. do Castilho 41; tel. 53 21 91, 39 r.
Miraparque, Av. Sidónio Pais 12; tel. 57 80 70, 110 r.
Novotel, Av. José Malhoa; tel. 7 26 60 22, 246 r.
Presidente, R. Alexandre Herculano 13; tel. 53 95 01, 59 r.
Rex, R. do Castilho 169; tel. 68 21 61, 41 r.
Roma, Av. da Roma 33; tel. 76 77 61, 263 r.
Torre, R. dos Jerónimos 8; tel. 3 63 73 32, 52 r.

Hotels
**

Borges, R. Garrett 108; tel. 3 46 19 51, 99 r.
Dom Alfonso Henriques, R. Cristóvão Falcão 8; tel. 8 14 65 74, 33 r.
Internacional, R. da Betesga 3; tel. 3 46 19 13, 54 r.
Portugal, R. João das Regras 4; tel. 87 75 81, 47 r.
Suíço Atlântico, R. da Glória 3; tel. 3 46 17 13, 82 r.
Vip, R. Fernão Lopes 25; tel. 3 52 19 23, 54 r.

Pensions

Alicante, Av. Duque de Loulé 20; tel. 53 05 14, 36 r.
Bragança, R. do Alecrim 12; tel. 3 42 70 61, 40 r.
Imperador, Av. 5 de Outubro 55; tel. 3 52 48 84, 43 r.
Nazareth, Av. António A. de Aguiar 25; tel. 54 20 16, 32 r.

Residência York House, R. das Janelas Verdes 47; tel. 3 96 24 35, 17 r.

Pousadas

See entry

Turismo de Habitação

See entry

Youth Hostels

See entry

Information

Information outside Portugal

The Portuguese tourist offices supply information about travel to Lisbon.

United Kingdom

Portuguese National Tourist Office
22–25A Sackville Street
London W1X 1DE. Tel. (071) 494 1441

Ireland

Portuguese National Tourist Office
Portuguese Embassy
Knocksinna House, Knocksinna
Fox Rock, Dublin 18. Tel. (01) 289 3569

USA

Portuguese National Tourist Office
919 North Michigan Avenue, Suite 3001
Chicago, IL 60611. Tel. (312) 266 9898

Portuguese National Tourist Office
590 Fifth Avenue (4th Floor)
New York, NY 10036. Tel. (212) 354 4403

Canada

Portuguese National Tourist Office
60 Bloor Street West
Toronto, Ontario M4W 3B8. Tel. (416) 921 7376

Office National du Tourisme Portugais
1801 McGill College Avenue, Suite 1150
Montreal, P.Q. H3A 2N4. Tel. (514) 282 1264

Information in Lisbon

"Turismo"
Palácio Foz, Praça dos Restauradores
Tel. 3 46 36 24, 3 42 52 31
Open: Mon.–Sat. 9am–8pm; Sun., pub. hols. 10am–6pm

Arrival hall, airport
Tel. 8 48 59 74, 89 36 89, 89 43 23. Open: daily 6am–8pm

Santa Apoleonia Railway Station
Tel. 86 78 48. Open: daily 9am–8pm

Estação Marítima de Alcântara (Alcântara Maritime Station/Conde de Óbidos)
Tel. 3 96 50 18

Miradouro de Santa Luzia (Santa Luzia vantage point)
Tel 87 07 20

Montra de Lisboa, shop 2016, Amoreiras Shopping Centre
Tel. 65 74 86

Direcção-Geral do Turismo
(principal tourist authority)
Av. António Augusto de Aguiar 86
Tel. 57 50 86

Insurance

General

Visitors are strongly advised to ensure that they have adequate holiday insurance, including loss or damage to luggage, loss of currency and jewellery.

Health

British citizens, like nationals of other European Community countries, are entitled to obtain medical care when on holiday in Portugal under the same basis as Portuguese people. Medical treatment is available at health centres (Centro de Saúde). It is necessary to show your passport, or if not a UK national, a medical care booklet exchanged for form E111 at the relevant regional health authority, the Administração Regional de Saúde. A charge may be made (apart from Casualty-type emergencies), but ask for the official (green) receipt to claim a refund at the nearest appointed bank. Only a small amount will be refunded, you will be responsible for the rest. For prescribed medicines you may be charged from 20–65%, for others you pay the full cost. Dental care is limited under the state scheme and charges are not refundable.

Additional private insurance

It is essential for visitors from non-EC countries. and advisable for EC nationals, to take out some form of short-term health insurance providing complete cover and possibly avoiding delays. Nationals of non-EC countries should certainly have insurance cover.

Vehicles

Visitors travelling by car should be ensure that their insurance is comprehensive and covers use of the vehicle in Portugal.

Language

Knowledge of foreign languages

The foreign languages most commonly spoken in Portugal are Spanish, English and French, and there are now also numbers of returned "guest workers" who have learnt some German while working in Germany. In any event, however, it is well worth having at least a smattering of Portuguese.

Portuguese

On first hearing Portuguese spoken a visitor may not quite know what to make of it, because it can sound rather like a Slav language (e.g. Polish). The written form of the language, however, can at once be recognised as a Romance language, and some knowledge of Latin or Spanish will be a great help in understanding it.

Grammar

Portuguese grammar is notable for the rich tense system of the verbs, in particular for the preservation of the Latin pluperfect (e.g. fõra, "I had been"). A further peculiarity is the inflected personal infinitive: "entramos na loja para comprarmos pão" = "we go into the shop to buy bread".
The plural is formed by the addition of "s", in some cases with the modification of the preceding vowel or consonant:

Singular	Plural
o animal	os animais
o hotel	os hoteis
a região	as regiões

The definite article is "o" (masculine) or "a" (feminine) in the singular, "os" or "as" in the plural. The declension of nouns and adjectives is simple. The nominative and accusative are the same; the genitive is indicated by "de" (of), the dative by "a" (to). The prepositions "de" and "a" combine with the definite article as follows:

de + o = do	de + a = da
de + os = dos	de + as = das
a + o = ao	a + os = aos
a + a = à	a + as = às

The Portuguese spoken in Portugal seems lacking in resonance, but is soft and melodious, without the hard accumulations of consonants and the rough gutturals of Castilian Spanish. It is notable for its frequent sibilants and for the nasalisation of vowels, diphthongs and triphthongs. Unstressed vowels and intervocalic consonants are much attenuated or disappear altogether. The stressed syllable of a word so dominates the rest that the vowels of the other syllables are radically altered in tone quality and not infrequently are reduced to a mere whisper. In the spoken language the boundaries between words are so blurred (in the phenomenon know as "sandhi") that the individual word within a group largely loses its independence: thus the phrase "os outros amigos" ("the other friends") is run together into a single phonetic unit and pronounced something like "usótrushamígush".

The nine vocalic phonemes used in Portuguese are represented by the five vowels a, e, i, o and u together with three diacritic signs or accents (´ ` ˆ), two of which (´ and ˆ) also indicate the stress. Nasalisation is indicated by the tilde (Portuguese "o til": ˜) or by the consonant "m" or "n".

The stress is normally on the penultimate syllable of a word ending in a vowel or in "m" or "s" and on the last syllable of a word ending in a consonant other than "m" or "s". Exceptions to this rule are marked by the use of an accent. It should be noted that "ia", "io" and "iu" are not treated as diphthongs as in Spanish but as combinations of separate vowels. Thus the word "agrário", for example, with the stress on the second "a", requires an accent to indicate this in Portuguese but not in Spanish where it is "agrario" without an accent.

Some peculiarities of Portuguese pronunciation

a	unstressed, like a whispered e
à	long "ah"
c	k before a, o and u; s before e and i
ç	s
ch	sh
e	unstressed, like a whispered i; in initial position before s, practically disappears ("escudo" pronounced "shkúdo"; Estoril pronounced "Shturíl")
ẽ	closed e
é	open e
g	hard g (as in "go") before a, o and u; zh (like s in "pleasure") before e and i
gu	hard g
h	mute
i	nasalised after u ("muito" pronounced "muínto")
j	zh
l	in final position as in English or, in Brazil, like a weak u ("animal" pronounced "animáu")
lh	ly (with consonantal y): cf. Spanish ll
m,n	in final position nasalise the preceding vowel
nh	ny (with consonantal y): cf. Spanish ñ
o	unstressed, like u
õ	closed o
ó	open o
qu	k
r	trilled

rr	strongly rolled
s	s before vowels; z between vowels; sh before hard consonants and in final position; zh before soft consonants
v	v
x	sh
z	in final position sh; otherwise z

The Brazilian pronunciation of Portuguese is markedly different from the Portuguese mainland. In particular final "s" and "z" are pronounced "s" and not "sh", and initial "r" sounds almost like "h".

Numbers

Cardinals

0 zero	22 vinte-e-dois (duas)
1 um, uma	30 trinta
2 dois, duas	31 trinta-e-um (uma)
3 três	40 quarenta
4 quatro	50 cinquenta
5 cinco	60 sessenta
6 seis	70 setenta
7 sete	80 oitenta
8 oito	90 noventa
9 nove	100 cem, cento
10 dez	101 cento-e-um (uma)
11 onze	200 duzentos, -as
12 doze	300 trezentos, -as
13 treze	400 quatrocentos, -as
14 catorze	500 quinhentos, -as
15 quinze	600 seiscentos, -as
16 dezasseis	700 setecentos, -as
17 dezassete	800 oitocentos, -as
18 dezoito	900 novecentos, -as
19 dezanove	1000 mil
20 vinte	2000 dois (duas) mil
21 vinte-e-um (uma)	1 million um milhão de

Ordinals

1st primeiro, -a	11th undécimo, -a; décimo primeiro
2nd segundo, -a	12th duodécimo, -a; décimo segundo
3rd terceiro, -a	13th décimo terceiro
4th quarto, -a	20th vigésimo, -a
5th quinto, -a	21st vigésimo primeiro, -a
6th sexto, -a	30th trigésimo, -a
7th sétimo, -a	40th quadragésimo, -a
8th oitavo, -a	50th quinquagésimo, -a
9th nono, -a	60th sexuagésimo, -a
10th décimo, -a	100th centésimo, -a

Idioms and Vocabulary

Forms of address

Men are usually addressed as "o Senhor", women as "minha Senhora". If you know a man's name you should address him by his name with the prefix "o Senhor"; younger women, particularly if they are unmarried, are addressed by their Christian name with the prefix "a Senhora", older ladies only by Senhora Dona and their Christian name. "You" in direct address is "o Senhor", "a Senhora" or "Vossê", in the plural "os Senhores", "as Senhoras" or "Vossês".
In Portuguese names, which are frequently very long, the maternal surname usually comes first.

Idioms

Good morning, good day	Bom dia
Good afternoon	Boa tarde
Good evening, good night	Boa noite
Goodbye	Adeus, Até à vista
Yes, no	Sim, não
Excuse me (apologising)	Desculpe, Perdão
Excuse me (e.g. when passing in front of someone)	Com licença
After you (e.g. offering something)	A vontade!
Please (asking for something)	Faz favor
Thank you (very much)	(Muito) obrigado
Not at all (You're welcome)	De nada, Não tem de què
Do you speak English?	O senhor fala inglês?
A little, not much	Um pouco, não muito
I do not understand	Não compreendo (nada)
What is the Portuguese for . . .?	Como se diz em português . . .?
What is the name of this church?	Como chama-se esta igreja?
Have you any rooms?	Tem um quarto livre?
I should like . . .	Queria . . .
A room with private bath	Um quarto com banho
With full board	Com pensão completa
What does it cost?	Quanto custa?
Everything included	Tudo incluído
That is very dear	E muito caro
Bill, please!	Faz favor, a conta!
Where is . . . Street?	Onde é a rua . . .?
the road to?	a estrada para . . .?
a doctor?	um médico?
a dentist?	um dentista?
Right, left	A direita, esquerda
Straight ahead	Sempre a direito
Above, below	Em cima, em baixo
When is it open?	A que horas está aberto?
How far?	Que distância?
Wake me at six	Chama-me às seis

Road signs

Alfândega	Customs
Alto!	Stop
Atenção!	Caution
Auto-estrada	Highway
Bifurcação	Road fork
Cuidado!	Caution
Curva perigosa	Dangerous curve
Dê passagem!	Give way/yield
Desvio	Diversion
Devagar!	Slow
Direcção única; Sentido único	One-way street
Estacionamento proibido	Parking prohibited
Grua	Tow-away zone
Ir a passo!	Dead slow
Ir pela direita, esquerda	Keep right, left
Nevoeiro	Mist, fog
Obras na estrada	Road works
Parque de estacionamento	Car park, parking place
Passagem proibida	No entry
Peões	Pedestrians
Perigo!	Danger!
Portagem	Toll
Praia	Beach
Proibido ultrapassar	No overtaking
Rebanhos	Beware of livestock

Language

Travelling	aircraft	aeroplano, avião
	airport	aeroporto
	all aboard!	partida!
	all change!	mudar!
	arrival	chegada
	baggage	bagagem
	baggage check	guia, senha
	bus	autocarro, camioneta
	conductor (ticket-collector)	revisor
	couchette car	furgoneta
	departure	partida
	fare	preço
	flight	vôo
	information	informação
	line (railway)	via férrea
	luggage	bagagem
	luggage ticket	guia, senha
	no smoking (carriage)	não fumadores
	platform	plataforma, gare
	porter	moço de fretes
	restaurant car	carruagem restaurante
	railway station	estação
	sleeping car	carruagem-cama
	smoking (carriage)	fumadores
	steward	comissário de bordo
	stewardess	hospedeira (do ar)
	stop	paragem
	ticket	bilhete
	ticket-collector (conductor)	revisor
	ticket office	bilheteria, guichet
	timetable	horário
	toilet	toilette
	train	comboio
	waiting room	sala de espera
Months	January	janeiro
	February	fevereiro
	March	março
	April	abril
	May	maio
	June	junho
	July	julho
	August	agosto
	September	setembro
	October	outubro
	November	novembro
	December	dezembro
	month	mês
	year	ano
Days of the week	Monday	segunda-feira
	Tuesday	terça-feira
	Wednesday	quarta-feira
	Thursday	quinta-feira
	Friday	sexta-feira
	Saturday	sábado
	Sunday	domingo
	day	dia
	holiday, feast-day	dia de festa, dia feriado

Holidays and Religious Festivals

New Year's Day	Ano-Novo
Easter	Páscoa
Ascension	Ascensão
Whitsun	Espírito Santo, Pentecostes
Corpus Christi	Festa do Corpo de Deus
All Saints	Todos os Santos
Christmas	Natal
New Year's Eve	Véspera do Ano-Novo, Noite de São Silvestre

At the post office

address	endereço
air mail	correio aéreo
by airmail	por avião
express letter	carta urgente
letter	carta
letter-box, post-box	marco postal
packet	embrulho
parcel	pacote
postage	porte
postcard	bilhete postal
poste restante	poste restante
postman	carteiro
post office	correio
registered letter	carta registrada
stamp	selo, estampilha
telegram	telegrama
telephone	telephone
telex	telex

Portuguese menu

açorda	garlic and bread soup
água	water
água mineral	mineral water
aguardente, brandy	brandy
alho	garlic
almoço	lunch
amêndoa	almond
antepastos	starter, horse d'oeuvre
arroz	rice
assado	grilled
aves	poultry
azeite	olive oil
azeitonas	olives
batatas	potatoes
batatas fritas	fried potatoes
bebidas	drinks
bife	beef
bolo	cake
cabrito	kid (goat)
caça	game
café	coffee
café com leite	coffee with milk
carne	meat
carneiro	mutton
carta (or lista, ementa)	menu
cebolas	onions
ceia	late-night snack, supper
cerveja	beer
chá	tea
chávena	cup
chocolate	chocolate
coelho	rabbit
colher	spoon

colher de chá	teaspoon
copo	glass
corço	venison
cordeiro	lamb
couve	cabbage
couve-flor	cauliflower
cozido	cooked
doces	sweets
ervilhas	peas
espargos	asparagus
espinafre	spinach
faca	knife
feijões	beans
frango	chicken
fruta	fruit
garfo	fork
gelado	ice cream
guardanapo	napkin
jantar	dinner, evening meal
javalí	boar
laranja	orange
lebre	hare
leitão	sucking pig
leite	milk
legumes (hortaliça)	vegetables
maçã	apple
manteiga	butter
massa(s)	pasta
molho	sauce
mostarda	mustard
óleo	oil
ovo (ovos estrelados)	egg (fried)
pão	bread
pãozinho	roll
pato	duck
peixe	fish
pepinos	cucumber
pequeno almoço	breakfast
pera	pear
perdiz	partridge
perua	turkey
pimenta	pepper
pimento	paprika, green pepper
porco	pork
prato	plate
prato do dia	dish of the day
presunto	ham
queijo	cheese
repolho	white cabbage
sal	salt
salada	salad
salame	salami
sobremesas	dessert
sopa	soup
sumo de fruta	fruit juice
talher	cutlery
tomates	tomatoes
uva	grapes
vaca	beef
vinagre	vinegar
vinho	wine
vitela	veal

Language courses

General

Some tour operators offer specialised language holidays to Portugal. In Lisbon there are various institutions offering language courses which are, on average, of between two and four weeks' duration. Some courses also include an additional programme of activities.

Language schools in Lisbon

Berlitz
Av. Conde Valbom 6; tel. 3 52 01 23

Cambridge School
Av. Guerra Junqueiro 8; tel. 8 48 45 44

CIAL Centro de Linguas
Av. da República 14; tel. 7 93 02 31

Prolinguas
Rua Saraiva de Carvalho 84 Pt 2; tel. 3 97 88 10

Faculdade de Letres da Universidade de Lisboa
Cidade Universitária; tel. 7 93 33 56

Language schools in Sintra

Mons Lunae
Língua e Cultura Portuguesa
Rua Almada Guerra 26
2710 Sintra. Tel. 01/9 23 49 41

Libraries

Lisbon has several libraries, some of which are very specialised. Books can usually be consulted in the reading rooms on production of a passport. English-language books are obtainable in the following libraries:

Biblioteca Nacional (National Library)
Campo Grande 83 (Metro: Entrecampos)
(See A–Z, Cidade Universitária)

Biblioteca da Fundação Calouste Gulbenkian
(Gulbenkian Foundation Library)
Av. de Berna 45 (basement of museum building)
(See A–Z, Fundação Calouste Gulbenkian)

Goethe Institute Library
Campo dos Mártires da Pátria 36

Lost Property

Police

Lost property can be collected from the central police lost property office: PSP – Secção dos Achados, Rua dos Anjos 56 A; tel. 3 46 61 41.

Public local transport

Lost property found on public transport belonging to the Carris company is collected at the office in Largo do Carmo, beside the Elevador do Carmo; tel. 3 46 50 35. For objects left on the Metro go to the lost property department in Restauradores Metro Station; tel. 3 42 77 07.

Airport

For items left at the airport; tel. 8 41 54 26.

Markets (mercado)

Lisbon

Markets are held daily in nearly every district of Lisbon. Altogether there are over 30 market halls.

Mercado de Ribeira Nova

Mercado da Ribeira Nova
Av. 24 de Julho. Mon.–Sat. 6am–2pm
(no meat or fresh fish for sale on Mondays). (See A–Z, Bica)

Rua de São Pedro
Outdoor fish market in the long, narrow Rua de São Pedro in Alfama district.
Mon.–Sat. mornings. (See A–Z, Alfama)

Feira da Ladra (flea market)
Campo de Santa Clara
Tues. and Sat. 9am–6pm. (See A–Z, Alfama)

Outskirts of Lisbon

Sintra (São Pedro district)
every 2nd and 4th Sunday of the month

Cascais
Wednesday mornings

Carcavelos
(chiefly clothes). Thursday mornings

Medical Assistance

Emergency

In an emergency medical assistance or an ambulance can be summoned by telephoning the charge-free number 115.

Lisbon hospitals' emergency service

The central exchange number for several Lisbon hospitals is 87 22 40. In emergencies contact the accident department (urgência) of the nearest hospital (see Hospitals).

British hospital

English is spoken at the British Hospital, Rua Saraiva de Carvalho 49; tel. 60 20 20 (day), 60 37 85 (night).

Red Cross

The emergency service of the Cruz Vermelha (Red Cross) can be contacted by telephoning 3 01 77 77. Charges are payable for house calls.

English-speaking doctors

Information concerning English-speaking doctors is available from the British Hospital (see above).

Medical cover

In accordance with EC regulations free or reduced-cost emergency medical treatment is available in Portugal for members of other EC countries, on production of your passport, or if not a UK national, form E111. In the event of treatment being necessary your passport or form E111 must be taken to the health centre (Centro de Saúde). Further information from the regional health service office (Administraçáo de Saúde).

Monuments and Sculpture

Historical personalities

Afonso de Albuquerque
(See A–Z, Belém)

Dom João I. (See A–Z, Praça da Figueira)

Dom José I. (See A–Z, Praça do Comércio)

Dom Pedro IV. (See A–Z, Rossio)

Duque de Saldanha
During the Miguelist Wars Commander Saldanha supported the Liberals under Pedro IV.
Tomás Costa, 1909. Praça do Duque de Saldanha

Duque de Terceira
One of the leaders in the war against the absolutist Miguel I.
Simões de Almeida, 1877. Praça do Duque de Terceira

Fernão de Magalhaẽs
Fernão de Magalhaẽs set off in 1519 to circumnavigate the world for Spain. In 1520 he rounded the tip of South America through the straits which were later named after him, the Magellan Straits. He died on the Philippine island of Mactan in battle with the natives. One of his ships returned to Europe thereby completing the first successful circumnavigation of the world. The monument was a gift from the Chilean government in 1950.
Guilherme Cordoba, 1950
Praça do Chile

Marquẽs de Pombal. (See A–Z, Praça Marquẽs de Pombal)

Marquês de Sá da Bandeira
Supporter of the Liberals under Pedro IV against the Miguelists.
Giovanni Ciniselli, 1884
Praça do D. Luis I.

Dr Sousa Martins
The monument in front of the old Medical Faculty is dedicated to a doctor and writer who was reputed to have miraculous healing powers, even after his death in 1897. The base of the monument is decorated with flowers, candles and parts of the anatomy made of wax and plaques, which are still placed there today in gratitude for successful recoveries.
Costa Mota, 1907
Campo dos Mártires da Pátria

Monuments and Sculpture

Cultural personalities

Júlia Lopes de Almeida
Born in Rio de Janeiro in 1862 the Brasilian author wrote novels, stories and plays. The monument is a gift from Brasilian women to the women of Portugal.
Margarida Lopes de Almeida, 1953
Jardim Gomes de Armorim, Praceta da Av. António José de Almeida

Rosa Araújo
(See A–Z, Avenida da Liberdade

Camilo Castelo Branco
Born in 1825 an author whose novels were renowned for their rich vocabulary and realism. Camilo Castelo Branco went blind and committed suicide in 1890.
António Duarte, 1950
Av. do Duque de Loulé

Luís de Camões
(See A–Z, Chiado)

Chiado
(See A–Z, Chiado)

Eduardo Coelho
(See A–Z, Bairro Alto)

Almeida Garrett
Almeida Garrett (1799–1854) is one of the most important Romantic novelists. Political criticism pervades his works. As a supporter of the Liberals he fought in the army of Pedro IV against the absolutist government of Miguel. He was politically active shortly before his death.
Barata Feyo, 1950
Avenida da Liberdade

Calouste Gulbenkian
(See A–Z, Fundação Calouste Gulbenkian)

Alfredo Keil
(See A–Z, Avenida da Liberdade)

Fernando Pessoa
(See A–Z, Chiado)

Rafael Bordalo Pinheiro
Rafael Bordalo Pinheiro (1846–1905) was famous primarily for his ceramics. He began his artistic career as a caricaturist, which is reflected in his ceramics. There is a museum dedicated to him (see A–Z, Museu Rafael Bordalo Pinheiro).

Raul Xavier, 1921
Campo Grande

Eça de Queirós
(See A–Z, Chiado)

Cesário Verde
A writer who lived in the second half of the 19th c. whose literary works centred on the town of Lisbon.
Maximano Alves, 1955
Jardim de Cesário Verde,
Rua de Dona Estefânia

Saints

Santo António
Not only is there a statue in front of the Museu Antoniano dedicated to the patron saint of Alfama (see A–Z, Museums) but also in the much newer suburb of Alvalade.
António Duarte, 1972
Praça de Alvalade

São Vicente. (See A–Z, Alfama)

Allegorical figures and symbolic monuments

Adamastor. (See A–Z, Bica)

Ardina. (See A–Z, Bairro Alto)

Neptuno
part of a fountain
Machado de Castro, 1771
Praça da Estefânia

Pelourinho de Lisboa. (See A–Z, Paços do Conselho)

Tejo and Douro
(See A–Z, Avenida da Liberdade and Praça do Comércio)

Monuments of historic events

Chão Salgado (salted ground); 1759
Rua de Belém
In a side alley off the Rua de Belém (near No. 118) there is an inconspicuous stone column commemorating an event in 1758. In September of that year an assasination attempt was made on King José I, for which members of the families of the Dukes of Aveiro and Távoras were held responsible. The Duke of Aveiro's property, which stood on this spot, was torn down and the earth mixed with salt to render it useless in the future.

Guerra Peninsular (See A–Z, Campo Grande)

Mortos da Grande Guerra (See A–Z, Avenida da Liberdade)

Padrão dos Descobrimentos
(See A–Z, Padrão dos Descobrimentos)

Restauradores
(See A–Z, Praça dos Restauradores)

Motoring

Automobile Club

Automóvel Clube de Portugal (ACP)
Rua Rosa Araújo 2426. 1200 Lisbon. Tel. 56 39 31

Breakdown

The breakdown service of the ACP can be contacted by dialling (01) 9 42 50 95 in Lisbon and the south and (02) 31 67 32 in the north. Should you breakdown on the Ponte 25 de Abril (on the southern approach to Lisbon), keep the vehicle as far to the right-hand side of the bridge as possible and hang a white handkerchief out of the window and wait for the patrol vehicle.

Emergency telephones

Orange emergency telephones are situated on the motorways.

Fuel

Petrol prices in Portugal are higher than in the rest of Europe. Lead-free petrol (gasolina sem chumbo) is not available everywhere. There are several petrol stations in the city which stay open until midnight.

Motoring

Traffic regulations

Traffic regulations in Portugal are more or less the same as in other European countries where vehicles travel on the right. Road signs and markings correspond to international standards.

Priority

Priority is given to traffic on roads which are signposted by a yellow diamond with a black and white border. Otherwise traffic coming from the right has priority, motorised vehicles having priority over unmotorised vehicles.

Speed limits

In built-up areas the speed limit for cars and motorcycles is 60kmph/37mph and 90kmph/55mph on ordinary roads. On motorways the speed limit is 120kmph/74mph
For lorries, buses and vehicles with trailers the speed limits are lower: in built-up areas 50kmph/ 31mph, on ordinary roads 70kmph/ 43mph and on motorways 90kmph/55mph. The minimum speed on motorways is 40kmph/24mph.
Drivers who have not held a full driving licence for a full year may not exceed 90kmph/55mph and must display a yellow disc bearing the figure "90" at the rear of the car, obtainable from any vehicle accessory shop in Portugal.

Seat belts

Seat belts must be worn outside built-up areas.

Alcohol

The blood alcohol limit is 0.5 grammes per litre. Driving under the influence of alcohol is forbidden.

Museums (museu)

General

It is often the case that one or other of Lisbon's museums is closed for renovation and so it is wise to check before visiting a particular museum at the tourist information office. Opening times are also subject to change. In general, however, most museums are open from 10am–5 or 6pm but are closed on Mondays, some close at lunchtime between 12.30–1pm and 2–2.30pm.
Unfortunately information boards and brochures in the smaller and more interesting museums are usually only written in Portuguese.

List of museums

Aquário Vasco da Gama (Vasco da Gama Aquarium)
Rua Direita, Dafundo (west of Belém)
Open: daily 10am–6pm (Wed. admission free)
Tram: 15 Direction Cruz Quebrada, Stop Aquário Vasco da Gama
Marine animals of all kinds are on display: fish from every ocean in the world, molluscs, sea anemones, sea horses, giant turtles, piranhas, electric eels. The main attraction is a giant octopus weighing 207kg (lula gigante) and 8.2m/26ft long, caught at a depth of 130m/426ft. On the upper floor are rooms containing shellfish, stuffed seabirds and preserved sea creatures.

Casa Museu de Dr Anastácio Gonçalves
(Dr Anastácio Gonçalves Musuem House) Av. 5 de Outubro 8
Open: Tues.–Sun. 10am–5pm (closed public holidays)
Metro: Picoas, Saldanha
The fur dealer and art lover José Anastácio Gonçalves bought the former studio and house of the Portuguese artist José Malhoa at the beginning of the 1930s. His collection includes many paintings by Malhoa, Columbano and other Portuguese artists from that circle, ceramics, Chinese porcelain, valuable furniture and carpets. Gonçalves was a friend of the oil magnate and art collector Calouste Gulbenkian (see Famous Personalities) who lived in the nearby Hotel Aviz.

Centro de Arte Moderna (See A–Z, Fundação Calouste Gulbenkian)

Museu d'Águã (Water museum)
(See A–Z, Museu d'Água Manuel da Maia)

Museu Antoniano (Museum of St Anthony)
Largo de Santo António da Sé 24
Open: Tues.–Sun. 10am–1pm, 2–6pm
Tram: 28, 28B; 37
This small museum houses the most varied and unusual exhibits of the patron saint of Lisbon, who was supposedly born on the site of the neighbouring church Santo António da Sé, named after him (See A–Z, Sé Patriarcal). Illustrations of the saint in the form of oil paintings, sketches, etchings, medallions, cushions, stamps, embroidered and hand-sewn collages are on display here, together with statuettes made from ceramic, wood and stone ranging from 2cm high to lifesize.

Museu Arqueológico (Museum of Archaeology)
(See A–Z, Igreja do Carmo)

Museu de Arte Decorativo (Museum of Decorative Art)
(See A–Z, Museu de Arte Decorativo)

Museu de Arte Sacra (Museum of Sacral Art)
(See A–Z, Igreja de São Roque)

Museu do Bombeiro R.S.B. (Fire brigade Museum)
Av. de D. Carlos I (Regimento Sapadores Bombeiros, R.S.B., building)
Open: Tues. and Fri. 3.30–5pm. Tram: 28. Bus: 39, 48
Miniature fire engines and equipment from the 19th c., commemorative medals and photographs of former firemen are on display in the four rooms of the museum. The original engines which served as models for the miniatures have been preserved but cannot be exhibited here for lack of space. Some major fires in Lisbon are documented by photographs and newspaper articles. There are collections of items from houses destroyed by fire (e.g. Chiado fire)

Museu Calouste Gulbenkian
(See A–Z, Fundação Calouste Gulbenkian

Museu da Cidade (City Museum).
(See A–Z, Museu da Cidade)

Museu da Cinemateca (Museum of Cinematography)
Rua Barata Salgueiro 39
Open: Mon.–Fri. 9.30am–12.30pm, 2–5.30pm
Bus: 39; tram: 20; metro: Avenida, Rotunda
This small collection in the Cinematica Portuguesa building came into being through the donations of private individuals and institutions. On show are equipment and materials from the beginning of film such as the laterna magica from the 19th c. with various colour celluloid strips, projectors, old cameras and lenses. Photographs depict scenes from old Portuguese and international films.

Museu dos CTT dos Comunicações (Postal Museum)
Forum Picoas, Av. Fontes Pereira de Melo
Open: Tues.–Sun. 10am–5pm (closed public holidays)
Metro: Picoas
Models of postal coaches, mail boats, postal cars, letter boxes, teleprinters, old and modern telephone equipment, photographs, etc. illustrating the development of the postal service.

Museu Etnográfico (Museum of Ethnography)
(See A–Z, Museu Etnográfico)

Museu de Etnologia (Museum of Ethnology)
(See A–Z, Museu de Etnologia)

Museu dos Serviços Geológicos de Portugal
(Museum of Geological Services of Portugal)
Rua da Academia das Ciências 19
Open: Mon.–Fri. 9am–12.30pm, 2–5.30pm
Tram: 20, 24. Bus: 15, 58
The Institute Museum houses a very extensive collection of geological and archaeological finds from Portugal, yet it is not very well documented. On view are bones and teeth of dinosaurs, fossils, rocks and prehistoric arrowheads and jewellery. A small modern section explains the geology of Portugal.

Museu Instrumental do Conservatório Nacional
(Museum of Musical Instruments)
Campo Grande 83 (National Library)
Open: Mon.–Fri. 10am–1pm, 2–5pm
Metro: Entrecampos
The conservatory's collection comprises musical instruments from the 17th–19th c. including some old fado guitars "guitarras portuguesas".

Museu João de Deus
Av. Alvares Cabral 69
Open: 10am–noon, 2.30–5pm
Bus: 9, 20, 22, 27, 28
Small museum and library established to commemorate the writer and pedagogue João de Deus. His pedagogical method, similar to the Montessori method, is still the basis for 29 kindergartens in Portugal.

Museu do Livro (Book Museum)
Campo Grande 83 (National Library)
Open: Mon.–Fri. 10am–7pm; Sun. 10am–5pm
Bus: 3, 7, 7B, 33, 46
This permanent exhibition sets out to provide a cross-section of the history of the book from the Middle Ages to the 19th c. One of the items on display is the first large book to be printed after Gutenberg invented book-printing.

Museu da Marinha (Maritime Museum)
(See A–Z, Mosteiro dos Jerónimos)

Museu das Marionetas (Puppet Museum)
(See A–Z, Museu das Marionetas)

Museu Militar (Military Museum)
(See A–Z, Museu Militar)

Museu Nacional de Arqueologia e Etnologia
(National Museum of Archaeology and Ethnology)
(See A–Z, Mosteiro dos Jerónimos)

Museu Nacional de Arte Antiga (National Museum of Ancient Art)
(See A–Z, Museu Nacional de Arte Antiga)

Museu Nacional de Arte Contemporânea
(National Museum of Contemporary Art)
(See A–Z, Museu Nacional de Arte Contemporânea)

Museu Nacional do Azulejo (National Tile Museum)
(See A–Z, Convento da Madre de Deus)

Museu Nacional dos Coches (National Coach Museum)
(See A–Z, Museu Nacional dos Coches)

Museu Nacional de História Natural
(National Natural History Museum)
(See A–Z, Jardim Botânico)

Museu Nacional do Teatro (National Theatre Museum)
(See A–Z, Parque do Monteiro-Mor)

Museu Nacional do Traje (National Costume Museum)
(See A–Z, Parque do Monteiro-Mor)

Museu Rafael Bordalo Pinheiro
(See A–Z, Museu Rafael Bordalo Pinheiro)

Museu de São Roque. (See A–Z, Igreja de São Roque)

Newspapers

International newspapers and magazines are on sale at various newspaper stands in the centre and at the airport.

Night Life

General

As is the case in many south European countries night life begins relatively late. Some bars and discos only begin to fill up after midnight. Many of them are not recognisable as such from the outside and there is a bell to ring to gain admission. Admission charges are high if there is live music but this usually includes a free drink.
The weekly magazines "Sábado" or "Se7e" publish an up-to-date list of bars, pubs and restaurants.

Bars

Café de São Bento
Rua de São Bento 212

Procópio
Alto São Francisco 21 (at the Jardim Amoreiras)

Bairro Alto Bar
Travessa Inglesinhos 50

Alcântara-Mar
Rua Cozinhaga Económica 11

Pé Sujo
Largo São Martinho 6
(Brazilian)

Chafarica
Calçada do São Vicente 81. (Brazilian)

Bipi-Bipi
Rua Oliveira Martins 6. (Brazilian)

Bora-Bora Bar
Av. Almirante Reis 194. (Indonesian)

	Cerca Moura Largo das Portas do Sol 4 (outside seating)
	Chapito Costa do Castelo 7 (outside seating)
	Ópera Travessa das Mónicas 65
Discos	Skylab Rua Artilharia Um 69
	Whispers Av. Fontes Pereira de Melo 35
	Plateau Rua das Janelas Verdes
	Kremlin Escadinhas da Praia 5
	La Folie Rua Diário de Notícias 122
Jazz	Hot Club de Portugal Praça da Alegria 39
Casino	Casino in Estoril (in Avenida Aida)

Opening times

Shops	Individual shops are generally open Mon.–Fri. from 9am to 1pm and from 3 to 7pm, Sat. from 9am to 1pm and some open on Saturday afternoons in the winter months. Tobacconists and food shops also open in the evenings and on Sundays.
Shopping centres	Most shopping centres do not open until 10am, remaining open until midnight and also at weekends.
Chemists	Opening hours are Mon.–Fri. 9am–1pm and 3–7pm, Saturdays 9am–1pm. The addresses of duty chemists outside of normal opening times are posted on the door.
Banks	Most banks open Mon.–Fri. from 8am to 3pm, some close between noon and 1pm. A few banks in the city centre open again from 6–11pm Mon.–Sat.
Post offices	Post offices generally open Mon.–Fri. 9am–12.30pm and 2.30–6pm. Most post offices open from 8.30am–6.30pm and are also open Saturday mornings. For exceptions see Post Offices.
Museums	Most museums open Tues.–Sun. from 10am to 5 or 6pm, some close at lunchtime for one or one and a half hours.
Churches	Smaller churches are usually closed during the day, usually opening for evening mass around 8pm and occasionally for one or two hours at lunchtime.
Restaurants	Many restaurants open at lunchtime for about two hours (mostly from midday) and again in the evening from 7pm.

Parks and Gardens (parques e jardins)

General

On account of the climate and the restricted size of living accommodation the many parks and public gardens in Lisbon provide a meeting place for groups and also entire families. The viewing points (miradouro; see entry) are also laid out as small parks.

Gardens

Jardim Alfredo Keil. (See A–Z, Avenida da Liberdade)

Jardim das Amoreiras. Praça das Amoreiras

Jardim Botânico. (See A–Z, Jardim Botânico)

Jardim Botânico da Ajuda. (See A–Z, Palácio Nacional da Ajuda

Jardim Braancamp Freire. Campo dos Mártires da Pátria

Campo Grande. (See A–Z, Campo Grande)

Parque Eduardo VII. (See A–Z, Parque Eduardo VII)

Jardim da Estrela. (See A–Z, Jardim da Estrela)

Jardim Fialho de Almeida. Praça das Flores

Parque Florestal de Monsanto
(See A–Z, Parque Florestal de Monsanto)

Jardim França Borges. (See A–Z, Bairro Alto)

Parque Gulbenkian
(See A–Z, Fundadcão Calouste Gulbenkian

Parque do Monteiro-Mor
(See A–Z, Parque do Monteiro-Mor)

Jardins do Palácio dos Marqueses de Fronteira
(See A–Z, Palácio dos Marqueses de Fronteira)

Jardins do Palácio Nacional de Queluz
(See A–Z, Queluz)

Jardim da Praça Afonso de Albuquerque
(See A–Z, Belém)

Jardim da Praça do Império. (See A–Z, Belém)

Tapada das Necessidades
(See A–Z, Palácio Real das Necessidades)

Jardim Tropical. (See A–Z, Belém)

Jardim Zoológico. (See A–Z, Jardim Zoológico)

Police

P.S.P.

The city of Lisbon is under the jurisdiction of the P.S.P. (Polícia de Segurança Pública). Tel. 3 46 61 41 (day and night).

Reporting theft

P.S.P., Rua Capelo 13 (Chiado); some of the police officers speak English.

Notice indicating sale of postage stamps

A post box

Post

Mail	Letters and postcards to Europe usually take between three and seven days. All mail is carried by air without any extra charges or formalities.
Postage stamps	Postage stamps (selos) are sold in post offices and shops displaying the sign "CTT Selos".
Postal charges	Letter (carta, up to 20g) and postcard (bilhete postal): to EC countries 65 escudos, to non-EC countries 85 escudos, outside Europe 120 escudos.
Letter boxes	Letter boxes in Portugal are red; there are small boxes on walls or free-standing pillars on the pavement.
Post offices	Post offices are generally open Mon.–Fri. 9am–12.30pm and 2.30–6pm. Main post offices open from 8.30am–6.30pm and are also open Saturday mornings. The main post office in the Praça do Comércio is open from 8.30am to 6.30pm. The post office at the Praça dos Restauradores 58 opens Mon.–Sun. 8am–1pm and the post office at the airport is always open.
Poste restante	Poste restante should be labelled "Posta restante" and sent to a particular post office. Mail not addressed to a particular post office can be collected from the main post office on the Praça do Comércio (side entrance in the Rua do Arsenal 27). A passport or identity card must be shown.
Telegrams	Telegrams can be sent from a post office, a hotel reception desk or by telephoning 183.

Pousadas

General

Pousadas are state-run hotels which have been converted from castles, palaces, monasteries and even modern buildings. The interior is always highly-appointed, sometimes antique. They are mostly found in places of cultural or historical interest, in regions of exceptional scenery or in popular towns. The length of stay in pousadas is usually restricted to five days. As there is a limited number of beds advance booking is recommended. Prices are high by Portuguese standards, the pousadas are classified in three categories: CH, C and B. Pousadas in category CH are always in historical buildings. A double room in this category with breakfast in high season (July to September) costs between £90 and £110.

Pousadas near Lisbon

There are three pousadas of CH category near Lisbon:

Pousada do Castelo, 9 r.
Paço Real, 2510 Óbidos; tel. (062) 95 91 05

Pousada de Palmela, 28 r.
Castelo de Palmela, 2950 Palmela; tel. (01) 2 35 12 26

Pousada de São Filipe, 14 r.
Castelo de São Filipe, 2900 Setúbal; tel. (065) 52 38 44

Public Holidays

January 1st	New Year
February/March	Carnival
March/April	Good Friday
April 25th	Dia da Liberdade (national holiday to commemorate the Carnation revolution on April 25th 1974)
May 1st	Labour Day
May/June	Corpus Christi
June 10th	Dia de Portugal (national holiday: anniversary of the death of the writer Camões on June 10th 1580)
June 13th	Dia de Santo António – St Anthony's Day, patron saint of Lisbon
August 15th	Assumption Day
October 5th	Dia da República (national holiday to commemorate the fall of the monarchy on October 5th 1910)
November 1st	All Saints' Day
December 1st	Dia da Restauração (national holiday to commemorate the restoration of Portugal's independence from Spain in 1640)
December 8th	Immaculate Conception
December 25th	Christmas

Public Transport

General

Public transport in the city and surroundings comprises buses, trams and lifts belonging to the "Carris" company, the Metro and boats owned by "Transtejo", local train services operated by the "Companhia dos Caminhos de Ferro Portugueses" and overland buses, operated by various companies.
To stop a tram or bus a hand signal must be given, bearing in mind that the bus stops are not used so much in the evenings. In Lisbon it is customary to queue for buses, trams and lifts. Passengers are admitted in turn.

Metro

The fastest means of transport in Lisbon is the Metro which operates from 24 stations. The only changeover station is the "Rotunda". With the rebuilding of the burnt-down Chiado district there are plans to extend the route to the Cais do Sodré and an extension northwards has long been under discussion. At peak periods the Metro is completely overcrowded and passengers are warned of increased thefts at this time.
The Metro operates from 6.30am to 1am, the average journey time between stations is 1½ minutes. Metro stations are signposted by a red "M" at the entrances.

Buses

The principal means of transport are the orange-coloured buses (autocarro) of the "Carris" company. Altogether there are 80 bus lines and five additional night services. Some bus services cease at about 9.30pm, some continue until about 1.30am. The night buses operate twice an hour. Bus stops are recognisable by the word "paragem" (bus stop) and the bus number.

Trams

The future of the old "eléctricos" is uncertain as they incur high losses for the "Carris" company. However, they are an important tourist attraction and removing the tramlines from the city's streets would be undesirable. Apart from which, they are the ideal means of transport for the many hilly routes. Line 28 is of particular tourist interest (see Sightseeing Programme). Altogether there are 18 routes. They operate a similar timetable to the buses but some lines do not operate on Sundays. The tram stops are difficult to recognise; unlike the buses they are marked by a sign with just the word "paragem" and no route number. The numbers hang unexpectedly high up above on the cable. (See also City Sightseeing – City tours by trams.)

Lifts

The lift (elevador) is a practical means of transport given Lisbon's topography. They were built at the end of the 19th c., four of them have been preserved and are operated by the "Carris" company. The Elevador do Carmo (See A–Z, Elevador do Carmo) is an interesting attraction, a lift with two cabins. The remaining three (Elevador da Glória, Elevador da Bica, Elevador da Lavra) are funicular railways each with one carriage. The lifts operate from 7am to 11pm, the Elevador da Glória from 7am to 1am.

Boats

Several boat services on the Tagus connect Lisbon's city centre with towns on the opposite bank: Cais da Alfândega, opposite Estação Sul e Sueste (passenger ferry): to Cacilhas (15 mins.); Cais do Sodré (car and passenger ferry): to Cacilhas (20 mins.); Estação Fluvial, Belém (passenger ferry): to Trafaria (25 mins.) and to Porto Brandão (20 mins.).

Local trains

Local trains of the CP depart from Estação Cais do Sodré to Cascais. Short-distance trains to Oeiras stop at all stations, trains to Cascais only stop at those indicated on the screen in the departure hall. They operate every 20 minutes between 5.30am and 2.30am (journey time to Cascais, 35 minutes).
Trains to Sintra depart from Estação Rossio. The first trains leave Lisbon at about 6am, the last around 2.40am.

Many Lisbon trams are almost museum pieces

Elevador da Bica

Elevador da Gloria

Overland buses

Buses to the suburbs depart mainly from the bus stations or from the Praça de Espanha, Entrecampos or from Areeiro.

Tickets

The fares for public transport are generally very favourable. Tickets can be purchased on the bus, in the tram or in the lift, but it is more economical to buy a booklet (caderneta) containing ten tickets in advance. The system of fares is rather complicated; a ticket is valid for a certain stretch of the route and before setting out the passenger must establish from the map at the stop how many tickets need to be stamped for the journey. Tickets have to be stamped again when changing. Special tickets are required for the Metro, boats and local trains, available from Metro and railway stations.

Tourist pass

For a longer stay it is simpler and cheaper to obtain a tourist pass (passe turístico). These are available for either four or seven days and are valid for buses, trains, lifts and the Metro. A passport must be shown at the time of issue and produced for ticket inspection.

Ticket offices

Tickets for buses and trams together with tourist passes are obtainable from the "Carris" kiosks (at Parque Eduardo VII, at the Areeiro, at the Elevador do Carmo). Tourist passes are also on sale at the metro stations. The ticket office at the rear of the Elevador do Carmo is also open on Sundays.

Finding the way

Finding the way around the public transport system is not always easy for strangers. There are some route maps at bus stops but no maps in buses or trams. Stops are generally not announced. The Metro is more straightforward: routes are displayed in the stations and in the carriages. Signs in the underground stations give the terminal station as the direction of travel or state which train goes to Rossio. The ticket and tourist information offices issue route maps for buses, trams, Metro and local train services (rede de transportes).

Radio and Television

Portuguese radio

Portuguese radio (RDP) broadcasts a short daily programme for tourists in German, English and French during the summer months. Times of broadcasts vary (usually between 8 and 10.30am).

S.O.S. messages

In very urgent cases Portuguese radio (RDP) transmits messages for travellers on the radio in English, German and French every hour during the news, from July to Sept. (on 95.7 or 99.4 medium wave in the Lisbon area).

Television

Portuguese television (RTP) has two channels and broadcasts almost all foreign films with the original soundtrack and Portuguese sub-titles. In many larger hotels satellite programmes can be received from other European countries.

Rail stations (estação)

Lisbon has four rail stations:

Estação de Santa Apolónia
Av. Infante D. Henrique
Santa Apolónia railway station is the terminus and departure point for all rail connections with northern and north-east Portugal and abroad.
There is a tourist information centre and a bank in the station. The "Linha Verde" (No. 90) bus line operates directly from here to the centre and to the airport.

Estação do Rossio
Praça Dom João da Câmara (near Rossio)
Local train services to Sintra and all rail connections in the direction of Figueira da Foz start from Rossio rail station.
Rail information and the ticket office for long-distance trains are situated on the ground floor. The ticket office for local trains together with the departure hall are on the third floor. The first trains depart around 6am, the last leave Lisbon at 2.40am.

Estação Sul e Sueste
Praça do Comércio
Ferries to Cucilhas, Barreiro and Montijo on the other bank of the Tagus leave from the Sul e Sueste station. Trains depart from here for the Algarve and the Alentejo. Ferry times are stated on the train timetable, the ticket price includes the ferry crossing.

Estação do Cais do Sodré
Av. Vinte e Quatro de Julho
The station at the Cais do Sodré is the destination and departure station for the local line to Cascais via Belém and Estoril. Not all trains stop at Belém station. Only the short-distance trains which terminate at Oeiras stop there, not the trains which terminate at Cascais. Further information is displayed on the screens in the departure hall. The first trains from Lisbon depart at 5.30am, the last at 2.30am.

Rail travel

Organisation

Portuguese railways are operated by the partly state-owned corporation Companhia dos Caminhos de Ferro Portugueses (CP).

Estação Sul e Sueste

Network

Apart from the region around Lisbon and Porto the network is fairly thin on the ground. The main lines with the fastest trains are Lisbon–Porto and Lisbon–Algarve. On the shorter routes speed and punctuality are not always of central European standards. In smaller towns the railway stations are often situated some distance from the town.

Tickets

Rail travel in Portugal is generally economically priced.
Children under four travel free, children between four and twelve pay half fare.
A tourist ticket (bilhete turistico) provides unlimited travel on the entire Portuguese network and is valid for one, two or three weeks.
Information on tourist tickets and reductions for families, groups and senior citizens is available from the tourist offices, information desks at rail stations or from the Companhia dos Caminhos de Ferro Portugueses, Santa Apolónia, Lisbon; tel. 87 60 27, 87 70 92.

Ticket sales

On local routes the journey must be made within two hours of purchasing a ticket. Single tickets are only valid on the day of issue. Advance purchase of tickets for longer journeys is possible from Santa Apolónia, Rossio and Sul e Sueste rail stations (see Rail Stations). In smaller towns the counters only open an hour before the departure of the train. Where there is no ticket counter payment can be made on the train.

Motorail

See Getting to Lisbon

Restaurants

General

Many restaurants close on Sundays and public holidays. Visitors are recommended to reserve a table in the higher category restaurants. In the Rua das Portas de Santo Antão in the city centre there is restaurant upon restaurant offering a wide selection of seafood and shellfish. These restaurants cater predominantly for tourists with the menu written in several languages. It is generally the case in Portugal that the simpler restaurants offer the most genuine Portuguese cuisine.

Selection

*Aviz, Rua Serpa Pinto 12 B; tel. 3 42 83 91 (international cuisine, elegant surroundings)

*Casa da Comida, Travessa das Amoreiras 1; tel. 3 88 53 76 (pretty courtyard, very pleasant atmosphere)

*Clara, Campo dos Mátires da Pátria 49; tel. 3 55 73 51(one of the top restaurants in Lisbon)

*Tágide, Largo da Academia de Belas Artes 18; tel. 3 42 07 20 (elegantly furnished with old tile pictures, fine view)

*Tavares Rico, Rua da Misericórdia 37; tel. 3 42 11 12 (luxurious and famous restaurant, founded 1784)

*Terraço do Monteiro-Mor, Largo Júlio Castilho (Lumiar); tel. 7 58 58 52 (attractive terrace in the middle of Monteiro-Mor Park, table reservation necessary)

Atira-te-ao Rio, Rua do Ginjal 69/70, Cacilhas (on the southern bank of the Tagus); tel. 2 75 13 80 (beautiful situation directly by the Tagus, creative cuisine)

Bénard, Rua Garrett 104/106; tel. 37 31 33 (good food, pleasant decor)

Bota Alta, Travessa da Queimada 35/37; tel. 3 42 79 59 (popular, small restaurant in the Bairro Alto, good Portuguese cuisine)

Brasuca, Rua João Pereira da Rosa 7; tel. 3 42 85 42 (Brazilian cuisine)

Casa do Alentejo, Rua das Portas de Santo Antão 58; tel. 3 46 92 31 (typical Alentejo cuisine)

Cervejaria da Trinidade, Rua Nova da Trinidade 20; tel. 3 42 35 06 (converted brewery, beautiful tile pictures on the walls, two hall-like rooms, smaller inner courtyard, hot meals until late)

Comida de Santo, Calçada Engenheiro Miguel Pais 39; tel. 3 96 33 39(Brazilian cuisine)

Espelho d'Agua, Av. Brasília; tel. 3 01 73 73 (by the water near the Padrãos dos Descodrimentos, Belém)

Gare Marítima, Gare Marítima de Alcântara; tel. 67 63 35 (by the water, view of the Tagus and Suspension Bridge)

Gõndola, Av. de Berna 64; tel. 7 97 04 26 (beautiful outside terrace)

Lanterna Verde, Rua São João da Praça 45; tel. 8 86 99 06 (simple restaurant, typical Portuguese cooking)

Marisqueira A Berlenga, Rua de Barros Queirós 35; tel. 3 42 27 03 (central, relatively large restaurant with pleasant atmosphere)

Mestre André, Calçadinha Santo Estêvado 6; tel. 87 14 87 (very small restaurant at the edge of Alfama with a pleasant atmosphere and good food)

Michel, Largo de Santa Cruz do Castelo 5; tel. 8 86 43 38 (French cuisine)

Miradouro de Santa Luzia, Miradouro de Santa Luzia; tel. 8 86 39 68 (terrace with lovely view of the Tagus)

O Galeto, Av. da República 14; tel. 3 56 02 69 (good fast food restaurant open until 2am)

O Polícia, Av. Conde Valbom 125; tel. 7 96 35 05 (simple restaurant, fish specialities)

Vicentino, Rua da Voz do Operário 1; tel. 8 86 46 95 (turn-of-the-century decor, Portuguese country cooking)

Shopping and Souvenirs

General

Shoes, leatherware, gold and silverware are particularly worth buying. Souvenirs from Portugal are on sale in numerous shops in the city centre.

Souvenirs, gifts

Typical souvenirs are hand-painted ceramics which vary in colour and pattern according to region. Particularly beautiful designs are sold in the smaller shops in Cascais or Sintra, for example. A popular souvenir is the well known cockerel of Barcelos. (According to the legend a cockerel saved the life of a condemned man. The condemned man trying to prove his innocence pointed to a roast chicken and said that if it came alive again he would really be innocent. The chicken supposedy flapped its wings and crowed, whereupon the man was set free.)
Azulejos, painted tiles, which date back to the Moors, are to be found all over Lisbon. New, mass-produced tiles are on sale alongside old, hand-

Azulejos: an ideal souvenir

painted azulejos in the original designs. (The original tiles can be seen in the Museu Nacional do Azulejo).

Typical textiles are embroidered table cloths and lacework from Madeira and Arraiolos carpets from Arraiolos in the Alentejo. Carved cork, dolls in costumes from the different regions, basketware and silver and gold filigree jewellery are examples of products characteristic of Portuguese craftwork.

Portugal's best known sweet wines are port wine from Porto in the north and Muscatel de Setúbal. Port is available at all prices from different producers and there are many vintages – up to 100 years old.

A special souvenir of a visit to Lisbon are records or music cassettes of Lisbon fado. The most famous interpretations of this typical urban music are by Alfredo Marceneiro and Amália Rodrigues. Carlos do Carmo composes some fados which frequently describe the Portuguese capital.

In the bookshops there are some attractively illustrated volumes about modern and historic Lisbon.

Shopping centres

Following the fire in Chiado, in which two department stores were destroyed, only two or three smaller stores remain but they do not have the same range of goods as stores in major European cities. Instead there are numerous shopping centres (centro comercial) which house branches of different shops. The largest and most well known is the Amoreiras Shopping Center (See A–Z) with over 300 shops where prices are rather high. There are many elegant and expensive shops in the classic shopping streets in the Baixa (See A–Z) and in the Chiado (See A–Z). A popular shopping area is the Praça de Londres and the adjoining streets Av. de Roma and Av. Guer. Junqueiro. Small, old-established shops are situated in the Bairro Alto (See A–Z) and in the less busy streets of the Baixa. The weekly markets (See A–Z, Markets) offer goods at reasonable prices.

Several small galleries can be found in the Rua do Século and the adjoining side streets and a few junk shops in the Rua de São Bento and in the Rua de D. Pedro V.

Antiquarian bookshops

Livraria Barateira, Rua Nova da Trinidade 16

Livraria Camões, Rua da Misercórdia

Livraria Olisipo, Largo Trinidade Coelho 7

Alfarrabista, Rua do Alecrim 44

Arraiolos carpets

Casa Quintão, Rua Ivens 30

Casa dos Tapetes de Arraiolos
Rua da Impresa Nacional 116 E

Azulejos

Santa Ana
Rua do Alecrim 95

Albuquerque e Sousa Lda.
Rua D. Pedro V. 70

Books

Livraria Bertrand
Rua Garrett 73

Livraria Sá da Costa Editora
Rua Garrett 100

Livraria Portugal
Rua do Carmo 70

In the Rua Garrett, with its many exclusive shops

Shopping and Souvenirs

	Livraria Ferrin LDA Rua Nova do Almada 72
Delicatessen	Manuel Tavares Rua Betesga 1 A–B
Ironmongers	Guedes, Ferragens Rua das Portas de Santo Antão 34
Prints, old engravings	O Mundo do Livro Largo Trinidade Coelho 11 (views of old Lisbon)
Gloves	Luvaria Ulisses Rua do Carmo 87 A
Interiors	Antiga Casa José Alexandre Rua Garrett 18
Cork goods	Casa das Cortiças Rua Escola Politécnica 4
Fashion	Spaghetti Rua dos Fanqueiros 258–260
Paper goods	Papelaria Fernandes Rua Áurea 145–149
	Papelaria da Moda Rua Áurea 167–169
Port, coffee tea, sweets	Casa Macário Rua Augusta 272–274 (port from 1890)
Records	Valentim do Carvalho Amoreiras Shopping Center, loja 2109
	Strauss Amoreiras Shopping Center, loja 1130
	Discoteca do Carmo Rua do Carmo 63
Jewellery	Ouvrivesaria Teixeira Rua da Prata 266
Shoes	Sapataria Charles Rua Augusta 275 A Rua do Carmo 105
	Sapataria hera Amoreiras Shopping Center, loja 1101 Av. de Roma 37 A
	Toot Amoreiras Shopping Center, loja 1072
Souvenirs	Artesenato Rua Castilho 67

Artesanato Arameiro
Praça dos Restauradores 62–64

Casa do Turista
Av. da Liberdade 159

Abreu
Praça D. Pedro IV (Rossio) 44

Madeira House
Rua Augusta 131–133

Maderia lace

Casa dos Bordados da Madeira
Rua 1. de Dezembro 137

Amoreiras Shopping Center
Av. Eng. Duarte Pacheco
(See A–Z, Amoreiras Shopping Center)

Shopping centres

Libersil
Av. da Liberdade 38

Centro Comercial Palladium
Av. da Liberdade 1–7

Centro Comercial Imaviz
Av. Fontes P. Melo 35

Centro Comercial Alvalade
Pr. de Alvalade/Av. da Igreja

Pollux
Rua dos Fanqueiros 276
(2nd entrance Rua da Madalena 251)

Department store

Sightseeing Programme

Note

The following suggestions are intended to give visitors to Lisbon who do not have a great deal of time at their disposal an initial impression of some of the sights and the character of the city.
Places for which there is an entry in the A to Z section are printed in **bold** type.

One day

Visitors with only one day to spend in Lisbon can get a marvellous view of the exceptional location of this Portuguese capital by climbing up to the **Castelo de São Jorge**. From a height of some 110m/360ft the view encompasses the city centre, the harbour, the estuary of the Tagus as far as the Atlantic, the **Ponte 25 de Abril** and the opposite bank with the **Monumento Cristo Rei**. On clear days the peaks of the Serra da Arrábida in the south (see Costa de Lisboa) are visible. A tiled picture up at the castle helps with orientation and explains other sights in the town centre. There is a pleasant walk through the castle grounds where there is a grassed area with a small zoo. The tour of the ruined walls should not be missed because of the view over the northern parts of Lisbon and the lake-like Tagus Bay "Mar de Palha" (sea of straw) together with the white cupola of the **Igreja de Santa Engrácia** and the two towers of the **Igreja de São Vicente de Fora** in the foreground.
The visit to the castle can be coupled with a walk through the **Alfama**. From Largo das Portas do Sol steps lead down to the oldest part of Lisbon where the street pattern with its winding alleys, steps and archways is of Moorish origin.
Returning to the Largo das Portas do Sol the route leads over the Rua do

Limoeiro/Rua Augusto Rosa towards the town centre to the beautiful **Miradouro de Santa Luzia** with another wonderful view over the rooftops of the Alfama down to the Tagus. At Largo da Sé stands Lisbon's oldest religious building, the **Sé Patriarcal** (cathedral). Follow the tramlines downhill, past the Igreja de Santo António da Sé, to the heart of the city.
Visitors interested in the history of Lisbon and its architecture can spend the afternoon out at **Belém** and see the **Mosteiro dos Jerónomis**, the **Padrão dos Descombrimentos**, the **Torre de Belém** and one of the numerous museums (see Practical Information, Museums). It is worth taking the time to catch the old tram into this historical suburb.
An alternative programme is to stroll through the shopping streets of the **Baixa** to the central square **Rossio** and along the **Avenida da Liberdade**. The trip by the Elevador do Carmo is recommended. From the platform there is a fine view over the Baixa, the castle opposite and part of the **Chiado** which was burnt down in 1988.
Those who wish to get an impression of the city away from the hurly-burly can take tram No. 28 and make a personal tour of the city. It departs from the centre in both directions through interesting parts of the city.
In the evening a walk through the lively **Bairro Alto** with its many restaurants, fado venues, bars and pubs makes interesting entertainment. From the Miradouro de São Pedro de Alcântara (see Bairro Alto) there is a magnificent view of the illuminated city of Lisbon by night.

Two days

During a two-day stay one day should be set aside for the above visit to the **Castelo de São Jorge** and the walk through the town centre. On the tour through the **Alfama** a visit to the Igreja de Santa Engrácia and/or the Igreja de São Vicente de Fora could be included. The afternoon walk through Lisbon's centre can be extended by a stroll through the **Chiado** district which can be reached from the **Baixa** directly over the Rua Garrett or by the **Elevador do Carmo**. An interesting route is through the Rua da Misericórdia/Rua de São Pedro de Alcântara/Rua de Dom Pedro V./Rua da Escola Politécnica to the **Jardim Botânico**. Pause to have a look inside the **Igreja de São Roque** at the Largo Trinidade Coelho before continuing past the Miradouro de São Pedro de Alcântara and the Praça Principe Real (see Bairro Alto). The spacious Botanical Gardens provide a calm retreat from the hurly-burly of the city.
The second day could begin with a visit to the **Fundacão Calouste Gulbenkian**. This should be followed by an excursion to **Belém** with its many places of interest. Should time permit the Museu de Arte Popular has exhibitions of Portuguese folk art. The somewhat setback **Museu de Etnologia** is worth a visit. Among other exhibits it has craftwork from former Portuguese colonies

Three days

On a three day trip it is suggested one day be spent on an excursion to **Sintra** and/or **Quelez**. Some tour operators offer bus tours to both places (see Practical Information, Excursions). For the independent traveller Sintra is easily reached by the suburban railway from Rossio station (see Practical Information, Rail Stations). The Palácio Nacional de Queluz can also be reached by the same line, with a half hour walk from Queluz-Belas station. When planning the day it should be remembered that the palace in Queluz closes at midday. Allow sufficient time at Sintra not just for the palaces but also for a walk around the town itself.

Sport

Bathing, Swimming

Aguaparque
Avenida das Descobertas, Restelo
Swimming pools, slides, waterfalls, etc.

Piscina do Ariero
Avenida de Roma

Piscina dos Olivais
Avenida Dr. Francisco Luis Gomes
Olivais

Piscina de Monsanto
Parque de Monsanto

The best bathing areas near Lisbon are listed under Beaches.

Fitness centres

Health Club Gemini
Rua Sousa Lopes, Campo Pequeno; tel. 7 96 37 78

Health Club Soleil
Centro Comercial Amoreiras, Amoreiras; tel. 69 29 07

Luz Health Club
Rua Adelaide Cabete 6, Benfica; tel. 7 15 30 53

Golf

Vimeiro Golf Club
Hotel Golf Mar, Praia do Porto Novo, Vimeiro; tel. (061) 98 46 21
9 holes
small, well tended course, on both sides of a stream

Estoril Palácio Golf Club
Estoril; tel. 4 68 01 76
18 holes
short but interesting course

Guia Estoril Sol
Estrada da Lagao Azul, Linhó, Sintra; tel. 9 23 24 61
9 holes

Guia Quinta da Marinha
Quinta da Marinha, Estrada do Guincho, Cascais; tel. 4 86 98 81
18 holes

Clube de Campo de Portugal – Aroeira
Herdade Quinta da Aroeira, Fonte da Telha, Monte de Caparica;
tel. 2 26 18 02
18 holes

Lisbon Sports Club
Casal da Carregueira, Belas; tel. 4 31 00 77
14 holes
tennis courts, swimming pool

Tróia Golf Club
Torralta Tróia, Setúbal; tel. (065) 4 41 12
18 holes

Riding

Centro Hípico da Quinta da Marinha
Areia (Cascais)
Tel. 4 68 92 33

Sailing

There are sailing clubs at several resorts near Lisbon, particularly Cascais, Estoril and Sesimbra, where boats can be rented and courses are available at beginners' and advanced levels.

Surfing

Surfing is becoming increasingly popular on the beaches of the Estoril coast. The beach at Carcavelos is ideal for beginners, Guincho beach is challenging to expert surfers.

Tennis

Clube de Ténis de Oeiras
Rua José Diogo da Silva, Oeiras; tel. 4 42 69 92

Carcavelos Ténis
Quinta do Junqueiro, Parede; tel. 2 46 36 68

Centro de Ténis de Monsanto
Monsanto; tel. 3 46 87 41

Clube de Ténis do Estoril
Praça de Casino Estoril, Estoril; tel. 2 68 16 75

In addition many of the larger hotels which are not located directly in the city centre have tennis courts, especially near Cascais and Estoril. The courts are predominantly sand.

Water skiing

Water skiing equipment can be rented in Cascais and Estoril and lessons booked.

Spectator sports

Football

There are two important football clubs in Lisbon: Sport Lisboa e Benfica (Estádio da Luz, Av. General Norton de Matos) and Sporting Clube de Portugal (Estádio José Alvalade, Rua de Francisco Stromp). The season begins in mid-August and ends in June.

Bullfighting

See entry

Taxis (táxi)

General

Portuguese taxis are black and have a green roof. Taxis available for hire can be recognised either by the sign "Livre" or a green light on the front windscreen or by the illuminated taxi sign on the roof, which is white at the front and red at the rear.
When the taxi is occupied the taxi sign is switched to green. A green light next to the sign denotes daytime tariff, two green lights denote night-time tariff.

Fares

Taxi fares in Portugal are generally quite reasonable. In the city the meter indicates the fare. Out of town the fare is calculated according to the number of kilometres travelled, the return fare is payable for a single journey. Supplements are charged for night journeys (20%) and for carrying luggage (50%).
A tip of 10–15% is normal on account of the low fares.

Ordering taxis

There are so many taxis around in the city centre and near the main sights of Lisbon that they can usually be hailed in the street. It is often necessary to wait a long time at the central taxi ranks (Rossio, Restauradores, Cais do Sodré, etc.). Taxis can also be booked from a hotel or pension or dialled direct (Rádio Táxis de Lisboa: tel. 82 50 61, Rossiotáxis; tel. 82 75 36).

Telephone

International calls can be made from public telphones which require 5, 10, 20 or 50 escudo coins. Newer telephones accept "Crediphone" cards. At

the post office or telephone exchange the call must be registered at the counter beforehand and payment made afterwards. A degree of patience is required when making international calls, especially during the day in the main holiday season, as all the lines may be engaged. There are no reduced rates for weekend or evening calls.
One unit costs 10 escudos. A telephone call to the United Kingdom costs about 160 escudos.
In addition to the normal telephone charges hotels apply considerable surcharges.
"Crediphone" cards are available for 1200 escudos with 120 units and for 500 escudos with 50 units from the post office or the TLP telephone exchange (Rossio 66). Calls can also be made from the telephone exchange. Opening times: 8am–11pm daily (closed public holidays).

Dialling codes to Lisbon

From the United Kingdom: 010 351 1

From the United States and Canada: 011 351 1

Dialling codes from Lisbon

To the United Kingdom: 00 44

To the United States and Canada: 097 1

Theatres, Concerts

Classical concerts

Many classical concerts take place in churches, the principal ones in the Church des Mosteiro dos Jerónimos, in the basilica da Estrela or in the Sé Patriarcal (for addresses see relevant entry in the A–Z section). The Fundação Calouste Gulbenkian houses several concert halls, in summer various events take place in the open on a stage in the adjoining park. During the summer months concerts are also held in the ruins of the Igreja do Carmo. Many concerts also take place in the halls of the Teatro Nacional de São Carlos and in the Teatro São Luís, summer festivals and series of concerts are held in Sintra and in the castle gardens at Queluz. Up-to-date information is available from the tourist offices.

Fundação Calouste Gulbenkian, Grande Auditório
Av. de Berna 45

Fundação Calouste Gulbenkian–ACARTE, Sala Polivalente
Rua Dr. Nicolau Bettencourt

Teatro Nacional de São Carlos
Largo de São Carlos

Teatro São Luis
Rua António Maria Cardoso 54

Theatre

Together with the state theatres there are several independent venues in Lisbon, which are very successful despite limited funds. Typical of Lisbon, are the so-alled *revistas* which combine humour and social criticism, and which are performed in the theatres of the Parque Mayer (See A–Z, Avenida da Liberdade).

State theatres:
Teatro Nacional Dona Maria II., Praça D. Pedro IV (Rossio)
Teatro São Luis, Rua António Maria Cardosa 54

Theatres in Parque Mayer:
Teatro ABC
Teatro Variedades

Theatres, Concerts

Teatro Maria Vitória
Teatro Capitólito

Independent theatres:
Teatro Aberto, Praça de Espanha
A Barraca, Largo de Santos 2
Chapitô, Rua da Costa do Castelo 7
Casa da Comédia, Rua S. Francisco Borja 24
A Comuna, Praça de Espanha
Teatro da Cornucópia, Cascais, Rua Tenente Raúl 1 A
Clube Estefânia, Rua Alexandre Braga 24 A
Teatro de Graça, Travessa de S. Vicente 11
Teatro Ibérico, Rua de Xabregas 54
Teatro Maizum, Rua dos Poiais 75 B

Dance, ballet

The Fundaçao Calouste Gulbenkian has established a very well known dance troupe in Portugal, which makes frequent appearances in the halls of the foundation. Dance and ballet performances also take place in the Teatro São Luís.

Jazz

The Lisbon Jazz Club (Hot Clube de Portugal, Praça da Alegria 39) also has a jazz school and gives regular concerts. Larger concerts are organised from time to time by the Fundação Calouste Gulbenkian.

Rock, pop chanson

Portuguese and international rock, pop and chanson concerts take place in the Coliseu, in the Tivoli, in the large stadia (Restelo, Alvalade) in Carlos Lopes sports pavillion or in the bullfighting arenas.

Coliseu dos Recreios, Rua das Portas de Santo Antão 92/104
Tivoli, Av. da Liberdade 188
Pavilhão Carlos Lopes, Parque Eduardo VII
Estádio de Alvalade, Rua Francisco Stromp
Estádio de Restelo, Av. da Ilha da Madeira
Bullfighting arena, Campo Pequeno

Fado

See entry

Programme of events

The "Agenda Cultural", a pamphlet giving details of events for the month, is circulated among hotels, pensions, tourist information offices and numerous official outlets.
Every Thursday "Se7e" appears with details of the week's events, at the weekend the magazine "Säbado" is published which also contains information about events for the coming week (Saturday–Sunday). The weekend editions of many daily newspapers also carry details of events.

Advance tickets

Tickets for many events are sold out and are unavailable at the door. Concert tickets, in particular, should be purchased in advance at one of the following ticket offices:

Kiosk
Praça dos Restauradores
(for all kinds of events)

Fundação Calouste Gulbenkian
in the main building and in the Centro de Arte Moderna
(for events of the Gulbenkian Foundation)

Valentim do Carvalho record shop
in the Amoreiras Shopping Centre
loja 2109
(classical concerts)

Programme commencement

Most events do not commence until 9.30pm, often early evening performances begin at 6.30pm.

Time

Greenwich Mean Time applies on the Portuguese mainland and on Madeira. Summer time in Portugal is from the end of March to the end of September so that tourists from Great Britain do not need to alter their watches

Tipping

Service is included in hotel and restaurant bills; however an additional tip (gorjeta) of around 10% is gratefully received. Gratuities are usually given to guides, hairdressers, chambermaids, porters and taxi drivers, or where an extra service has been provided. It is also usual to tip the usherette in theatre or concert halls.

Toilets

Public conveniences are to be found in the city centre in several Metro stations, in all shopping centres, in some parks and at rail stations. Sometimes a small charge is fixed, otherwise a small tip is left for the staff.

Traffic Regulations

See Motoring.

Travel Agents (agência de viagem)

Selection

Marcus & Harting
Praça D. Pedro IV (Rossio) 45/50
Tel. 3 46 92 71

Quasar Viagens e Turismo
Rua Artilharia Um 39 A
Tel. 69 19 19

Wagons-Lits Turismo
Av. da Liberdade 103
Tel. 3 46 53 44

TAGUS Travel
Rua Camilo Castelo Branca 20
Tel. 35 25 09
(full range of holiday, business and youth travel)

Empresa de Navegaçao Madeirense
Rua de São Julião 5/4
Tel. 87 01 21
(bookings and information about cargo boat service between Lisbon and Funchal, Madeira)

RN Tours – Viagens e Turismo
Av. Fontes Pereira de Melo 14; tel. 3 55 67 64
Av. de Roma 4 B; tel. 8 48 61 57

Travel Documents

Personal documents

Visitors to Portugal from the UK, United States and Canada can stay for up to 60 days with a valid passport. Children must either have their own passport or be entered in one of their parent's passports.

Car documents

British driving licences and vehicle registration documents are recognised and should be carried. Visitors driving a car which is not their own must be able to produce evidence that they have the driver's permission to drive it. In case of accident the international Green Card is required. Nationality plates must be displayed on the vehicle.

Turismo de Habitação

In recent years, many of the owners of Portugal's manor houses, castles and family estates have begun to offer a delightful alternative to staying in hotels. Known as Turismo de Habitação, rooms are let with breakfast included, and lunch and dinner optional. The houses are nearly always in splendid countryside locations and offer a high standard of comfort. The houses can be booked direct with the owners, or with an organisation taking central bookings. In the Lisbon area contact: PIT (Promoções e Ideias Turísticas, SA), Alto da Pampilheira, Torre D2 8A, 2750 Cascais (tel. 4 86 79 58 or 2 84 44 64).

Viewpoints (miradouro)

Owing to the hilly terrain over which the Portuguese capital extends there are numerous points which offer a marvellous view over the city and river. Many of these so-called miradouros have been attractively laid out as small parks.

Castelo de São Jorge
Comprehensive view from the square in front of the castle and from the castle walls
(See A–Z, Castelo de São Jorge)

Miradouro de Santa Luzia
Largo de Santa Luzia
(See A–Z, Alfama)

Miradouro de Santo Estêvão
Church forecourt
(See A–Z, Alfama)

Miradouro da Graça
Square in front of the Igreja da Nossa Senhora da Graça
(See A–Z, Graça)

Miradouro Senhora do Monte
Largo da Senhora do Monte
in front of the small Ermida Nossa do Monte
(See A–Z, Graça)

Miradouro Torel
Travessa do Torel

Miradouro de Santa Luzia, one of the finest viewpoints of Lisbon

Alto de Santa Catarina
Rua de Santa Catarina
(See A–Z, Bica)

Parque Eduardo VII
Viewing point at the north end of the park
(See A–Z, Parque Eduardo VII)

São Pedro de Alcântara
Rua de São Pedro de Alcântara
(See A–Z, Bairro Alto)

Jardim Botânico da Ajuda
Calçada da Ajuda
(See A–Z, Palácio Nacional da Ajuda)

Ermida de São Jerónimo
Rua Pero da Govilha
(See A–Z, Belém)

Elevador do Carmo
upper platform of the lift
(See A–Z, Elevador do Carmo)

Water

Lisbon water is heavily chlorinated so it is drinkable but not particularly pleasant. There are several brands of still mineral water which are preferable (see Food and Drink, Drinks).

Weather

See below

When to Go

Lisbon typically enjoys long dry summers with pleasantly warm temperatures. In July and August the temperatures can rise to 30°C/86°F and above but the proximity to the Atlantic results in a little breeze. Even during these months it can become quite cool in the evenings. The period from November to March can be mild but very wet.

Climatic table Months	Temperature in °C		Hours of sunshine	No. of days of rainfall	Precipitation in mm
	Average maximum	Average minimum			
January	13.9	7.8	4.7	15	111
February	15.2	8.1	5.9	12	76
March	17.3	10.0	6.0	14	109
April	19.6	11.5	8.3	10	54
May	21.4	12.9	9.1	10	44
June	24.8	15.4	10.6	5	16
July	27.4	17.0	11.4	2	3
August	27.7	17.3	10.7	2	4
September	25.9	16.5	8.4	6	33
October	22.3	14.2	6.7	9	62
November	17.2	11.0	5.2	13	93
December	14.5	8.5	4.6	15	103
Annual	20.6	12.5	7.7	113	708

The best times to visit Lisbon are in the spring and autumn. Swimming from the beaches in the region is possible from June to October. In July and August the coast becomes very busy. Even in August the water temperature only averages 18°C/64°F. Many inhabitants leave the city to go on holiday during the two hottest months when large numbers of tourists come to stay.

In June the saints' festivals are celebrated, in July and August numerous concerts and festivals of classical music take place and in September the annual Avante Festival (see Events). The concert and theatre season begins again in the winter after a break in September and October.

Youth Hostels (pousadas de juventude)

Youth hostels (pousadas de juventude) offer accommodation at reasonable prices. They are particularly suitable for young people, but Portuguese hostels have no upper age limit.

Because there are relatively few hostels it is absolutely necessary to book in advance, particularly in the summer months; this can be done via the Portuguese Youth Hostels Association, the Associação Portuguesa de Pousadas de Juventude (see below)

Information

Associação Portuguesa de Pousadas de Juventude
Rua Andrade Corvo 46
1000 Lisbon
Tel. (01) 57 10 54

Youth hostels

Lisbon Youth Hostel
Rua Andrade Corvo 46
Tel. 01/53 26 96
124 beds
Metro: Picoas

Youth hostel in Oeiras: "Catalazete"
Estrada Marginal (Junto ao Inatel)
Tel. (01) 4 43 06 38
104 beds
Suburban train to Cascais from Cais do Sodré station

Index

Notes

Notes

Notes

Notes

Notes

Notes